MW00770463

wild +
whole

wild+whole

Seasonal Recipes for the Conscious Cook

Danielle Prewett

PHOTOGRAPHS BY **ANGIE MOSIER**

RODALE
NEW YORK

Published in the United States by Rodale Books, an imprint of Random House, a division of Penguin Random House LLC, New York.
RodaleBooks.com | RandomHouseBooks.com

RODALE and the Plant colophon are registered trademarks of Penguin Random House LLC.

LIBRARY OF CONGRESS CATALOGING-IN-PUBLICATION DATA
Names: Prewett, Danielle, author. | Mosier, Angie, photographer.
Title: Wild + Whole / Danielle Prewett ; photographs by Angie Mosier.
Other titles: Wild plus whole
Description: First edition. | New York : Rodale, 2024. | Includes bibliographical references and index.
Identifiers: LCCN 2023036415 (print) | LCCN 2023036416 (ebook) | ISBN 9780593578582 (hardcover) | ISBN 9780593578599 (ebook)
Subjects: LCSH: Seasonal cooking. | Cooking (Game) | LCGFT: Cookbooks.
Classification: LCC TX714 .P764 2024 (print) | LCC TX714 (ebook) | DDC 641.6/91—dc23/eng/20240212
LC record available at https://lccn.loc.gov/2023036415
LC ebook record available at https://lccn .loc.gov/2023036416

Printed in China

Interior and cover design by Amy Sly, The Sly Studio
Jacket photographs by Angie Mosier and Matt Gagnon (mushroom)
Prop styling by Thom Driver
Illustrations by Stephanie Singleton

10 9 8 7 6 5 4 3 2 1

First Edition

*For Travis, who inspired me to step out
of the kitchen and into the wild*

Contents

Spring

Summer

Fall

Winter

Things Better Homemade

INTRODUCTION

I believe that every meal tells a story, if you're willing to look for it. To me, the key to finding those stories is by connecting to my food, and to do that, I rely on the inherent rhythms of nature, the ebbs and flows tied to the year's changing seasons. I anticipate each season as it comes, knowing I have only a small window of opportunity in which to harvest its offerings myself. These fleeting chances make the food of each season all the more special, something that's easy to forget when we can find nearly anything we want any time of year at the grocery store.

I've spent the past decade seeking out the stories of the foods on my plate and letting what I've learned guide me to make more sustainable choices. Over the years, this has evolved into a holistic practice I call eating consciously, which has deepened my understanding of how everything we eat is connected to the world around us—to the soil, the sun, wildlife, plants, even time. Cooking and eating seasonally compels me to stay in tune with the natural world and appreciate the moment in which I'm living, and approaching food with curiosity and thoughtfulness brings me a deep sense of joy and fulfillment.

But every story has a beginning and eating with this mindset is a far cry from how I ate growing up.

I was raised in Texas, in a very small town out in the country. Over the years, we kept a variety of animals—dogs, cats, goats, chickens, ducks, geese, guinea hens, parrots, and even one cow—most of which we considered pets. We also operated a small hobby emu farm, and I was fortunate to learn at such an early age that there are more animals to eat than the ones you find on the menu at McDonald's. We often had emu burgers and steaks for dinner, and just one emu egg made an omelet that could feed our family of five!

As a little kid, I was enchanted by our life in the country surrounded by animals, but as I got older, things changed. My mom was diagnosed with a debilitating form of blood cancer. With bigger priorities demanding our time, we were forced to simplify our lives. My mom's illness took a heavy toll, limiting her ability to eat, let alone cook. It was a traumatic time for our family, and while my dad stepped up to the plate, grilling steaks for us or heating up TV dinners, meals were just meant to fill our stomachs. For us, food was about convenience. Cooking wasn't something I was interested in learning—I didn't care where the food I was eating came from or if it was healthy. I just wanted something that tasted good and satisfied my hunger. Food was the least important element in my life.

This attitude caught up with me in college, and my health took a hit. I felt sick when I didn't eat and sick when I did. Looking for a solution, I tried an elimination diet and learned to cook for myself. Preparing food became a form of self-care; the more I cooked, the better I felt, and the more I wanted to learn about cooking. These experiences inform my approach to ingredients in my recipes today—after growing up eating processed and fast foods, cooking and eating real foods feels like a luxury.

Wild game came into the picture in college, when I met my future husband, Travis. On our first date, he took me to a gun range to sight in a rifle; on our second, he cooked me a venison steak dinner. I remember the way he handled the meat with reverence, and as our relationship progressed, I came to understand that reverence. I fell in love with cooking the game Travis brought home—making stock from whitetail deer, searing mallard breasts—and working with ingredients you can't buy from the grocery store continues to fascinate me.

I eventually took this a step further, learning how to butcher and break down whole animals, but Travis was still the one doing the hunting—I knew how to process an entire deer before I ever squeezed the trigger on anything bigger than a dove. Completing the circle was important to me, but I felt as if I had to earn my way into hunting, that I didn't deserve to take an animal's life until I was ready. And eventually, I was. I picked up a shotgun (a very special vintage Browning 20 gauge that had belonged to Travis's grandfather) and started bird hunting.

The first bird I shot was a pheasant, flushed from the cattails by my golden retriever, Marina. That night, I made pheasant coq au vin. Though I'd cooked pheasant many times before, this meal was different—it was *my* bird. I savored each bite with an appreciation I had never felt before. In that moment, I understood not only the significance of the bird's life but also the significance of the habitat that had sustained its life. My memories of that experience—of hunting the bird, breaking it down, preparing it, and sharing it with Travis—are ones I'll treasure forever. From that meal on, eating was no longer about filling my stomach or exciting my taste buds. Food had meaning, and it became a way to create a life *with* meaning. I wanted to feel that way every time I sat down to eat.

It was important to me to know that every time I cooked, it was done with full consciousness, so between hunts, I educated myself on the sustainability of our food system. I wanted to understand how the food I was eating affected the natural world, and this inevitably drew me closer to its source. I became fascinated with the idea of living off the land. Eventually, my husband and I made the decision that all protein we cooked at home would come solely from game and fish we

hunted ourselves, and we later added a small flock of chickens to provide us with eggs.

Natural periods of scarcity throughout the year inspired a more thoughtful approach to using meat, and I came to appreciate it more as an ingredient, balancing it on the plate with seasonal vegetables and using meatless meals to stretch what we had. Dishes that did include wild game came to feel all the more special. We ate this way for nearly a decade, and it was a deeply rewarding experience. (The dishes I cook still lean heavily on wild game and fish for protein, but these days we've started to reintroduce domestic meat into our meals as a way to support farmers who share my goal of protecting and restoring our environment.)

My blog, *Wild + Whole,* started as a way to capture this lifestyle and share it with others—

a creative outlet where I could explore recipe development and food photography—but it unexpectedly set me on a path that led me to where I am today and, ultimately, to the book you're reading now. I hope it encourages you to eat consciously, and that doing so brings you the same deep joy it brings me.

Eating was no longer about filling my stomach or exciting my taste buds. Food had meaning, and it became a way to create a life *with* meaning. I wanted to feel that way every time I sat down to eat.

EATING CONSCIOUSLY

Our relationship with nature is broken. We rely on Earth's resources for survival, just like every other species on the planet, but we view ourselves as somehow set apart or isolated from nature—and on a global level, the way we eat is destroying our home. Food production is using resources faster than we can replace them (when we bother to replace them at all) and at the cost of essential wildlife populations and habitats. We should be striving for a food system where our resources can not only sustain what we take but regenerate themselves and thrive. But how can we make this happen—where should we even start?

In recent years, topics like sustainability and regenerative farming have increasingly become a rallying cry against the depletion and destruction of Earth's natural resources. We hear about these issues often, but the conversation is broad and frequently confusing, and the media loves to polarize and emphasize extremes in the interest of getting more clicks. Even if you understand the call to action, you might find that the suggested changes just don't fit your life, lifestyle, or budget. Should you feel guilty if you don't shop at the farmers' market? Or if you're not buying beef from a regenerative farm?

I'm not here to make you feel guilty, and I don't pretend to have the answer to fixing our broken food system. So instead of telling you to swear off processed foods or weighing in on the farmed seafood debate, I'm going to suggest you start eating consciously. Those big-swing changes have their benefits (and their drawbacks), but I truly believe the first step to finding a solution is to reconnect with the natural world. This means seeking a deeper understanding of the foods you eat—not just where they come from, but their effects on the environment as a whole, on the local communities where they're raised or grown, and on the people who work to produce them. It means learning the stories of those foods in order to make better and more informed choices.

How Did We Get Here?

Eating consciously starts with understanding the story that underpins all others: biodiversity, all the biologically varied organisms that make up an ecosystem—plants, insects, amphibians, reptiles, mammals, even microscopic organisms living in water and soil.[1] Biodiversity keeps the cycles of nature regenerating and breathing life into our world; it's a beautiful, tremendously intricate system, and one we depend on to sustain life.

Our food system, on the other hand, is one of the most significant drivers of biodiversity loss; instead of sustaining life, modern agriculture threatens ecosystems around the world—and all the organisms that have uniquely adapted to thrive in those ecosystems. Since the 1970s, we've lost 68 percent of our wildlife populations worldwide,[2] a terrifying rate of decline. We've traded rich and vibrant ecosystems for monocrops (more on those in a minute), and Earth is suffering for it. How did we get here?

Learning how farming has evolved over the course of human history has helped me make more thoughtful decisions about the foods I eat. Until the mid-1800s, agriculture was a holistic process, and almost all farms grew a variety of crops and used crop rotation to keep the soil healthy and protect against pests and plant diseases. Farmers also raised animals like cows, pigs, and chickens, and the manure from these animals was used as fertilizer, making them an essential part of the farm ecosystem.

As we entered the twentieth century, policymakers in the US were eager to capitalize on new farming technologies and pushed for rapid expansion, fundamentally changing our agricultural system. My grandparents had a farm in South Dakota and, like millions of other farmers, were encouraged to plant "fence row to fence row," destroying the majority of our native grasslands in the process—and leaving the country with more grain than we knew what to do with. Farmers received less and less money for their crops, and the value of farmland bottomed out. Thousands of family farms—including my grandparents'— went under, and many of those acres were bought cheaply and consolidated into large-scale operations that focus on monoculture, the planting of a single crop year after year. This might not sound so bad in itself, but the intensive agricultural practices associated with monoculture, like heavy tilling and pesticide use, can render the soil lifeless and dead

I'm going to suggest you start eating consciously. . . . This means seeking a deeper understanding of the foods we eat—not just where they come from, but their effects on the environment as a whole, on the local communities where they're raised or grown, and on the people who work to produce them. It means learning the stories of those foods in order to make better and more informed choices.

(this is how we ended up with the Dust Bowl, a devastating natural disaster in the US and Canada during the 1930s). Industrial farms then have to use excessive amounts of synthetic fertilizer to enrich the soil, creating runoff that pollutes our estuaries and causes harmful algae blooms that kill marine life.

Since the 1950s, food crop production in the US has nearly tripled.[3] Despite this massive jump in agricultural output, humans aren't the end consumers of most of the food produced. A huge portion is fed to animals in concentrated animal feeding operations (CAFOs), industrial farms that house and process high volumes of livestock. In addition to the resources these farms require—and the admittedly awful conditions for the animals they house—CAFOs emit significant amounts of greenhouse gases, and the animal waste they generate pollutes soil and water systems in the surrounding area, further contributing to biodiversity loss.

Of the crops that *are* destined to feed the human population, the policies of the past century have incentivized the farming of just four ingredients—corn, wheat, rice, and soy[4]—a disheartening situation that drives the production of highly processed food (contributing to the rise of the standard American diet, or SAD) and weakens crop diversity, which has fallen by 75 percent in the past twenty years alone.[5]

Regenerative Agriculture:
Restoring the Cycles of Nature

I learned about regenerative agriculture from the best: Will Harris of White Oak Pastures. Regenerative agriculture seeks to improve the land by focusing on soil health, which, in turn, draws carbon from the atmosphere into the ground and improves the health of local watersheds and biodiversity. While there are no set rules or definitions of regenerative agriculture, many farmers incorporate some of the following practices:

- Integrating livestock with carefully managed grazing habits

- Reserving a portion of land for native grasses and wildflowers that benefit wildlife and pollinators

- Implementing cover crops

- Mimicking forest systems in tropical regions by interplanting trees and shrubs with crops (agroforestry)

- Minimizing ground disturbance by avoiding the use of tilling, pesticides, and synthetic fertilizers

This type of farming is labor-intensive, which is reflected in the cost of the food, but you're paying for a higher-quality product that benefits the earth.

As President Franklin D. Roosevelt once said, "The nation that destroys its soil destroys itself," and today, we've reached a tipping point. On a national scale, an important part of the solution is to change *how* we farm, so that we can regenerate the land and coexist with wildlife in a more harmonious way while also ensuring that farmers can turn a profit. This requires revisions to the US Farm Bill, the largest piece of legislation funding our food and agricultural system, which influences what farmers grow and in what quantities, and which farming practices are implemented. Through the Conservation Reserve Program (CRP), the Farm Bill also provides incentives for landowners to conserve habitat for fish and wildlife by taking marginal croplands out of production and planting cover crops instead. Thankfully, there are numerous coalitions and nonprofits advocating for policy changes that will protect farmers' livelihoods, rural America, and our environment (see page 263 for some examples). And today, increasing numbers of farmers are working with conservation organizations to learn how to employ regenerative farming practices by integrating animals and diversifying crops.

Advocacy and policy change at a legislative level is great, but you're probably wondering what you can do as an individual. Well, quite a lot, actually, because every day, we vote with our forks. Conscious eating is a grassroots effort that, if embraced by a large enough population, can make a major impact.

SO YOU WANT TO EAT MORE CONSCIOUSLY— NOW WHAT?

As I mentioned earlier, I truly believe the first step to improving our broken food system is to reconnect with the natural world. It's hard to understand the massive implications and importance of biodiversity loss when you don't see it. Part of the problem is that when we buy packaged foods, they're so distorted from their original form that we don't even think about the plants or animals from which they came. How can we address issues in our food system if we don't know where our food comes from?

Connecting with our food enables us to understand its value. By going to its source, you can see the hidden costs of that food—not just how much you paid for it, but all the things that have to happen to get it to your table and the effects those steps have on your health and the environment. You know whether pesticides were sprayed on your vegetables and the resources required to raise the beef that goes into your burgers. If you eat meat, the most difficult cost to grapple with is the life of the animal that died to become your meal. It's not an easy thing to think about, let alone witness, but it taught me respect for the meat on my plate and made me appreciate it in a way I hadn't ever before.

Eating with intention and appreciation means making thoughtful decisions about the way you approach food—it doesn't mean making "perfect" choices 100 percent of the time. You should feel empowered to implement this mindset in ways that benefit the earth but also fit your life, lifestyle, and individual resources. In my journey, I made small changes to my eating habits over the course of a few years, which eventually led to a major shift in my lifestyle—and I made plenty of slips and course corrections along the way. Having self-compassion in those moments and making choices that fit my life has enabled me to stick with it long-term. It's easy to feel pressured to do the "best" thing, but instead, think about what's important to you, do some research, and let that guide your choices. Take a look at the six ways to eat—and live—more consciously on the following pages, and think about how these might fit into your life.

1. Become an Active Participant in Sourcing Your Food

Being an active participant means involving yourself directly in the life of your food, whether by growing or raising it or being individually responsible for acquiring it, without a farmer or retail outlet as the middleman. Right now, I love to source ingredients by hunting, fishing, foraging, and gardening. You may be interested in some combination of those, or even in raising your own animals for food—a journey I'm diving into now with my first flock of chickens. This isn't the fastest or easiest way to put meals on the table, but it's by far the most rewarding. Here are some ways to get up close and personal with the ingredients on your plate.

HUNTING AND FISHING

Humans have interfered with the natural world so much that we've passed the point where nature can "take care of itself," and now, without our intervention, animal populations would become increasingly unbalanced, leading to possible species loss and damage to the ecosystems in which they live. Hunting and fishing can be an effective way to conserve and manage these populations, and most hunters and anglers have an intimate understanding of nature and are fiercely protective of the wildlife we care so much about.

Thanks to visionaries like Theodore Roosevelt (who founded the National Wildlife Refuge system and is considered the father of conservation), we have an effective and sustainable wildlife management structure in the US. The money that outdoorsmen and outdoorswomen spend on hunting and fishing is also allocated to the conservation of these animals. Licenses and tags fund state game and fish offices, which manage and implement conservation projects. In addition, an excise tax on equipment and firearms established by the Pittman-Robertson Act of 1937 is apportioned to states for conservation and public access projects. According to the US Fish and Wildlife Service, in 2022 alone the excise tax garnered a record-breaking $1.6 billion, and since the act was established, it has distributed more than $27 billion!

However, I want to stress that hunting and fishing isn't a realistic or sustainable way for most people to get their food, which is why I've included recipes for sustainably raised domesticated animals in this book alongside those that feature game.

If you're interested in learning how to hunt or fish, I want to be very frank: It's not always easy, and you're never guaranteed success, but don't be discouraged by failure! You learn the most from your failures, and you'll get better and better each time. If you've never hunted before, the first thing you should do is study the rules and regulations outlined by your state's game and fish agency. You'll need to be able to identify what types of wildlife and fish (including sex, species, and size) are available and legal to hunt or catch in your area. You'll also need to get your hunter safety and education certification and purchase a hunting and/or fishing license.

When it comes to the nuts and bolts of hunting, *The Complete Guide to Hunting, Butchering, and Cooking Wild Game, Volume 1: Big Game* and *Volume 2: Small Game and Fowl*

are great resources for in-depth information about firearms, gear, and how to hunt for all manner of large and small game animals. And keep in mind that it's just as important to learn *where* to hunt as it is to learn *how* to hunt. Generally speaking, fishing is a good place to get started because it's so accessible. For hunting, if you have permission from the landowner, you can go on private land following your state's regulations, but there are also opportunities to hunt on public land managed by state and federal governmental entities. All lands, whether private or public, are divided into units and managed very carefully. Checking state guidelines will outline whether you can purchase an over-the-counter (OTC) tag or apply for a tag through a lottery system for a given land unit. You can also contact your state's game and fish office to see if there are any mentored hunts available, or join a conservation group, such as Backcountry Hunters & Anglers, to get connected with the community around you. Check out page 262 for more resources to help you get started.

GARDENING

It's not uncommon to find me walking around my garden in the early morning hours, watching pollinators buzzing around, helping delicate curling bean tendrils climb their trellis, and hopefully picking a few ripe vegetables. That's because my garden is more than just a place to grow food—for me, it can be a place of refuge, despite whatever plant diseases or insects might be lurking in the leaves. There's always something to challenge me in the garden, and I feel that I, like an unruly cucumber plant, am always growing.

One of the great things about gardening is the world of vegetable varieties it opens for you. Seed catalogs and online sources offer an amazing array of heirloom varieties that you won't find at the grocery store, and planting some of these in your garden helps preserve and encourage seed diversity.

When it comes to learning how to garden, the best advice I have is to just get started! I've learned mostly by trial and error, but there are so many wonderful resources out there (including the ones on page 262). One of the most helpful things I did was join a Facebook group for gardeners in my immediate area.

You'll learn from others the best time to plant and what varieties work well where you live, and you'll get tips for dealing with common local plant diseases and pests (there's a good chance that if you're getting a sudden swarm of tomato hornworms, other gardeners in your community are, too).

I've had a lot of ups and downs in gardening, and every experience—good or bad—has been an opportunity to learn. Here are a few things I've picked up along the way.

- Soil is the foundation of your garden, and it's the most important thing you can invest in. If you're building a raised bed, use the best soil you can get your hands on. If you're planting straight in the ground, amend the existing soil with lots of organic compost. Your soil should be alive! To that end, it's a great idea to get your soil tested so you know what you're working with. Don't just guess and start adding fertilizer. You can find kits online that give you results within a couple of weeks and advice for how to amend your soil based on those results.

- Invest in a drip-irrigation system with a timer. In my first garden, I used a combination of hand-watering and cheap rotary sprinklers. This splashed water on the lower leaves of all my plants, resulting in a lot of soilborne diseases and then the dreaded powdery mildew. Drip irrigation uses less water and keeps your plants clean and healthy.

- Plant flowers—lots of them! Flowers attract pollinators, which you'll need to have around if you want to grow actual vegetables, not just vegetable plants (plus, they're pretty to look at). It's most economical to start flowers from seed; then, as you deadhead spent flowers, you

can save their seeds to plant next year. I like to plant a mix of native wildflowers, ornamental cutting flowers, and edible blossoms.

FORAGING

Foraged foods can add so much to a meal, whether that's a beautiful color or shape, a distinct flavor that cultivated varieties just don't have, or a special reminder of how amazing our Earth is. And there are so many edible wild ingredients to discover by foraging—mushrooms, berries, and alliums are just a few of my favorites. I even love the physical act of foraging—spending time outside can be so relaxing, and it gives me the chance to immerse myself in nature. It's truly rewarding to find a seasonal ingredient that has emerged from its slumber at the right place and the right time, just as nature intended.

Foraging is a fun way to collect food, but proper identification is incredibly important. Never *ever* eat anything if you aren't 100 percent sure what it is. If you're interested in foraging, I encourage you to gather a collection of identification books. There are lots of books on foraging in general (see page 263 for recommendations), but I prefer to use regional resources; these have more specific examples of native plants and fungi local to your area, as well as examples of what topography to look for. You can also sign up for mentored foraging forays all across the US—just spend a little time researching what is available near you and when.

2. Shop Responsibly

If you don't have access to wildlife or room in your budget for a hunting tag, or if your apartment is a few miles from the nearest patch of soil fit for planting, you can still make conscious decisions about where you're getting your ingredients. Here are some tips on sourcing domestic meat and eggs, wild game, seafood, produce, and grains.

DOMESTIC MEAT AND EGGS

When it comes to buying domestic meat and eggs, buy the best-quality products you can when your budget allows and when you have time to seek them out. This might not be every time you shop but doing it every once in a while can make a difference. If you've never bought meat outside the grocery store, you might be surprised by what's available. Start local by supporting ranchers and farmers in your area; look for those who are working to restore the land using either regenerative farming practices (see page 16) or by raising grass-fed and grass-finished animals. These practices are less resource intensive than those used by factory farms, as they don't rely solely on agricultural production for feed; instead, they work in harmony with the cycles of nature to grow healthy grass for their animals to eat.

Today, many of these farmers use social media to market their products, and you can see videos and photos of the farm and the animals. You may be able to order their products online and have them delivered to your doorstep or arrange to meet them at your local farmers' market for a pickup. Another cool way to support your community is to buy a livestock animal at a county fair or local rodeo that was raised by a 4-H or Future Farmers of America (FFA) student. Although you'll be paying above market value, the money goes toward college scholarships and education (and the animal will be sent to a butcher shop to be processed for you). A quick Internet search should tell you if that option is available near you.

If you can't find a farmer locally, look online for a farm that uses regenerative practices or pasture-raises their animals and sells direct to consumers, or find a distributor who does the hard work for you, sourcing responsibly raised meat and shipping it directly to your door. See page 262 for resources.

Whole, Half, or Individual Cuts?

When you're purchasing meat directly from a farm or farmer, you'll usually have the option to buy a half or quarter animal, the whole damn thing, or (less often) individual cuts of meat. If you opt for a whole, half, or quarter, the farm will break that portion down for you into a variety of cuts and vacuum-seal the meat so it's ready for you to freeze and eat throughout the year. It's a big cost up front, but in the end it's cheaper than buying the same amount of meat piece by piece over the course of a year. It's worth the investment if you have the budget and the freezer space. Most farmers prefer selling animals this way because it's much harder for them to sell individual cuts the way grocery stores can, and this is the only way some small-scale ranchers can distribute their meat.

We've gotten used to the standardization of meat; we read a recipe that calls for a specific weight of a specific cut, then go to the store and get exactly what we need. When I started hunting and butchering meat, I had an aha moment when I realized each animal yielded a limited number of steaks and a lot of other cuts that I hadn't worked with before. I didn't get to be picky about which cuts I wanted—I got the whole dang animal whether I liked it or not, and I had to learn how to cook the odd bits so they wouldn't go to waste. Farmers and ranchers often have this same dilemma—they need to sell the whole animal, not just the choice cuts. If you're going this route instead of buying a whole, half, or quarter animal, think about ordering some nontraditional cuts, like beef flank or neck or turkey drumsticks, or even the odd bits and offal, such as the tongue, heart, and liver. (And if you don't know how to

Do What You Can, When You Can

Eating consciously isn't about perfection, but it does require some commitment, and it's not without its challenges. You might find yourself short on time, or money, or even energy, and needing to fall back on foods or food sources you've been trying to avoid. If you're low on produce on Thursday but the farmers' market only opens on weekends, don't martyr yourself—stop by the store and pick up something locally grown, if you can (and if nothing fits that bill, maybe opt for something without packaging). Don't overcommit yourself by trying to do everything all at once or feel guilty when you aren't able to make the choices you think are best. A little goes a long way, and taking small steps—when you can—can lead to big lifestyle changes. We'll start to see global change when a lot of people make small changes, not when a few people make perfect choices all the time.

cook with those, you'll find recipes throughout this book.) Better yet, call the farmer and ask what cuts they have an excess of.

WILD GAME

Many of the recipes in this book call for wild game, and if you don't hunt or fish, you're probably wondering where to buy it. In the United States, it's illegal to sell truly wild game (with a few special exceptions). You might find species like elk on restaurant menus and in specialty stores, but these animals aren't actually wild—they're farmed like livestock. And as with anything related to our food system, choosing whether to buy farmed "wild" game species is a complex issue. Many hunters strongly disagree with the sale of truly wild game because it goes against one of the tenets of the North American Model of Wildlife Conservation, which opposes commercializing wild game based on lessons learned from our nation's past of market hunting. Hunting wild game for trade and profit took populations of buffalo, whitetail deer, and turkey to the brink of extinction, and species such as the passenger pigeon were wiped out completely. Thanks to the Lacey Act of 1900, which prohibits illegal taking of wild game (effectively outlawing market hunting), and a century of regulated licensed hunting, many game animal populations are now thriving at sustainable levels. One successful example? At the turn of the century, the population of whitetail deer in the US had plummeted to 300,000—today, there's an estimated 5.3 million in Texas alone.

A strong argument against farmed game is the potential for disease to spread from captive populations into the wild. Farmed deer and elk, for example, may be infected with chronic wasting disease (CWD), a fatal neurological disease similar to mad cow but transmissible only among cervids (deer, elk, and moose), which can easily make the jump to wild deer or elk in the area.[6] The first case of CWD was identified in a captive deer in Colorado in the late 1960s, and the first case in a wild deer was discovered in 1981. Today, CWD affects wild herds of migratory elk, whitetail deer, mule deer, and moose in twenty-nine states. (At this time, CWD has not jumped the species gap to humans, but if you hunt in an area known to have CWD cases, always have your deer tested before eating its meat.) Instead of buying farmed venison, I suggest farm-raised bison. Private, sustainably raised herds are largely responsible for saving bison from extinction.

If you're interested in trying truly wild game but aren't a hunter yourself, invasive species may (surprisingly) be the way to go. When we introduce a new organism to an existing ecosystem—whether intentionally or unintentionally—they can outcompete native species for resources and destroy habitats. I've seen firsthand the damage a group of feral hogs can do to pastures here in Texas, and the huge patches of grass-barren land in Molokai, Hawaii, where nonnative axis deer have eaten every bit of green within reach. Keeping these populations in check is essential to the protection of native species.

To control populations and mitigate damage, some states license companies to hunt, butcher, and sell truly wild invasive game species, such as feral hog, and nonnative introduced species such as nilgai and axis deer. To do this legally, a US Food and

Drug Administration (FDA) inspector must be present for every step from the kill to butchering. It's an intense and often difficult process (and isn't without some controversy of its own). This factors into the price of the meat, but in return, you're getting truly wild animals and aiding conservation in the process. See page 262 for some reputable companies providing this sustainable solution to the problem of invasive species.

SEAFOOD

The seafood industry is incredibly complex, and trying to figure out which choices are

sustainable can be overwhelming. As with anything else, it's best to source fish that are as local as possible, and preferably from within the US, since we have high standards and management laws. (Although shockingly, the US imports over 60 percent of its seafood!)[7] If the fish is unlabeled or the label doesn't list a place of origin, don't be afraid to ask your fishmonger. Some companies, such as Gulf Wild, have implemented trackers that tell you exactly where, when, and by whom their fish were caught, helping to crack down on seafood fraud. And finally, there are several certification and rating labels that will inform you if a fish is the best choice, a good alternative, or something to avoid. These labels were introduced by the Monterey Bay Aquarium Seafood Watch program, a reputable resource for information on sustainable seafood. For additional resources on where and how to shop for sustainable seafood, check out page 262.

Commercial Wild-Caught Fish

We have strong fishery management laws and systems in place here in the US, and wild-caught US seafood can be one of the most sustainable sources of protein. Many wild fisheries are abundantly stocked, and their populations can regenerate quickly enough to sustain commercial fishing. The National Oceanic and Atmospheric Association (NOAA) and Monterey Bay Aquarium Seafood Watch are good resources for finding sustainable options, as well as navigating which imported wild-caught fish to avoid.

Farmed Fish

Although farmed fish is typically more affordable than wild-caught, making it an accessible protein for many, it's not without some trade-offs. The farming of seafood is intended to relieve pressure on our wild fish populations, but it can end up harming those populations, and the environment, in the process. In the early days of aquaculture (and in many places today), salmon farms that utilized natural resources (like oceans and rivers) were a breeding ground for parasites like sea lice, which impacted native fish, and the waste produced by these farms polluted the surrounding area. Adding insult to injury, the farmed salmon started to escape and crossbreed with native fish, and their offspring act much like invasive species, outcompeting the wild population for resources!

That said, not all farmed seafood is bad. Today, improvements have been made that limit damage to wild populations; for example, some farms have moved their operations to isolated tanks on land. There are also many different methods of farming, each with its own impact. To make an informed choice, research the farmer or ask your fishmonger where the fish was farmed. I've found that the best choices you can make when it comes to farmed seafood are bivalves—scallops, mussels, clams, and oysters. These aren't just sustainable food sources—they're actually regenerating our oceans by increasing species diversity, filtering nitrogen, and sequestering carbon. It's pretty amazing—and these are ingredients you can get pretty much all year long! One promising development in aquaculture is the adoption of agricultural polyculture practices to seafood, which means farming shellfish, edible seaweed, and fish together in a healthier, more symbiotic relationship.

PRODUCE, GRAINS, AND PANTRY ITEMS

When it comes to produce, I start by looking locally. The easiest ways to connect to nearby farmers are to shop at farmers' markets, swing by roadside stands, and join a CSA (a community supported agriculture) program. CSA is a system that has been used by farmers for many years that allows consumers to purchase a "share" of the farm's output ahead of the season, guaranteeing a regularly scheduled (often weekly) delivery of in-season fruits and vegetables. It's a way to cut out the middleman, provide financial support to farmers ahead of the growing season, and get plugged into your local community.

Because CSA boxes are usually filled with a variety of seasonal ingredients—and sometimes an abundance of the same fruit or vegetable—you'll have to decide what to cook based on what you get and not the other way around. This inspires creativity in the kitchen, forcing you to utilize different ingredients or find clever ways of cooking a vegetable you've been eating a few weeks in a row.

Sourcing local grains and pantry items can be a little trickier. I had no idea what kind of pantry items were being grown around me until I started searching a couple of online directories for local farmers in Texas. Once I sifted through the meat and produce, I was surprised by the other goods I found: There's a stone mill near my home that sources local grains from small-scale farmers and grinds them into flour. And in my former hometown, I found a small farm that grows and sells Carolina Gold rice; they even sell the "middlins," or broken pieces of rice that can be cooked like grits, instead of discarding them as waste. I recently learned about a family off Padre Island who hand-harvest sea salt from the Texas coast, and there are numerous olive orchards throughout Texas that produce olive oil and house vinegars.

If you can't find local producers of grains and pantry items, there are some wonderful distributors out there who do the sourcing for you so that you can order online with confidence. For example, King Arthur Baking has committed to sourcing 100 percent of their flour from regeneratively grown wheat by 2030. Check page 262 for more resources.

3. Eat Locally and Seasonally

The best way to start eating seasonally is to eat locally. Choosing foods grown in your area will automatically mean you're eating in season. You'll also be putting money into your local economy, which provides security to farmers and resiliency in our food system and encourages positive land stewardship. When you buy packaged foods marketed as "sustainable" options at the grocery store, your money is going in the pockets of large corporations, not the farmer who grew or raised it—in fact, only about sixteen cents of every dollar spent on food goes back to the farmer.[8] Sourcing locally is a step toward decentralizing our food system, a change that comes with significant benefits. When the next

global pandemic hits, for example, or there's another major interruption in the supply chain, knowing how to source food locally will give you security and peace of mind.

One of the most common questions I hear is "How do I find a local farmer?" Today, it's easier than ever—just type "vegetable farmers near me" or "pasture-raised chicken near me" into a computer search engine, and you'll have results instantly. There are also online directories for each state and some national ones to help you connect with a nearby farmer (see page 262 for some examples). If you'd rather meet your farmer in person, a trip to the farmers' market is your best bet!

When you're grocery shopping, look for stores that stock goods from small-scale producers in your area. One of the supermarkets near my home sells fruits, vegetables, spices, jams, wine—you name it—from nearby communities, products easily identified by a Texas-shaped label that says "Texas Roots" and sometimes even gives the name of the county the food is from. I can't always shop at the farmers' market, so when I do shop at the grocery store, I know buying these local products is the next best thing.

4. Eat a Diverse Diet of Real Foods

It's important to eat real, whole foods in as close to their original form as possible, and to cut out packaged and processed foods that contribute to intensive farming as often as you can. Right now, the biggest recommendation for change in our food system is to eat less meat and more plant-based foods to reduce our reliance on factory-farmed meat. I'm not here to tell you whether you should eat meat—that's a choice you'll need to make for yourself (and if you take the time to connect with your food, the answer will be clear to you). Whichever side of the fence you land on, more vegetables is a very good thing, and you'll find a number of meatless recipes in this book. There are also wonderful alternatives to factory-farmed meat that can actually help reverse climate change (see page 262).

If you opt to go meatless, keep in mind that most plant-based meat substitutes are processed foods derived from monocrops, and this type of agriculture only exacerbates environmental issues. Instead, focus on eating a wide variety of whole foods. Choosing new varieties of vegetables, fruits, and grains helps preserve crop and seed diversity and adds excitement to your plate. The recipes you'll find

Ugly Food

Another great option is to order food from third-party companies that sell produce and other foods that don't meet grocery store standards: the ugly, misshapen, slightly bruised, or out-of-date (but still safe to eat) items that would otherwise be tossed in a landfill. Companies such as Misfits Market, Hungry Harvest, and Imperfect Foods allow you to shop online, typically at prices lower than you'd find in-store, and have your order shipped directly to your home. The items offered typically change from week to week, which might encourage you to add more variety to your plate.

in this book are a celebration of the incredible variety of foods available to us, both cultivated and in the wild. If you've been afraid to try working with something like fennel, rabbit, oyster mushrooms, or buckwheat, this is your invitation to try new things and have fun in the kitchen!

5. Reduce Food Waste

Food production in America takes up roughly 50 percent of the country's land and uses 40 percent of our fresh groundwater. But according to a 2019 report from ReFed, 35 percent of the food we produce each year goes to waste—which translates to 18 percent of that land and 14 percent of that water.[9]

Food waste happens at many points in the supply chain: at the farm, during transportation and distribution, at retail points of sale, and in the food service industry. But shockingly, the greatest amount of food waste happens within our homes! That now-slimy bunch of celery you only used a few stalks from might not seem like much on its own, but imagine millions of people around the world throwing out their slimy celery, and those wasted resources start to add up.

For most of us, reducing food waste boils down to a few best practices:

- **Buy only what you need and only when you need it.** I try to buy only as much food as my family can finish within a week and refrain from buying more until we've eaten what we have or preserved it by freezing, pickling (see page 250), or dehydrating.

- **Store it with the aim of prolonging its shelf life.** Keep your pantry items in sealed containers to keep out moisture and bugs and prevent them from going stale. Store produce in microfiber bags designed to retain moisture to keep them fresh in the crisper drawer. Get to know your fridge and learn which spots are too cold for your vegetables to avoid accidentally freezing them. Label and date the containers you use for leftovers, and keep them where you'll see them in the fridge so you'll eat them before they spoil. For packaged items, check the "use by" date, not the "sell by," before throwing them out—they may be perfectly fine for longer than you think.

- **Use what you already have and as much of it as possible.** I try to use the whole fruit or vegetable, or as much of it as possible—if I have a bunch of carrots, I use the leafy green tops in verde sauce (see page 62), for example. The same applies to animals, whether that means making stock with bones and silver-skin trimmings or cooking with offal—when I process a deer, for example, I save the heart to skewer and grill (see page 158).

6. Support Organizations Working to Restore Nature

Getting involved with nonprofit organizations that aim to protect our environment, conserve our wildlife, and support farmers using holistic methods of agriculture is a great way to donate your time and money to something you care about. There are numerous organizations doing important research to help us understand more about our wildlife and implementing projects to restore nature. See page 263 for a list of nonprofits you can support.

Composting: From Food Waste to Garden Gold

Some of my veggie and fruit scraps are given to my chickens, who happily eat what I can't, but everything else gets composted. I keep a bucket on my counter for collecting all those bits and line the bottom with torn paper or used paper towels to absorb excess moisture and minimize unwanted smells. I've composted many different ways over the years: vermiculite (using worms to break down food waste), a large three-bin system for garden and yard waste, and even an electric countertop composter! Do some research to find out what works best for you based on your needs and living space. If you live in a city, you might be able to pay for a composting service, much like a trash service, that will pick up your green waste each week. For more resources on composting, check out page 262.

ABOUT THE RECIPES

Perhaps you picked up this book because you want to learn more about cooking with wild foods, or maybe you're looking for new ways to cook with the abundance from your garden. My biggest hope is that this book serves as more than just a place to find a great recipe—I hope it inspires you to become more connected to your food.

As you scan through this book, you'll notice two things right away: The first is that the recipes are organized by season, not by meal. There is no better way to experience food than to eat it at the peak of its perfection, and my recipes are heavily inspired by the ingredients I find at the particular time of year I'm cooking them. The second thing you'll see is that the recipes are very whole-food driven, with a lot of emphasis on fruits and vegetables. (That's not to say you should consider this a diet book—if you don't believe me, try the Bourbon Butternut Squash Pie on page 196!)

Part of what makes conscious eating so rewarding is that it's very inclusive. Instead of catering to a specific diet or category of ingredients, this book looks at meals more holistically; you'll find recipes that feature wild game, some that use domestic animals, and some wholly vegetarian recipes. And you might find ingredients you didn't even know you could eat, like squash blossoms and beef cheeks. That's not meant to be intimidating but rather to celebrate the vastly diverse and beautiful foods, both wild and cultivated, available each season. I let nature inspire my recipes—as the saying goes, what grows together goes together. As you search this book, you'll find some tried-and-true combinations, like bacon and tomatoes (see page 122), but also some rather unexpected pairings, like mushrooms and chocolate (see page 193). This is what excites me most about food—there are endless possibilities and opportunities to have fun experimenting

in the kitchen. If you usually don't like stepping outside your comfort zone, don't let the unfamiliar intimidate you—keep an open mind as you're looking for new recipes to try.

Dinner won't always be extravagant, but when you decide to go the extra mile (or pay the extra money) for a special ingredient, it should be celebrated. Many of the recipes in this book acknowledge those rare moments when we have access to a seasonal ingredient

Let these shifts in nature, not the dates on a calendar, guide you into each season, and know that we won't all experience them at the exact same time. This is Mother Nature's timing.

we may only get once a year (or even once in a lifetime), like a Périgord black truffle or a wild spring turkey, and I love to do it justice by turning it into a delicious meal my loved ones and I will remember.

Some recipes, like the Broiled Salmon with Miso-Peach Jam and Crispy Fried Rice on page 111, were developed for those busy weeknights when you want to get dinner on the table in under an hour, but a handful require more time and energy—I love to slowly braise a tough venison neck for several hours, and I'm a fan of taking the extra step to brine chicken and pheasant for a day or two before cooking to ensure maximum juiciness. Read each recipe through before getting started so you'll know whether it fits the time—and ingredients—you have available. To help you on the ingredient

side, I've listed substitutions whenever possible. I like to think of recipes as guidelines or road maps, not rigid sets of rules, and you should feel free to make the most of what you have on hand. If you want to cook a dish but the recipe calls for a vegetable that's not in season where you live, swap it out for one that is. The same goes for proteins: Don't have venison or pheasant? I'll tell you how to replace it with beef or chicken (respectively). I believe in cooking what you love and with what you have.

One of the most important things to keep in mind as you skim these pages is that nothing in this book should be too challenging for the average home cook. If you're new to cooking or worried whether you can successfully make these recipes, just remember that I was once a terrible cook. (It was common for me to burn pizzas in college, and I once tried to make fried rice without cooking the rice first.) *Anyone* can learn how to cook! It just takes a willingness to learn from your mistakes and to keep trying. With that in mind, I've done my best to be as descriptive as possible so you'll know what you should be seeing, smelling, or hearing as you work through a recipe. I want you to feel as if you're in the kitchen with me—together, we're going to make some damn good food.

A Few Notes on Ingredients and Equipment

Seasonal Ingredients

In the introduction to each season, you'll find a list of fruits, vegetables, and wild foods available throughout the US. Although I attempt to capture the essence of each season in this cookbook in a way that applies to everyone, the best way for you to truly eat seasonally is to source your food locally.

Generally speaking, fruits and vegetables are categorized into warm season (foods that need higher temperatures and longer sunlight hours to grow, like peppers and tomatoes) and cool season (plants that need cooler temperatures to grow, such as root vegetables and brassicas). Because every region has its own microclimate, changes in the weather will determine when these ingredients are available to you. This also applies to foraged wild foods; for example, in Texas, we start finding chanterelles as early as May, whereas they might not appear until fall in Montana or the Pacific Northwest. Let these shifts in nature, not the dates on a calendar, guide you into each season, and know that we won't all experience them at the exact same time. This is Mother Nature's timing.

While domestic animals are available any time of year, wild game and fish are seasonal, and their availability varies by species. The season in which I've chosen to highlight them is based on the time of year that hunting or fishing that species is legal; for the most part, these regulations are standard from state to state.

Pepper

All pepper, black or white, is freshly ground. I keep my pepper mill on its coarsest setting because I like the texture of the coarsely ground peppercorns, but if you prefer a finer grind, just use a bit less pepper than called for to start and then adjust to taste. For recipes that call for large amounts of pepper (like the spice blends on page 254), I blitz a handful of whole peppercorns in a spice grinder until coarsely ground.

Salt

Coarse salt—either coarse sea salt or kosher salt—is a workhorse in my kitchen, and I love keeping a variety of others on hand, especially salts I've collected while traveling and hand-harvested artisanal salts (see page 262). Different brands of salt vary in density per teaspoon, which makes them seem more or less salty in relation to one another. I use Morton's, so if you're using a different brand, adjust the quantity called for in these recipes as needed to avoid over- or undersalting. The best way to do this is to start with less salt than you think you need and then taste as you go along, adding more as you like. I also highly encourage you to have some flaky finishing salt around to sprinkle on food just before eating; I like Maldon and Jacobsen Salt Co.

Cooking Fats and Oils

I often call for "neutral oil"—this means oil with very little flavor of its own and usually a higher smoke point than more robust oils like extra-virgin olive. I've suggested avocado and grapeseed oils as options, but you could also use canola or even refined coconut oil (the refining process strips out the coconut flavor you find in unrefined or virgin coconut oil). If you want a buttery flavor without the risk of burning, try clarified butter (or ghee), pure butterfat from which the milk solids have been removed. If I'm using olive oil, it's an extra-virgin variety.

Rendered animal fats can add wonderful flavor. In recipes for cooking red meat, you could substitute tallow (rendered beef fat) for neutral oil; in poultry/fowl recipes, try schmaltz (rendered chicken fat) or duck fat. You'll see lard in a couple of baked recipes. Check out page 261 for tips on how to render animal fats at home.

Herbs and Spices

Fresh herbs grow pretty much year-round where I live, and I use them as much as possible. The herbs and spices in your pantry should be fragrant and flavorful, so every spring, I toss out anything stale or that hasn't been used within a year, then give my herbs a good haircut and dry out the leaves to refill those empty jars. I use these "freshly dried" herbs and spices to make homemade salt blends and spice rubs. Having these on hand makes cooking easier and faster, and you'll find recipes for some of my favorites on pages 254 and 256.

Equipment

The items I count as essential in my kitchen include a sharp chef's knife, a scale, a well-seasoned cast-iron skillet, a wide stainless-steel skillet, a large enameled cast-iron Dutch oven, and saucepans in a couple of different sizes. I also find myself reaching often for a fine-mesh strainer. For food safety and to avoid overcooking meat, invest in a couple of good-quality instant-read thermometers. You'll want one that's oven-safe so you can leave it in the meat and monitor the temp as it cooks, and a regular one to check meat after you've seared it. And while I've always preferred to do things

by hand (I whip cream with nothing but a whisk and the will to keep my arm moving), a few key small appliances can come in handy, including a stand mixer, a high-powered blender, an electric spice grinder, and a heavy-duty meat grinder.

WORKING WITH WILD GAME

I'm a firm believer that the secret to cooking wild game isn't the ingredients you pair with it—those just complement the flavor—but the techniques you use to prepare it. In this section, I dive a little further into the specifics of cooking with wild game, breaking down the differences between game animals and their domestic counterparts and why those differences matter, and outlining the best ways to cook wild game so you can enjoy this special meat.

Before we get into all that, let's talk about what, exactly, wild game is.

What Is Wild Game?

When I say "wild game," I mean truly wild animals—birds, fish, and mammals that live without direct human intervention. The wild species we hunt and eat in North America are established and highly regulated by each state's game and fish department and the US Fish and Wildlife Service, in cases like migratory waterfowl species. In most cases, hunting is limited to a specific period during the year to protect populations (see page 20 for more on hunting and wildlife conservation), and many animals are wholly off-limits to hunters.

The following pages outline the most common species of big game, small game, waterfowl, and upland birds hunted and eaten across North America.

BIG GAME SPECIES

"Big game" means just what it sounds like: bigger-bodied mammals. These include hooved animals, black bear, and wild hog.

Hooved Animals

Hooved animals include species in the cervid and bovine families and fall within a category I refer to as "venison," as the meat from these animals can be treated similarly in the kitchen. Venison is by far the most popular category of big game, since these species are widely accessible across the United States. These include:

- Axis deer
- Bighorn sheep
- Bison
- Caribou
- Elk
- Moose
- Mountain goat
- Mule deer
- Nilgai
- Oryx
- Pronghorn antelope
- Whitetail deer

These species can be used interchangeably in any recipe that calls for venison. Note that there will be some differences in flavor from one species to another based on the animals' diets and lifestyles. Uncontrollable variables such as age, diet, and overall health play a significant role in texture and flavor of an individual animal, just as much (or more so) than the animal's species. There can also be dramatic differences in size among these animals—a bison loin is several times larger than that of a whitetail doe. To account for this, the recipes in this book call for meat by weight whenever possible. If there's one thing I've learned about wild game cooking, though, it's that you've got what you've got. It's not like going to the grocery store and picking out the exact amount of meat you need—there's no more or less meat on the particular animal you have than what's there, and you learn to make do. Depending on how much meat you have, you might want to double a recipe or divide it in half, and you should feel free to do so.

Wild Hog

Wild hogs (also called feral hogs or wild pigs) are similar to farm-raised pigs but have a lot less fat. When cleaned properly, they're delicious, and a hog taken during the fall in an oak forest full of acorns almost guarantees you some pretty incredible-tasting meat. They're also very invasive and very destructive to the landscape, and they multiply quickly. In some southern states (like Texas) and in Hawaii, there's no regulation on hunting these animals, and doing so can provide an opportunity to improve food security and the health of the ecosystem—as my friend and fellow wild game chef Jesse Griffiths says, "Eat a hog, save the world."

It's important to follow food safety guidelines when cooking wild hog because it can, in rare cases, harbor *Trichinella,* the parasites that cause trichinosis. They typically contract the parasite by eating infected animals, so hunting hogs in an area with an ample food supply, like acorns, will give you some peace of mind. (A good maxim to remember is "You are what you eat eats.") Cooking to an internal temp of *at least* 140°F will kill *Trichinella* provided that all the meat—every part of the cut you're cooking—reaches that temperature but note that the CDC recommends cooking to 160°F.[10] I prefer cooking wild hog to 145° to 150°F but use your discretion and do what makes you feel most comfortable.

Bear

Historically, bears were a valuable resource for Native Americans and early pioneers in North America. Today, black bears are particularly valued by hunters for their fat, which makes

a savory substitute for lard in cooking. There are no recipes for bear in this book, but if you have some on hand, you can use it in any recipe that calls for braising or stewing red meat. Note that bears commonly carry *Trichinella*, the parasites that cause trichinosis. Since the risk of infection is much higher, always cook bear meat to 160°F for safety—don't try to cook a bear roast medium-rare like you would with venison.

SMALL GAME SPECIES

Small game species are small-bodied furred mammals commonly hunted in the US. Commonly consumed species include:

- Rabbits and hares: cottontail, snowshoe hare, jackrabbit

- Squirrel

Even though small game is widely available, these species are underutilized as a food source, which is unfortunate. Their meat is every bit as tasty as the dark meat of a chicken. (It's worth repeating that "you are what you eat eats," so the meat of a squirrel that lived in the woods and ate acorns will taste very different from that of a squirrel in an urban area that got its meals by rummaging through trash in the park.) Other small game species include beaver, raccoon, porcupine, and opossum, but these are consumed less often and fall outside the scope of this book.

WATERFOWL SPECIES

Waterfowl like ducks, geese, swans, and sandhill cranes spend most of their lives in and around water, though many species of waterfowl are also frequent visitors to agricultural crop fields. Generally speaking, they're fantastic birds to eat.

Duck

Duck species can be divided into two categories based on what they eat: *Dabbling (puddle) ducks* get their food near the surface of the water and will also head to shore to find plants to eat. These ducks are the best tasting, since their diet is varied and includes things like acorns, corn, and rice. *Diver ducks*, in comparison, eat mostly fish and other aquatic species and can taste muddy as a result. If you're cooking a diver duck, give it a good brine first (see page 66) and feature it in a strongly spiced recipe, such as curry or gumbo. Duck species include:

- Dabbling: gadwall, mallard, pintail, teal, wigeon, wood duck

- Diver: bufflehead, canvasback, coot, redhead, sea ducks (scoters and eiders)

Geese and Other Waterfowl

Geese and other waterfowl can be just as delicious as a dabbling duck, and both specklebellies and sandhill cranes are tasty enough to have earned the nickname "rib eye in the sky." Species include:

- Greater and lesser Canada geese

- Light geese (blue, snow, and Ross's geese)

- Sandhill cranes

- Specklebellies (white-fronted geese)

- Tundra swans

Larger species and older birds (such as Canada geese, which can live up to twenty-five years!) are tougher, so their meat is best cooked with low-and-slow methods (see page 46) or ground (they make great sausages; see page 253). The breast meat of smaller species and younger geese can be cooked hot and fast (see page 49) and can be interchanged with duck in recipes.

UPLAND BIRD SPECIES

Upland birds (a category that encompasses all game birds not classified as waterfowl) have a special place in my heart, and I'm fortunate to have hunted, cooked, and eaten a huge variety. Each species has its own unique characteristics, however subtle or obvious those might be. I've divided upland birds into two categories: those with light-colored breast meat and those with dark (truly, this should be a scale, since some species fall somewhere in the middle, but let's keep things simple). This is important, because it affects how their meat should be cooked. Dark-breasted birds have eggplant-purple meat and are best cooked medium-rare to medium so they're still pink in the middle, similar to duck. (When hunters complain about the taste of these birds, it's generally because they've been overcooked to well-done.) Light-breasted birds are best treated similarly to domestic poultry like chicken, but I like to leave them ever so slightly blush pink at the center. Species include:

- Light-breasted: forest grouse (blue, spruce, and ruffed), partridge (chukar and Hungarian), prairie chicken, pheasant, quail (bobwhite, California, Gambel's, Mearns's, mountain, and scaled), turkey (eastern, Gould's, Merriam's, Osceola, and Rio Grande)

- Dark-breasted: dove, sage grouse, sharptail grouse, woodcock, ptarmigan, and pigeon (although not classified as an upland species, I've included them here since they can be cooked similarly)

Essential Techniques for Wild Game

There are some similarities between wild game and farmed animals; you can easily swap red meat for red meat, for example, so that tried-and-true beef recipe would also work with deer. The same is true for white meat—a chicken dish in your weekly rotation would also work with wild turkey. But there are also some big differences between domestic and wild animals. Instead of spending their lives in pens or fenced pastures, wild animals migrate long distances and use their wings or legs to escape predators, and they consume a widely varied diet, not just grass or grain or standardized feed. These factors make wild animals strong and lean, and their meat incredibly flavorful, and no two animals are exactly alike. We often scorn these qualities when we should be appreciating them.

I like to describe wild game as having a more enhanced meatiness, the way beef tastes meatier after it's been aged and chicken is more flavorful after being brined. (I avoid the term *gamey*, a word with negative connotations; the flavors associated with gaminess are likely caused by poor care in the field or during processing, not something inherent to the animal.) In addition, the meat of wild game animals is embedded with layers of aromatic compounds imparted by what the animal ate, such as sage, grass, or acorns. These are nuances that make wild game special, and recipes for wild game should reflect that. Understanding the characteristics that make wild species stand out from domestic will help you work with those inherent qualities to make the best meals possible.

One of the questions I'm asked most often about wild game is "How do you know how to cook each cut?" Knowing which cuts are tender and which are tough is a good guideline for how you should cook them. And this might sound like a dramatic overgeneralization, but there are essentially only two ways of cooking: low and slow, and hot and fast. With some exceptions, tough cuts benefit most from low-and-slow cooking, while tender cuts

There are essentially only two ways of cooking: low and slow, and hot and fast.

are best cooked hot and fast. In this section, I'll break down the cuts from big game, small game, and fowl, and share my favorite cooking techniques.

TOUGH OR TENDER?

As an animal ages, the muscle fibers and connective tissue (tendons, ligaments, and silver skin) interwoven in their working muscles grow bigger and stronger to accommodate movement. In cooking, this is what makes a cut of meat inherently tough. The muscles that do the least work are the most tender. For detailed visuals on the cuts

Testing Steak for Doneness

To check for doneness, you can use a meat thermometer or check the density of the meat with tongs. If you're new to cooking wild game or not comfortable assessing the meat's density, I suggest taking out the guesswork and using a thermometer—it's worth getting the temperature right! Use the following ranges as a guideline when cooking venison steaks (if you're used to cooking with beef, you'll notice the temperatures here are a few degrees lower).

- Rare: 123° to 127°F

- Medium-rare: 128° to 132°F

- Medium: 133° to 137°F

I love my steaks cooked to 128°F, which is on the rare side of medium-rare, but if you like a true medium-rare, aim for 130°F.

To learn how to feel for doneness based on density, use your hand as a guide: With one hand relaxed, press the soft, fleshy area of your palm at the base of your thumb with the other—the firmness of this area resembles that of a raw steak. If you press your thumb and index finger together, the muscle will tighten and feel as firm as a rare steak. The thumb and middle finger will feel like a medium-rare steak, the thumb and ring finger like a medium steak, and the thumb and pinkie like a well-done steak. Knowing what this feels like, you can press into an actual steak with tongs to judge its doneness. Check the meat's density throughout the cooking process to better gauge the rate at which it's cooking so you'll always know when it's time to drop that butter in!

Big Game Butcher Chart

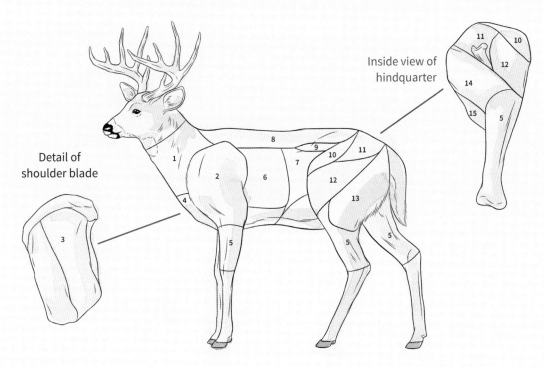

Inside view of hindquarter

Detail of shoulder blade

1. neck
2. shoulder
3. flat-iron steak
4. brisket
5. shanks

6. ribs
7. flank
8. loin or backstrap
9. tenderloin
10. tri-tip

11. rump or top sirloin
12. sirloin tip
13. outside or bottom round
14. inside or top round
15. eye of round

Upland and Waterfowl Butcher Chart

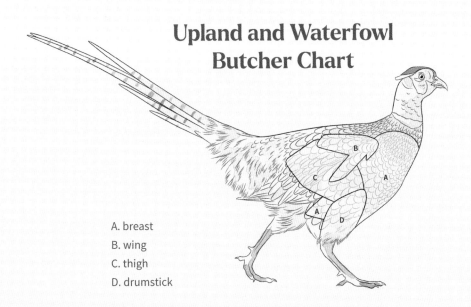

A. breast
B. wing
C. thigh
D. drumstick

described here, *The MeatEater Fish and Game Cookbook* and *The Complete Guide to Hunting, Butchering, and Cooking Wild Game*, both by Steven Rinella, are excellent resources.

Big Game

In big game animals, tough cuts include the shank, neck, and shoulder roasts (except the flat-iron steak on the shoulder blade), as well as the cheeks, tongue, ribs, and outside (bottom) round. The brisket, flank, and skirt also belong in this category because they're encased in a thin but tough layer of silver skin, which can be tedious to remove; I usually leave it attached and slow cook the meat to tenderize it. If you do take the time to remove every bit of silver skin, these cuts can be very tender. They're great when flash-seared and cut against the grain for carne asada or fajitas (see page 112).

The two most common tender cuts are the loin (backstrap) and the tenderloin, but there are several others. In a hindquarter, I consider the top (inside) round (my favorite cut for venison steaks), eye of round (excellent when butterflied and stuffed with a savory filling), sirloin tip, tri-tip, and top sirloin (rump) as tender cuts, as well as the flat-iron steak inside the shoulder blade. I also include the heart in this category; it's a working muscle just like the others, and it's very tender.

Small Game

In small game animals, the loin (saddle) is the most tender cut, and the tough cuts are similar to those of big game. But because wild rabbits and squirrels are so small, it's silly to cook their tough and tender cuts separately; I typically cook the whole animal in a soup or stew.

Fowl

For fowl, the thighs, drumsticks, wings, necks, and gizzards are tough, while the breast, heart, and liver are tender.

LOW AND SLOW

Low-and-slow cooking is the secret to turning a tough cut of meat into the most succulent meal ever. Have you ever eaten a rich osso buco where the meat slides right off the bone? This effect comes from slowly braising the animal's shank over gentle heat (that's the "low") for a long period of time (that's the "slow").

If you've ever wondered why your pot roast is tender but dry as cardboard, high heat is likely the culprit. Heat twists and contracts the muscle fibers in meat, squeezing out moisture much like you'd wring water from a wet towel; the higher the heat is, the more juices run out, resulting in dryness. Low heat means less moisture loss, and retaining moisture is critical for wild game since it lacks fat, which can give meat the impression of moistness even if you've overcooked it.

Certain low-and-slow methods can be used for some tender cuts and help keep them juicy and evenly cooked, but low and slow is *essential* when you're working with really tough cuts. You can always opt to grind tough cuts to instantly tenderize the meat (more on that on page 252), but low-and-slow cooking will transform them. The primary protein in those tough bits of connective tissue is collagen, which breaks down into gelatin as it cooks, lending succulence to the meat.

My favorite low-and-slow cooking techniques are braising, stewing (and soup making), confit, smoking, sous vide, pan-

How to Cut the Perfect Steak

I always save the tender muscles of big game animals to cut into steaks—they're the quickest way for me to put dinner on the table. These muscles come in all shapes and sizes, so the first thing to consider is how you'll break them down into serving portions. Luckily, you have lots of options.

The tenderloin, tri-tip, flat-iron, top sirloin (rump), and eye of round are smaller and best cooked whole. Make sure you trim off all the silver skin on the outside of these muscles, and remove the thick tendon running through the center of the flat-iron (similar to how you would skin a fish fillet). I like to cut bigger muscles like the inside round and sirloin tip into 1½- to 2-inch-thick steaks. You'll notice that the sirloin tip is actually three muscles combined into one, each encapsulated with silver skin. I trim this on the outside of the muscle, but leave everything on the inside (trust me—don't cut it out before cooking or you'll lose lots of really flavorful fat and juices!). If you want something similar to a prime rib, you can cook the sirloin tip whole (as I do in the Mushroom-Rubbed Roast Venison au Jus on page 162).

When it comes to the loin (backstrap), I like cutting the end portion (near the hips) where the loin is much wider and slightly thinner into 4- to 6-inch segments for individual steaks. The narrow center and front portions of the backstrap near the neck can be cut into individual fillets. To do this, cut the meat into segments of equal length and width, then flip them on one cut side and tie them with kitchen twine to create tall, evenly round portions. These make for a beautiful "filet mignon" presentation . . . and if you substitute bacon for the twine, no one will complain.

roasting, and reverse searing. See page 267 for a list of recipes in this book that use each technique.

HOT AND FAST

Cooking tender cuts of meat from wild game animals is just like cooking their domestic counterparts, except the cook times are typically shorter. In meat, fat acts as an insulator or barrier of sorts, which slows down the transfer of heat to the center of the cut. Since wild game is very lean, heat travels through the meat much faster, making it easy to overcook if you're not very careful. Cooking tender cuts quickly over high heat ensures you're getting the flavor developed when meat is browned without overcooking it.

My favorite hot-and-fast cooking techniques are searing, pan-frying, and grilling. See page 267 for a list of recipes in this book that use each technique.

Spring

Renewal, Turkey Gobbles, Flower Blooms

TO ME, SPRING IS THE MOST BEAUTIFUL TIME OF YEAR. *The warmth of the sun and moisture from the clouds fulfill the season's promise of renewal and growth. I pay close attention to the transition from winter to spring; it comes and goes so fast that if I'm not careful, I'll miss it.*

Here in Texas, I consider it spring when I see the first bluebonnet bloom, a sign that tells me the thorny, low-growing dewberry vines will soon bear fruit. You might mark the arrival of the season differently wherever you live: by the budding of redbuds and dogwood trees in Arkansas; patches of ground covered in clusters of ramps in the Upper Midwest; buckets hung on tapped maple trees, waiting to be filled with sweet sap in Vermont.

No matter where you live, a sure sign of the changing season is the unmistakable gobble of a wild turkey searching for a hen to mate with. To most Americans, turkey is a cold-season food, likely because of the myth that it was served at the first Thanksgiving (it wasn't), but in the natural world, spring is when they make their presence known. The flavor of a wild turkey is richer and more developed than that of the Butterballs you can get from the grocery store year-round, and spring is the best season to hunt them.

Opportunities to forage are in full swing, and you'll find a variety of mushrooms (such as morels, oysters, and giant puffballs), wild alliums like ramps, beautifully curled fiddlehead ferns, and sunchoke roots ready to be dug up. Spring also brings a bounty of edible flowers—like spicy nasturtiums, oniony chive blossoms, tart redbuds, and delicate strawberry flowers—that add beauty and texture to any recipe. I particularly enjoy picking the blossoms that shoot up from the bolted winter brassicas and herbs in my garden—they're delicious.

Lettuce grows profusely in my garden in the cool weeks before the Texas heat kicks in. I do my best to hold on to those fleeting moments, and fresh crisp salads adorned with beautiful red radishes find their way into most of my meals. At the farmers' market, I look forward to seeing fennel and asparagus and other vegetables I haven't quite mastered growing myself.

Spring always seems too short, but I think that's a wonderful reminder of how important it is to slow down and smell (or eat) the flowers. ◆

Spring Ingredients

PRODUCE (GENERALLY)

Alliums: chives, spring onions

Artichoke

Asparagus

Celery

Edible flowers

English peas

Fennel

Herbs: perennials (chives, rosemary, thyme, oregano, sage); cool-season annuals/biennials (cilantro, cutting celery, dill, parsley, sorrel, tarragon)

Lettuce

Long-storing vegetables: dried beans, peas, corn, onions, garlic, potatoes

Overwintered greens: collards, kale, spinach

Overwintered roots: beets, carrots, parsnips, turnips

Radishes

Rhubarb

Sugar snap peas

FORAGED FOODS

Dandelion

Fiddlehead ferns

Maple sap (for syrup)

Mushrooms: morel, oyster, pheasant back

Nettles

Ramps

Spruce tips

Sunchokes

Dewberries (in parts of the southern US)

Wild onion and garlic

WILD GAME AND FISH

Wild turkey

Black bear

Wild hog

Light geese: snow, blue, Ross's

Freshwater fish: white bass, northern pike, walleye, trout, catfish

Saltwater fish (inshore and deepwater)

SOUTHERN US

New potatoes

Strawberries

Swiss chard

Note: *Overwintered vegetables* are frost-tolerant varieties planted in the fall and left in the ground over the winter. The process converts the starches in root vegetables and bitter greens into sugars, making them sweeter.

Cheesy Fried Morels with Rustic Tomato Sauce

SERVES 4 TO 6

Neutral oil, such as avocado or grapeseed, for frying

1 cup whole-milk ricotta cheese

¼ cup grated Parmesan cheese

2 garlic cloves, grated

¾ teaspoon coarse sea salt

8 ounces medium to large morels (2 large handfuls), cleaned, dried, and stemmed (see Prepping Morels, page 55)

2 slices plain white bread

1 cup plain bread crumbs

¼ teaspoon freshly ground black pepper

1 teaspoon dried oregano

1 teaspoon dried basil

3 large eggs

1 tablespoon whole milk or water

Tomato Sauce (recipe follows), warmed, for dipping

The idea for this recipe came about one evening when I was craving an upgraded, adult version of a mozzarella stick. I thought about the deliciously earthy flavor of morels and how their hollow insides would make the perfect vessel for stuffing. Choose wide morels that are large enough to pipe filling inside but small enough that they can be eaten in one or two bites, and avoid mushrooms with gaping holes, which will leak filling into the oil as they fry.

1 Fill a deep cast-iron skillet or wide pot with about 1½ inches of oil and heat over medium-high heat to 350° to 375°F. Line a plate with paper towels and set it nearby.

2 In a small bowl, stir together the ricotta, Parmesan, garlic, and ¼ teaspoon of the salt until well blended. Fit a piping bag with a large plain tip, stand it tip-down in a tall cup, and fold the top of the bag down around the outside of the cup (this makes it easier to fill). Transfer the ricotta mixture to the bag, then unfold the top and twist it to move the filling down toward the tip. Pipe the ricotta mixture into each mushroom, filling them completely without overstuffing them and setting them on a plate as you work.

3 This next step requires you to get a little crafty: Tear off very small pieces of the bread and use them to plug the hole in the end of each mushroom to keep the filling inside.

4 Spread the bread crumbs out on a large plate and stir in the remaining ½ teaspoon salt, the pepper, oregano, and basil. In a small bowl, beat together the eggs and milk. Dip each morel into the egg mixture, then roll it around in the bread crumbs until fully coated. Transfer the breaded morels back to the plate as you finish them and set aside until you're ready to fry.

5 Carefully drop the breaded morels into the hot oil in batches and fry for 2 to 3 minutes, until golden brown on the bottom, then flip and fry until golden brown on the second side, 1 to 2 minutes more. Turn the mushrooms and repeat until golden brown on all sides, then use tongs or a slotted spoon to transfer the fried morels to the paper towel–lined plate to drain.

6 Serve very warm, with the tomato sauce alongside for dipping.

Prepping Morels

Morels are known for their distinct honeycomb texture, but all those holes can harbor a lot of grit, and sometimes even insects, so you'll want to clean them really well before using them. Give them a quick rinse under cold running water, then drop them in a bowl of lightly salted cold water and soak for 10 to 15 minutes to remove debris and kill any bugs. Drain the morels and shake them dry, or use a salad spinner to extract as much excess moisture as possible, then carefully blot with paper towels before cooking.

Tomato Sauce

MAKES ABOUT 3 CUPS

Extra-virgin olive oil

½ small yellow onion, finely diced

2 garlic cloves, minced

1 (28-ounce) can crushed San Marzano tomatoes

½ teaspoon dried oregano

½ teaspoon dried basil

¼ teaspoon red pepper flakes

⅛ teaspoon sugar

Big pinch of coarse sea salt

1 bay leaf

Serve this sauce alongside Cheesy Fried Morels (opposite) for dipping or spoon it over pasta.

Heat a 2-quart saucepan over medium-high heat. Pour in enough olive oil to lightly coat the bottom of the pan and let it get hot, then add the onion. Cook, stirring occasionally, until the onion is soft and translucent, 4 to 5 minutes, then add the garlic and cook for 1 minute, stirring just once or twice. Stir in the tomatoes and season with the oregano, basil, red pepper flakes, sugar, and a heavy pinch of salt, then add the bay leaf. Reduce the heat to its lowest setting and simmer, stirring occasionally to keep things from sticking, until thickened, about 30 minutes. Remove from the heat and let cool, then transfer to a jar or other airtight container and store in the fridge for 3 to 5 days.

Caramelized Fennel Soup with Gruyère Toast

SERVES 4 AS A STARTER
OR SIDE

2 fennel bulbs

2 tablespoons unsalted butter, plus more for the toast

1 medium sweet onion, halved through the root end and thinly sliced

Coarse sea salt

1 teaspoon sugar

⅔ cup dry white wine, such as a sauvignon blanc

3 cups Vegetable Stock, homemade (page 259) or store-bought

1 teaspoon fennel seeds, coarsely crushed with a mortar and pestle or spice grinder

Freshly ground black pepper

4 slices sourdough bread, toasted

1 heaping cup grated Gruyère or Comté cheese

Note: Want to get the most out of your fennel? The fronds are great in salads—I add them by the handful! The stalks are excellent in a chunky stew like the Midwest Cioppino on page 234 or save them for making Vegetable Stock (page 259).

I've always hated anything with a licorice or anise flavor, so it took me a while to come around to fennel—and I didn't become a *true* fan until one chilly spring evening when I decided to roast it with some root vegetables. I was blown away by how the heat of the oven caramelized the natural sugars in the fennel, giving it a subtly sweet taste—and I've been hooked ever since.

That caramelization gave me the idea for this riff on French onion soup. In the classic recipe, the onions are cooked for over an hour, until they're dark in color and deeply caramelized—and a bit too rich for me. This "blond" version, with a lighter and brighter broth and just the right balance of sweet and sour from the addition of white wine, is the Betty to the traditionally "brunette" soup's Veronica. After a winter of heartier, comforting foods, this refreshing soup is perfect for chilly spring evenings like the one that inspired it.

1 Cut the stalks off the fennel bulbs, reserving a handful of the fronds (see Note). Halve the bulbs through the root and core them, then cut them into ⅛-inch-thick slices (use a mandoline, if you have one). Chop the reserved fronds and set aside for garnish.

2 Melt the butter in an extra-wide pot or Dutch oven over medium-high heat. Stir in the fennel and cook, stirring only occasionally, for 4 to 5 minutes, until the fennel begins to caramelize at the edges and soften. Add the onion, season with a few pinches of salt and sugar, and stir to incorporate. Cook, stirring only occasionally, for several minutes more, until the onion begins to soften and caramelize.

3 Cook, giving things a stir every once in a while, until the fennel and onion have cooked down to about half their original volume and everything is super soft and sticky, about 40 minutes, depending on how wide your pot is; reduce the heat as needed so nothing burns or dries out (but keep in mind that you need enough heat to caramelize the vegetables, so don't lower it too much). Don't let the onions reach a deep brown, as you would for traditional French onion soup—you're looking for a really nice medium-gold color, like a wheat field at sunrise.

4 Pour in the wine and stir, scraping up the browned bits from the bottom of the pot. If you lowered the heat, return it to medium-high

to cook off the alcohol, then cook until almost half the liquid has evaporated. Add the stock and fennel seeds, bring to a simmer, and cook for 15 to 20 minutes to concentrate flavors. The soup should have a sweet and savory fragrance. Taste and adjust the seasoning with more salt, if needed, and a few good cranks of pepper.

5 Preheat the broiler. Set four ovenproof soup bowls on a rimmed baking sheet and ladle the soup into the bowls. Top each with a piece of toast, sprinkle evenly with the cheese, and broil until the cheese has melted, 1 or 2 minutes. Garnish with the reserved fennel fronds and serve immediately.

Jammy Eggs with Smoky Fried Bread Crumbs and Spring Aioli

SERVES 2 TO 4

Fried Bread Crumbs
(makes about ½ cup)

1 tablespoon neutral oil, such as avocado or grapeseed

½ cup bread crumbs (panko or homemade; see Note)

1 teaspoon smoked paprika (optional)

Pinch of coarse sea salt

8 large eggs

½ cup Spring Aioli (page 249)

Flaky sea salt and freshly ground black pepper

Nasturtium leaves or flowers, for garnish (optional)

Note: Making your own bread crumbs using stale crusty bread is a great way to avoid food waste. Tear the bread into large chunks and spread them over a baking sheet. Toast in the oven at 300°F until fully dry, 20 to 30 minutes, tossing once halfway through. Allow them to cool. Working in batches, pulse the dry bread chunks in a food processor until you reach a coarse consistency. Store in an airtight container in the refrigerator for up to 2 weeks.

I could eat these jammy, custardy soft-boiled eggs every day. In fact, I pretty much do, enjoying them for lunch or in a number of different iterations as a snack several times a week. I like to think of this dish as a deconstructed deviled egg. The combination of crunchy bread crumbs and soft aioli is a perfect complement to the humble eggs. This can be served as a starter and is also great for a light brunch.

1 **Make the fried bread crumbs:** Heat a skillet over medium-high heat and add the oil. When the oil is hot, add the bread crumbs and cook, stirring occasionally, for a few minutes, until golden brown and crunchy. Remove from the heat and transfer to a paper towel–lined plate to drain and cool.

2 Pour the cooled bread crumbs into a small bowl and mix in the paprika (if using) and salt. Use immediately or store in an airtight container at room temperature and use within a couple of days.

3 Remove the eggs from the refrigerator just before cooking. Bring a large pot of water to a rolling boil over high heat. Fill a large bowl with ice and water to make an ice bath and set it nearby. *Very carefully* add the eggs to the boiling water (use a ladle or a large spoon to gently place them in the pot—don't drop them in!). As soon as all the eggs are in the water, set a timer for 6 minutes 30 seconds for large eggs or 6 minutes 45 seconds for extra-large eggs. When the timer goes off, immediately use a slotted spoon to transfer the eggs to the ice bath and let them cool slightly.

4 As soon as the eggs are cool to the touch, start peeling: Pull one egg out of the ice bath and lightly tap the shell on the counter to make little cracks, rotating the egg as you tap until the whole shell is fractured. Peel back a little piece of shell and grab the tissue between the egg and the shell—once you have ahold of that, you can practically peel the whole egg in one fell swoop. Set the eggs aside on a plate as you peel them. Just before serving, slice them in half.

5 Spread a generous swipe of the aioli on each plate, top with the halved jammy eggs, and scatter the fried bread crumbs over the top for crunch. Garnish with a pinch of flaky salt, a pinch of pepper, and some nasturtiums, if you like, then serve.

Charred Carrot Hummus with Pecan Dukkah

MAKES 3 CUPS

2 pounds carrots, scrubbed

6 tablespoons extra-virgin olive oil, plus more as needed

Kosher salt and freshly ground black pepper

1 head garlic

2 tablespoons tahini

Juice of 1 lemon (about 2 tablespoons), plus more if needed

½ teaspoon ground cumin

½ teaspoon ground coriander

⅛ teaspoon cayenne pepper, plus more if needed (optional)

Pecan Dukkah (page 181), for serving

Flatbread, such as naan or pita, cut into bite-size pieces or wedges and warmed, for serving

I have so much appreciation for the humble carrot and its ability to transform when roasted. One day after cleaning out the fridge, I found myself with a half-empty bag of carrots to use up. I decided to roast them but got a little distracted and forgot all about them—by the time I pulled them out, they were charred on the outside. This would've been a bummer, but I thought about the smoky flavor a little char lends to dips like Romesco Sauce (page 137) and opted to throw them in the blender instead of giving up on them. The result of that mistake was a complex-flavored carrot puree that was just begging for some garlic, lemon juice, and tahini. I love serving this with baked flatbread like naan or pita for dipping and topping it with a generous sprinkle of pecan dukkah, a full-flavored blend of nuts and toasted spices.

1 Preheat the oven to 400°F.

2 Cut the carrots in half crosswise where they begin to narrow, then slice the thicker portions in half lengthwise. You want them to cook as evenly as possible, so try to cut pieces that are roughly the same size. Lay the carrots in a large baking dish, coat them with 2 tablespoons of the olive oil, and season with a couple pinches of salt and some black pepper. Pour in ¼ cup water and cover with aluminum foil. Place the head of garlic on a separate piece of foil and drizzle it with olive oil. Bring the edges of the foil up and crimp tightly to enclose the garlic.

3 Slide the carrots and garlic into the oven. Roast the garlic for 30 minutes, until the cloves are golden and soft, then remove it from the oven and set aside to cool. Roast the carrots for 45 minutes, then remove the foil and roast for 15 minutes more, or until they're very tender when pricked with a fork and most of the water in the baking dish has evaporated. Switch the oven to broil on high and let the carrots char for 3 to 4 minutes, then give them a toss and broil for 3 to 4 minutes more. Remove from the oven.

4 Using a spatula, scrape the carrots and any juices from the baking dish into a high-powered blender or food processor. Squeeze the roasted garlic cloves out of their skins into the blender or food processor and add the remaining ¼ cup olive oil, the tahini, lemon juice, cumin, coriander, cayenne (if using), ½ teaspoon salt, and ¼ cup water. Puree until smooth. Add a little bit more water to thin the hummus to the desired consistency, if needed. Taste and season with additional salt as desired. The hummus should have a complex blend of sweet, tangy, and smoky flavors. If it tastes a bit flat, add another squeeze of lemon. If you want more heat, add another ⅛ teaspoon cayenne.

5 Scrape the hummus into a bowl and garnish it with a generous sprinkle of pecan dukkah. Serve with warm flatbread for dipping. Any leftover hummus will keep in an airtight container in the fridge for up to 5 days.

Mustard Pan–Fried Fish with Carrot Top Verde Sauce

Carrot Top Verde Sauce

½ cup packed minced carrot leaves or fresh parsley

1 garlic clove, minced

2 anchovy fillets, minced

1 tablespoon capers, coarsely chopped

¼ cup fresh lemon juice (from 1 to 2 lemons)

½ cup extra-virgin olive oil

Coarse sea salt

Fish

4 (6-ounce) thin white-fleshed fish fillets (1-inch thick or less), such as white bass, crappie, walleye, or catfish

Coarse sea salt and freshly ground black pepper

¼ cup spicy Dijon or Creole mustard

¼ cup all-purpose flour

Neutral oil, such as avocado or grapeseed

Flaky sea salt

Coating a delicate fillet of fish with mustard and then dredging it in flour is a classic way to prepare seafood. Like all good things, it's generational—I learned it from Travis, who learned it from his father, who learned it from his father! Around here, it's a common preparation for speckled sea trout, but it works equally well with other thin fillets of white-fleshed freshwater fish like white bass, crappie, catfish, and walleye. The fish should be floured lightly and cooked in a small amount of oil, not thickly coated and deep-fried—you're aiming for a beautiful, delicate golden crust.

This chunky verde sauce is one I make often with parsley to serve on top of a seared venison steak, and it works seamlessly with the tops from a bunch of carrots instead. Carrot greens have a similar flavor profile to parsley, but with just a teeny bit of extra spice. The leaves tend to be very coarse; when minced, they lend a beautiful texture to the sauce. Save any verde you have left over (or make a standalone batch!) to mix into grains by the spoonful, scoop on top of roasted potatoes, or serve with the schmaltzy roasted vegetables on page 88. It also doubles as a great salad dressing.

---

1 **Make the verde sauce:** In a medium bowl, combine the carrot leaves, garlic, anchovies, capers, and lemon juice. While whisking continuously, slowly drizzle in the oil in a thin stream and whisk to emulsify. Season with a couple pinches of salt and set aside until ready to serve. (This can be made several hours in advance and stored, covered, in the refrigerator. Whisk to re-emulsify before serving.)

2 **Make the fish:** Remove the fish from the refrigerator and season generously on both sides with coarse salt and pepper. Rub about 2 teaspoons of the mustard on each side of each fillet until fully coated. Set aside for about 30 minutes to come to room temperature before cooking.

3 Spread the flour in a shallow dish. Just before cooking, dredge each fish fillet in the flour to coat on both sides, then shake off any excess flour and set it aside on a plate.

4 Heat a large skillet over medium-high heat. Add enough oil to coat the bottom of the pan in a thin layer. When the oil begins to shimmer and slide across the pan like water, lay 2 fillets down (the oil should gurgle and sputter when the fish makes contact, but not scream—reduce the heat as needed if it does). Cook for 2 to 3 minutes, until a crust has developed on the bottom and the flesh about halfway up the side of the fillets turns opaque, then use a fish spatula to gently flip it. Cook on the second side for 2 to 3 minutes. The fish should be golden brown on both sides and flake easily with a fork. Be careful not to overcook it. Use the spatula to transfer the fish to a plate and repeat to cook the remaining fillets. Add more oil to the skillet between batches if needed and reduce the heat if the pan gets too hot.

5 Just before serving, season the fish with flaky salt and some pepper. Serve with a spoonful of the verde sauce on top and your preferred sides.

Perfect Pan-Roasted Turkey Breast with White Wine and Tarragon Sauce

SERVES 4

1½ to 2 pounds boneless, skinless turkey breast (thick upper portions only; see Getting the Most Out of a Wild Turkey, page 67)

Coarse sea salt and freshly ground black pepper

Neutral oil, such as avocado or grapeseed, or clarified butter

3 tablespoons unsalted butter, cubed

3 garlic cloves, minced

½ cup dry white wine

1 cup turkey stock or chicken stock, homemade (see page 257) or store-bought

4 teaspoons coarsely chopped fresh tarragon leaves

I shot my first turkey ever, a long-beard Rio Grande, among the wild bluebonnets in the beautiful hill country of Texas. I was guided by MeatEater's Janis Putelis, an expert in hunting and calling wild turkeys. Unlike most sit-and-wait turkey hunts, we spent a lot of time hiking and listening for males responding to our crow calls with what's known as a shock gobble. After several miles of walking, one finally did—but he was roughly 300 yards away across a river. I was pessimistic about our chances, but Janis didn't miss a beat. We hid behind his handmade turkey tail–feather fan, and after some back-and-forth dialogue that sounded like an old wooden chair being dragged across the floor (a language only turkey fanatics can understand), I realized this tom was committed. We watched him waddle down a steep hill, fly across the river, and then strut within shooting range. Within moments, I had him on the ground. It was the coolest turkey encounter I've ever had, and it put a special place in my heart for hunting, cooking, and eating these birds.

I usually get just one wild turkey each year, so I try to make the most of it. Pan-roasting is hands down my favorite cooking method for the tender breast meat, and I like to dry brine the meat at least a day in advance to ensure it stays juicy (to do the same, see Dry Brining on page 66). Starting the turkey on the stovetop creates a delicious brown crust, and the low oven temperature ensures the meat cooks evenly. The buttery white wine and tarragon sauce, made in the same pan you use to cook the bird, is the perfect complement to a spring turkey.

1 At least 30 minutes before cooking, pull the turkey breast out of the fridge to let it come to room temperature. Preheat the oven to 250°F.

2 Season the turkey with salt and pepper on both sides. Heat a large skillet over medium-high heat; the pan should be big enough to fit all the meat in a single layer without crowding (if it doesn't fit, work in batches). Add enough oil to lightly coat the bottom of the pan. When the oil is hot, lay the turkey in the pan—it should sizzle but not sputter and kick out oil; if it does, reduce the heat a bit. Cook for 2 to 3 minutes, until the bottom is a nice golden brown and lifts freely from the pan. Flip and cook for few minutes more to brown the second side.

continued

Dry Brining

You're probably most familiar with wet brining, where you submerge meat in a solution of salt and liquid. I use a wet brine for cuts of meat I plan to smoke, but for everything else, I prefer dry brining, which uses salt (and sometimes spices and herbs), but no liquid, to keep meat moist. To dry-brine, sprinkle the meat with coarse sea salt, using a little more than you'd typically use for seasoning, then set it on a plate or baking sheet and cover (if you're dry-brining a plucked bird and aiming for crispy skin, leave it uncovered to let the skin dry out). Slide it into the fridge and let it stand for at least 6 hours or up to 2 days before cooking. As the meat sits, you might notice liquid beading on the surface, probably prompting you to think, *But you said this helps* retain *moisture!* The salt *does* initially draw out some moisture, but that liquid dissolves the salt to form a brine, which the meat then reabsorbs. Unless the recipe specifies it, there's no need to rinse the meat after dry brining; just pat the surface dry with a paper towel before cooking.

3 Transfer the turkey to a baking sheet (set the skillet aside) and stick an oven-safe meat thermometer into the thickest part of the turkey, then immediately slide the baking sheet into the oven. Roast the turkey until it registers 150°F for a slightly blush-pink color (my favorite) or 155°F for well-done meat. This could take between 30 and 45 minutes, depending on the size of the breast, so keep an eye on the thermometer.

4 When the turkey is nearly finished, return the skillet to the stovetop, add a piece of the butter, and let it melt over low heat. Add the garlic and cook until slightly golden but not toasted, about 1 minute, then add the wine and stir, scraping up the browned bits from the bottom of the pan. Raise the heat, if needed, to bring the liquid to a low boil to burn off the alcohol and reduce the wine. Pour in the stock and bring to a boil, then cook until the sauce has reduced to between ⅓ and ½ cup (just eyeball it). Reduce the heat to medium-low, or low enough that the sauce is just barely simmering, and drop in the remaining butter—the sauce should be plenty hot, so just shake the pan to emulsify the butter as it melts and cook until the sauce is thick enough to coat the back of a spoon, but don't let it get so hot that the butter and oil separate. Taste and season with salt and pepper, then sprinkle in the tarragon.

5 Remove the turkey from the oven and transfer to a cutting board to rest for about 8 minutes. Thinly slice the turkey at a 45-degree angle against the grain and serve immediately with the sauce.

Getting the Most
Out of a Wild Turkey

Most people treasure wild turkey for its breast meat, and all too often I hear of hunters taking only the breast and leaving the rest of the bird behind. This is such a shame, because there are delicious uses for nearly the whole bird: The legs and wings are wonderful when cooked slowly, as they are in the Vinegar-Braised Turkey on page 70 or Coq au Vin on page 174. The heart and liver are great when fried with eggs, and the gizzard and neck can be used to make giblet gravy. The carcass makes an incredible stock. If you're lucky enough to shoot a mature tom (adult male), you might notice a strange yellow blob of tissue at the top of its chest. This is called the sponge, and it's used for storing fat during mating season. It looks frightening, but try throwing that in the stockpot, too, and trust me when I say it adds a delicious buttery texture and golden color!

The size of a wild turkey can vary drastically depending on its age, and a young male turkey (called a jake) is going to be much smaller than a tom. Despite their age, one thing they all have in common is that their breast meat is quite thick toward the top where it meets the wishbone and tapers to become dramatically thinner as it reaches the bottom. The problem with cooking the breast whole is that it doesn't cook evenly. To make the most out of this muscle, I like to cut it in half at a slight angle where it begins to thin out so I'm left with a thinner triangular portion from the bottom, which is perfect for making cutlets (like those on page 68) and a thicker portion from the top that's great for pan-roasting. The upper portion of one breast from a jake is usually enough to serve two people, so if you're planning to serve four, you'll need to use both breasts. Adult turkeys can be quite a bit bigger, and you may be able to serve three or four people per breast.

Turkey Cutlet with Morels and Asparagus

SERVES 2

Handful of morels or other wild mushrooms (4 to 6 ounces), cleaned and dried (see Prepping Morels, page 55)

1 pound boneless, skinless turkey breast, thin lower portions only (see Getting the Most Out of a Wild Turkey, page 67), or 2 boneless, skinless pheasant breasts or small chicken breasts

Coarse sea salt and freshly ground black pepper

2 teaspoons smoked paprika

1 cup all-purpose flour

1 cup panko bread crumbs

2 large eggs, beaten

Neutral oil, such as avocado or grapeseed, or clarified butter

4 tablespoons (½ stick) unsalted butter, cut into tablespoons

2 garlic cloves, minced

1 bunch asparagus, cut at a 45-degree angle into ¼-inch-long pieces

2 tablespoons fresh lemon juice (from 1 lemon)

2 tablespoons chopped fresh parsley

Shaved Parmesan cheese, for garnish

Chopped fresh chives, for garnish

Note: If it's not morel season, substitute other wild mushrooms, shiitakes, or creminis (baby bellas).

I found my first morel ever while turkey hunting in Tennessee with my friend Ryan Callaghan and chef Michael Hunter. It was a successful trip for everyone, and the outing enabled me to taste morels and turkey together—a treasured springtime pairing.

This recipe turns the thinner lower portions of the turkey breasts into crispy cutlets. I love the satisfying crunch of the panko coating and the way the fried turkey is balanced with lemony asparagus and garlicky morels. To double this recipe, use the thicker upper portions of the breast, cut in half horizontally, and simply double the other ingredients.

1 Slice the mushrooms (with their stems) crosswise into ¼-inch-thick rings or halve them lengthwise; you should have about 1 cup. Set aside.

2 Using a meat mallet, pound the meat to an even thickness. Season generously with salt, pepper, and the paprika.

3 Put the flour on one plate, the panko on another, and the eggs in a shallow bowl. Dredge a cutlet in the flour and shake off any excess, next dip it in the egg, letting any excess drip off, then dredge it in the panko to coat both sides. Set aside on a plate and repeat with the second cutlet.

4 Fill a large skillet with about ⅛ inch of oil and heat over medium-high heat. When the oil is hot, fry the breaded cutlets, leaving some room between them (work in batches if needed) for 2 to 3 minutes, then flip and cook for 2 to 3 minutes more, until golden brown on both sides. Transfer to a plate.

5 Pour out all but 1 tablespoon of the oil from the pan, add the morels, and toss to coat. Cook over medium-high heat, undisturbed, for 1 minute, then stir and drop in 1 tablespoon of the butter. Cook for another couple of minutes, then add the garlic and a pinch of salt. When the garlic is fragrant, add the asparagus and toss to combine. Add the lemon juice and remaining 3 tablespoons butter. Cook, stirring, until the asparagus is tender but still vibrant green and snappy; this shouldn't take more than a few minutes. Taste and season with salt, then finish with the parsley.

6 Serve the morels and asparagus with the fried turkey cutlets, garnished with shaved Parmesan and chives.

Vinegar-Braised Turkey with Fennel, Leeks, and Preserved Lemon

SERVES 4 TO 6

3 pounds turkey thighs, drumsticks, and/or wings (see Notes)

Coarse sea salt and freshly ground black pepper

Neutral oil, such as avocado or grapeseed, or schmaltz (rendered chicken fat)

2 tablespoons unsalted butter

1 small fennel bulb, bulb and stalks sliced ½ inch thick (reserve a handful of the fronds for garnish)

2 large leeks, sliced into ½-inch-thick half-moons and rinsed well to remove grit

¼ cup white wine vinegar

2½ to 3 cups unsalted turkey stock or chicken stock, homemade (page 257) or store-bought

½ teaspoon freshly ground white or black pepper

2 tablespoons golden raisins

1 teaspoon minced fresh rosemary

1 teaspoon minced fresh thyme

1 preserved lemon, or zest of 1 lemon

I often say comparing the flavor of a wild turkey to a farmed one is like comparing dark leg meat and white breast meat: the former is much more flavorful—and the flavor of the leg or wing meat of a wild bird is even darker and richer. That's because their muscles are constantly working—and that's also why they can be notoriously tough. Don't let that turn you off! After dry brining (see page 66) and a few (hands-off) hours of cooking low and slow, these parts of the bird become tender—and so delicious.

This recipe calls for braising in vinegar because I find that cooking turkey legs and wings in acidic liquids really brightens their overall flavor. The fennel and leeks are lovely aromatics that feel appropriate for spring, and they make a nice change from the standard mirepoix-based stews we've been eating all winter. And the little golden raisins, plump from the meaty juices they've absorbed? They're a delightful surprise to bite into! This hearty meal would be excellent on top of couscous, with some crusty bread to soak up the juices, or served alongside Schmaltzy Roasted Carrots, Celery, and Leeks (page 88).

Whenever you're cooking wild game, keep in mind that there's so much variability from animal to animal, so cooking times may vary. I've made this recipe with an old tom that took about 8 hours to break down, and with a young jake that took only 3 hours. Don't get discouraged if it's taking a while—that's just the turkey's way of getting the last laugh. Keep on braising!

1 Preheat the oven to 250°F.

2 At least 30 minutes before cooking, pull the turkey out of the fridge, season it generously with salt and pepper, and let it come to room temperature.

3 Heat a large (5- to 7-quart) Dutch oven over high heat. Add enough oil to lightly coat the bottom of the pot, about 2 teaspoons. When the oil is hot, add the turkey pieces in batches and cook until golden on all sides, about 4 minutes. Transfer the turkey to a plate as you finish each batch and continue with the remaining turkey.

Notes: Don't have turkey legs? You can use 2½ pounds of breast meat (the bones weigh at least ½ pound) or the leg meat from other birds, such as pheasant or chicken.

Pheasant and turkey drumsticks are unlike anything I've ever cooked with before. Their tendons harden like bones instead of tenderizing after a long cooking time. With some elbow grease and a pair of needle-nose pliers, you can remove most of the tendons while the meat is raw; just snap the foot at the joint (don't cut it—you don't want to break the tendons in half) and use the pliers to pull them out. If you struggle to remove them, they're easy to pull out of the meat after cooking.

4 Reduce the heat to medium, add the butter to the pot, and let it melt. Add the fennel and a few pinches of salt and stir to coat with the melted butter. Cook, stirring only occasionally, for about 10 minutes, until the fennel is soft and turning golden brown at the edges. Stir in the leeks and cook, stirring more frequently, for 5 minutes, or until the leeks resemble soft ribbons. Season with another pinch of salt. Pour in the vinegar and half the stock and stir, scraping up the browned bits from the bottom of the pot. Stir in the white pepper, raisins, and herbs.

5 Carefully nestle the meat in the pot (in an even layer, if you can), then add enough of the remaining stock to come halfway up the sides of the meat. Bring to a simmer, then cover with a lid and transfer to the oven. Braise for 3 to 4 hours for wild turkey, or 2 to 3 hours for domestic. When it's done, the meat should slide off the bone with no effort; if it doesn't, keep braising until it does (see Notes). Remove the pot from the oven and let the turkey rest uncovered for 20 minutes.

6 Meanwhile, remove and discard the pulpy flesh of the preserved lemon so you're left with just the yellow rind. Thinly slice the rind into ribbons, then cut the ribbons crosswise into ⅛-inch cubes.

7 Transfer the turkey from the pot to a cutting board and set aside until cool enough to handle. Set the pot with the braising liquid over a burner on its lowest setting to keep it hot. Add the cubes of lemon rind to the pot and stir to incorporate. Taste and season with salt and/or pepper, if desired.

8 Remove and discard the bones and hardened tendons from the turkey (this step is particularly important for wings and drumsticks, but it's optional for thighs; see Notes). The meat should naturally shred apart into smaller pieces, perfect for serving.

9 To serve, divvy up the meat among bowls and spoon the hot braising liquid and veggies from the pot over the top. Garnish with the fennel fronds and serve immediately.

Sous Vide Maple-Butter Wild Hog Loin

SERVES 4 GENEROUSLY

½ cup plus 1 tablespoon pure maple syrup

½ cup coarse sea salt

½ teaspoon Prague powder #1 (pink curing salt; see Note below; optional)

2 teaspoons whole peppercorns

1 bay leaf

6 cups ice-cold water

2 to 3 pounds trimmed wild hog or pork loin, halved (to make it more manageable)

Unsalted chicken stock, homemade (see page 257) or store-bought, as needed (optional)

Neutral oil, such as avocado or grapeseed

1 tablespoon finely diced shallot

2 sprigs thyme

1 small sprig rosemary

1½ teaspoons apple cider vinegar

2 tablespoons unsalted butter

Note: The curing salt adds a rosy color to the meat and a hint of hamlike flavor, but feel free to leave it out.

The Wild + Whole community is spread across the country, and I love hearing about each person's unique experience of the changing seasons. For my friends in the north, the symbolic transition from winter to spring is when they tap sugar maples and boil the sap into syrup. That sweet, delicious syrup is a wonderful complement to domestic pork and, of course, to the invasive wild hogs that run rampant across the South.

---

1   In a small pot, bring 2 cups water to a boil over high heat. Stir in ½ cup of the maple syrup, the salt, Prague powder (if using), peppercorns, and bay leaf and cook until the salt has dissolved, 2 to 3 minutes. Remove from the heat and pour the brine into a large bowl. Add the ice-cold water and let cool completely. Add the meat to the cooled brine (it should be submerged in the liquid; if not, add more water as needed) and cover the bowl. Refrigerate for 24 hours.

2   The next day, set up a water bath with an immersion circulator and heat the water to 145°F (see Note on next page).

3   Remove the hog loin from the brine and rinse it under cool water. Place the meat in a heavy-duty resealable bag and seal the bag securely. Drop the bag into the heated water bath and cook the meat for 30 minutes for every ½ inch of thickness (for example, a 2-inch-thick loin needs 2 hours of cook time). You can add an extra 30 minutes to ensure it's thoroughly cooked all the way through just to be on the safe side, but don't go too long, or the meat can get mushy.

4   Remove the meat from the bag and measure ¼ cup of the juices (if needed, add chicken stock or water to reach ¼ cup). Set the juices aside. Pat the loin very dry with paper towels.

5   Heat a large skillet over high heat. Drizzle in enough oil to lightly coat the bottom of the pan. When the oil is smoking hot, add the hog loin and quickly sear for about 1 minute on each side, until you have a golden brown crust. Use tongs to transfer the meat to a plate and set aside.

Note: Since wild hog can carry parasites that cause trichinosis (see page 40), it's important to cook every bit of the meat to at least 140°F, which will kill the parasite. Cooking sous vide ensures the meat reaches this temperature all the way through, and also keeps the meat very tender and incredibly juicy; searing after cooking sous vide will raise the internal temperature just a little bit more. If you substitute bear for hog, set your immersion circulator to 160°F.

6 Reduce the heat to medium and add the shallot, thyme, and rosemary. Cook, stirring occasionally, until the shallot is soft and starting to caramelize, 3 to 5 minutes. Pour in the reserved juices, the vinegar, and the remaining 1 tablespoon maple syrup and use a spoon to scrape up any browned bits from the bottom of the pan. Bring to a simmer, then add the butter and shake the pan to melt the butter and emulsify the sauce. Cook for a couple of minutes to thicken the sauce a little, then remove from the heat.

7 Slice the hog loin across the grain and serve immediately with the pan sauce.

Spring Farro Salad with Jammy Eggs

SERVES 4 AS A MAIN COURSE

2 cups uncooked pearled farro

Coarse sea salt and freshly ground black pepper

Creole Mustard Dressing

½ cup mayonnaise, store-bought or homemade (see page 249)

¼ cup Zatarain's Creole mustard or other spicy stone-ground mustard (see Note)

1 garlic clove, grated

Coarse sea salt

Salad

8 cups mixed spring greens

2 cups thinly sliced snap peas (sliced at an angle)

8 globe radishes, thinly sliced into matchsticks

4 scallions, thinly sliced

Coarse sea salt and freshly ground black pepper

8 jammy eggs (see page 58)

Handful of edible spring flowers (optional)

Shaved Parmesan cheese, for garnish

Flaky sea salt

Note: Zatarain's Creole mustard has a tangy zip that I love.

I love that I can grow lettuce in my garden from October to April, and since some farmers grow it hydroponically, it's available all year long. This is great for me because I could eat a salad every day of my life, but I take particular enjoyment in salads come spring.

When it comes to making a really great salad, especially one I plan to eat as a meatless meal, I follow three rules: First, make sure there are layers of different shapes, colors, and textures. Here I use two of spring's most irresistible vegetables, crunchy sugar snap peas and crisp radishes, and the flowering tops of bolted veggies. Second, pack in a variety of flavors. The farro in this dish adds just the right amount of heartiness, and I love the nutty taste you get from toasting the dry farro before cooking it, an optional but highly recommended step. Finally, always season the salad just as you would any other dish to bring all those flavors to life. A little flaky salt and cracked black pepper go a long way!

1 Heat a 3-quart saucepan over medium-high heat. Add the farro and let it toast for a minute, undisturbed, then give the pan a shake to redistribute the grains. Cook, shaking the pan occasionally, until the farro smells nutty, almost like popcorn, 3 to 4 minutes more. Transfer the farro to a colander, give a quick rinse to cool it off, then drain and return it to the pan. Pour in 8 cups water and bring to a boil over high heat. Reduce the heat to maintain a simmer, cover, and cook until al dente, about 25 minutes. Drain any remaining water and transfer the farro to a large bowl to cool, then season with salt and pepper.

2 **Meanwhile, make the dressing:** In a small bowl, whisk together the mayo, mustard, garlic, and 2 tablespoons water until combined. Season with a pinch of salt.

3 **Assemble the salad:** Stir a few spoonfuls of the dressing into the farro to coat, then add the mixed greens, snap peas, radishes, scallions, and more dressing to taste and toss to combine. (You might not use all the dressing; store the remainder in an airtight container in the refrigerator for up to 3 days.) Divide the salad among four individual bowls and top each with 2 jammy eggs and some edible flowers (if desired). Garnish with shaved Parmesan, a sprinkle of flaky salt, and some pepper and serve.

Hot Italian Venison Steak Sandwich

SERVES 4

4 (6-ounce) venison steaks (see Note)

Italian Dressing

2 tablespoons red wine vinegar

¼ cup plus 1 tablespoon extra-virgin olive oil

2 garlic cloves, minced

¼ teaspoon dried oregano

Coarse sea salt and freshly ground black pepper

Sandwiches

4 (½- to 1-inch-thick) slices focaccia or Italian bread

Neutral oil, such as avocado or grapeseed

Hot Italian Seasoning (page 254)

Bacon and Pickled Pepper Aioli (page 249)

2 cups shredded romaine lettuce

¼ medium red onion, or 1 shallot, thinly sliced

4 peperoncini peppers, sliced

Note: Any tender steak cut will work here, but I particularly enjoy using the thin flat-iron steak, or a cut with a strong grain line like the inside round (see page 49 for instructions on cutting the round into steaks). If you're substituting beef for venison, use flank steak (or fake it—see page 113) or skirt steak.

I love a good open-faced steak sandwich, which is how this recipe is meant to be served: piled high with thin slices of medium-rare venison and all the delicious toppings called for here. The steak is seasoned with an Italian spice blend similar to one used in hot Italian sausage, and the bread is slathered with an irresistible bacon aioli studded with pickled peperoncini. But what's really great about this recipe is how evergreen it is—it can be made any time of the year!

1 At least 30 minutes and up to 1 hour before cooking, pull the venison out of the fridge to let it come to room temperature.

2 **Make the dressing:** In a small jar, combine the vinegar, olive oil, garlic, and oregano. Season to taste with a few pinches of salt and some pepper. Cover and shake to emulsify. (Alternatively, whisk the dressing ingredients together in a bowl.) Set aside.

3 **Assemble the sandwiches:** Lightly toast the bread in a toaster or under the broiler; set aside.

4 Heat a large skillet over medium-high heat, then add about 1 tablespoon neutral oil. Season the steaks generously on all sides with Italian seasoning. When the oil is hot, lay the steaks down in the pan, leaving some room between each (work in batches, if necessary). Cook, undisturbed, for 1 to 2 minutes, then flip and cook for 2 minutes on the second side. Flip again (this helps the meat cook more evenly) and cook for a minute or two more, or to your desired doneness. (You can use the finger test on page 44 to check for doneness or use a meat thermometer and pull the steak when it reaches a couple of degrees below the target final temperature listed in the chart on the same page.) Transfer the steaks to a cutting board and let rest for 10 minutes, then slice them as thinly as you can at a 45-degree angle against the grain.

5 Spread some aioli over each slice of bread, then pile on the lettuce and top with some onion and peperoncini slices. Season with a small spoonful of the dressing, then arrange some of the sliced venison on top and season with a pinch of Italian seasoning. Eat immediately.

Shepherd's Pie with Any Greens Colcannon

SERVES 6 GENEROUSLY

3½ cups Any Greens Colcannon (page 86, with reserved cooking liquid) or mashed potatoes

3½ teaspoons coarse sea salt, plus more as needed

1 teaspoon freshly ground black pepper, plus more as needed

2 large egg yolks, beaten (if using colcannon; optional)

Neutral oil, such as avocado or grapeseed

2 pounds 80% lean ground venison or lamb

1½ teaspoons minced fresh rosemary

1½ teaspoons fresh thyme leaves

1 large yellow onion, cut into small dice (about 2 cups)

3 or 4 carrots, chopped into ½-inch pieces (about 2½ cups)

4 garlic cloves, minced

¼ cup tomato paste

¼ cup all-purpose flour

2 cups venison stock or chicken stock, homemade (see page 257) or store-bought

¼ cup Worcestershire sauce

1½ cups shelled fresh English peas (or use frozen peas)

2 tablespoons salted butter, cubed

Spring weather can be unpredictable, and you never know when a cold snap might hit. When it does, this hearty classic is ultra comforting.

I give traditional shepherd's pie an upgrade by swapping out the plain mashed potato topping for kale and leek colcannon, another classic Irish dish. It's an easy way to get in some extra veggies while still indulging in a satisfying meat-and-potatoes meal. If you prefer (or you're worried what kind of reception your kids will give the greens), feel free to use the creamy mashed potatoes on page 155 in place of the colcannon; just let them cool before topping the filling.

1 Preheat the oven to 375°F.

2 If using colcannon, add enough of the reserved cooking liquid to keep it moist (it will continue to dry in the oven), then taste, season with salt and pepper as needed, and let cool. Stir the egg yolks into the cooled colcannon until combined, then set aside.

3 Heat a Dutch oven or large (at least 12-inch) ovenproof skillet over medium-high heat. Add a tablespoon of oil and swirl to coat the bottom of the pan. When the oil is hot (you'll know by the way it slides across the pan like water and starts to shimmer but not smoke), add the ground meat and pat it down into an even layer. Cook, undisturbed, until the bottom is starting to caramelize and brown and the meat lifts freely from the pan without sticking, about 2 minutes. Flip the meat, break it up, and season with the salt, pepper, rosemary, and thyme. Stir to incorporate the seasonings, then cook until the meat is completely browned, about 5 minutes more. Transfer the meat to a bowl or plate and set aside.

4 Add a splash of oil to the pot if it looks dry, then add the onion and cook until golden in color and soft, 4 to 5 minutes. Add the carrots and cook for a few minutes more, until they start to soften, then add the garlic. You don't want the garlic or any of the browned bits at the bottom of the pot to burn, so reduce the heat to medium-low or low if needed. Stir in the tomato paste, then sprinkle in the flour and mix well. Cook, stirring often, for about a minute to toast the flour and cook out its raw flavor (the mixture will thicken and clump up, but that's okay). Pour in the stock and immediately start stirring really well to make sure there are no lumpy bits of flour and scraping the

Note: This recipe serves six people or more, depending on how hungry they are. If you're not cooking for a crowd, transfer half the filling to a freezer-safe baking dish (I use a 9-inch square foil pan) and top it evenly with half the potatoes. Dot with half the butter, then cover with plastic wrap and a layer of foil and freeze for up to 6 months. Assemble and bake the remaining portion as directed. When you're ready to cook the frozen portion, let it defrost in the fridge overnight, then remove the foil and plastic wrap and bake as directed.

bottom of the pot with your spoon to release those browned bits. The flour should take in the liquid pretty quickly. Return the ground meat to the pot, add the Worcestershire, and stir until everything is well blended into a very thick, gravy-like sauce (it will thin as it bakes). Stir in the peas, taste, and season with salt, if needed.

5 Use a spatula to scoop the potatoes evenly over the filling in the pot, then scatter the butter across the top. (If your skillet isn't large enough to accommodate the topping, lightly grease a 9 by 13-inch baking dish with oil, then transfer the filling to the baking dish before topping.) Cover with aluminum foil, pop it in the oven, and bake for 15 minutes, then remove the pot from the oven and switch the oven to broil on low. Remove the foil and slide the shepherd's pie back into the oven. Broil until the top is golden brown and the filling is bubbling around the sides, about 5 minutes. Remove from the oven and let cool before serving.

Rib Eye Steak with Radish Chimichurri and Strawberry Salad

SERVES 4

Steaks

4 (8- to 12-ounce) rib eye steaks or venison steaks (see Testing Steak for Doneness, page 44)

Neutral oil, such as avocado or grapeseed

Coarse sea salt and freshly ground black pepper

Radish Chimichurri

¼ cup fresh lemon juice (from 1 to 2 lemons)

½ cup neutral oil, such as avocado or grapeseed, plus more if needed

Coarse sea salt

Pinch or two of sugar (optional)

½ cup packed fresh parsley leaves, minced

½ cup packed fresh cilantro leaves, minced

4 red globe radishes, finely chopped

3 tablespoons finely chopped shallot

I've been making this spring-inspired chimichurri for years, and I love everything about it. The idea came to me one day in March when I found myself wanting to spice up some chimichurri, my favorite condiment for steak. I had no chiles on hand for the job, but my garden had produced an abundance of radishes, so in the spirit of using what I had, when I had it, the radishes found their way into the mix—to great success. I love how they lend a textural crunch and a peppery note, and as a bonus, if left to sit for a couple of hours, they'll give the chimichurri a beautiful pink color!

Not only do I love the flavors, but the process of making the dish brings so much joy to my day. I step outside and snip fresh cilantro and parsley, which grow well in cool spring weather, and look forward to subduing the pungency of the vibrant pink radishes with a simple squeeze of lemon. Finely chopping all the ingredients is very meditative for me, a way to unwind from a busy workday and create a beautiful, nourishing meal in the process.

I typically serve this chimichurri with venison steak, but on a recent trip to White Oak Pastures, a renowned regenerative farm in Bluffton, Georgia, a grass-fed and finished beef rib eye was the way to go.

1 **Cook the steaks:** Between 30 minutes and 1 hour before cooking, pull the steaks from the fridge to let them come to room temperature.

2 Find a cast-iron skillet big enough to fit two of the rib eyes (or use two pans and cook them all at the same time) and heat it over medium-high heat. Add enough oil to lightly coat the bottom of the pan. When the oil is hot, pat 2 of the steaks very dry with a paper towel, season generously with salt and pepper, and lay them in the pan. Sear, undisturbed, for 2 minutes, then flip and sear for 2 minutes on the second side. Flip again and repeat, cooking for a total of 2 to 4 minutes more. Aim for an internal temperature between 125° and 130°F for rare, 130° and 135°F for medium-rare, or 135° and 140°F for medium (if you're cooking venison steaks, refer to the chart on page 164). Transfer to a cutting board and repeat with the remaining steaks. Let the cooked steaks rest for 8 to 10 minutes before slicing.

To Serve

2 cups ripe strawberries, halved or quartered

Handful of nasturtium leaves and flowers (optional)

1 head butter lettuce, torn into pieces

3 **Just before serving, make the chimichurri:** Put the lemon juice in a medium bowl. While whisking continuously, slowly pour in the oil in a thin stream and whisk until emulsified. Season with a pinch of salt. Taste and add another tablespoon of oil, if desired. If the lemon juice is extra tart, add a pinch or two of sugar, if you like, and stir until it has dissolved. Add the parsley, cilantro, radishes, and shallot and stir to combine.

4 To serve, put the strawberries, nasturtiums (if using), and lettuce in a large bowl, add some of the chimichurri, and toss. Slice the steaks at a 45-degree angle against the grain and serve with the rest of the chimichurri and the strawberry salad alongside.

Pan-Fried Radishes and Rosemary

SERVES 4

2 bunches of radishes (about
1 pound total)

1½ tablespoons neutral oil, such as
avocado or grapeseed

1 teaspoon minced fresh rosemary

Coarse sea salt and freshly ground
black pepper

2 tablespoons salted butter

Flaky salt, for finishing (optional)

Have you ever thought about cooking radishes? I only ever imagined eating them raw in a salad or the chimichurri on page 80, but one spring I had an abundance of radishes in my garden and had to think outside the box to use them all.

Radishes make an amazing, more flavorful substitute for potatoes and can even develop crispy brown edges when cooked. I like to keep a portion of their little tails and green stems intact; I know it seems weird, but they get really crispy and crunchy in the pan. Radishes contain a surprising amount of water, so use a skillet large enough to leave a little room between each one when you add them to the pan—they shouldn't be piled on top of one another, or they'll steam as they release liquid instead of browning.

Serve these radishes as is, or on a bed of the tangy Parmesan and Horseradish Crème Fraîche on page 152.

1 Slice the radishes in half; if they're really large, cut them into quarters so you have even-size pieces.

2 Heat a large (14-inch) stainless-steel skillet over medium-high heat. Add the oil to the pan and when it shimmers, add the radishes, placing them cut-side down. Leave them alone for a few minutes, resisting the urge to mess with them, until they stop releasing steam and you start to smell them browning. Take a little peek under one of the radishes to see what the bottom looks like. If it's starting to turn golden, give the pan a really hard shake to move the radishes around, then add the rosemary, a couple pinches of coarse salt, and a good crank of pepper.

3 Cook, stirring or shaking the pan every minute or two, for a good 15 to 20 minutes. You want to hear a really nice sizzle but no popping from the oil, so reduce the heat as needed to keep the radishes from burning. In the last 5 minutes of cooking, drop in the butter and let it melt. When it starts to foam, give the radishes a toss to coat them with the butter, then cook until the butter is browned and the radishes are cooked through. You should be able to pierce the radishes easily with a fork, but they should still have some firmness and texture; you don't want them to be mushy.

4 Pull the pan from the heat, sprinkle with a little flaky salt, if desired, and serve.

Radishes, the Spice of Life

The first year I grew radishes, I must've planted fifty seeds, and to my delight (and—let's be honest—surprise), all of them germinated and grew to full size. But when I pulled up my first one and bit into it, it had more eye-watering horseradish flavor than the gentle bite of a store-bought red radish. What I didn't know at the time was that a high soil temperature or inconsistent watering can make radishes extra spicy, and I had planted mine a little bit late. That season, I learned that homegrown vegetables, like wild game, don't always taste like their counterparts from the grocery store; they vary greatly in flavor and texture based on their growing conditions. And instead of throwing out those extra-spicy radishes, I found creative ways to use them.

Pickle: Pickling will tame their pungency and heat. I also love soaking diced radishes in lime juice to use as a substitute for jalapeño in pico de gallo.

Cook: You can tone down the heat by *applying* heat! I love pan-frying radishes with a good dollop of clarified butter or duck fat, then adding some fresh woody herbs, such as rosemary or thyme, and a good pinch of salt and pepper.

Grate: If your radishes are as spicy as fresh horseradish, why not use them as a substitute for it? I like to grate radishes and add the vibrant pink pulp to mayo or sour cream to use as a sandwich spread or condiment for steak.

Crispy Smashed Potatoes with Dill and Capers

SERVES 4

2 pounds baby red or gold potatoes

Coarse sea salt

¼ cup extra-virgin olive oil

3 tablespoons capers, drained

Freshly ground black pepper

1½ cups crème fraîche

2 garlic cloves, grated with a Microplane

Zest and juice of 1 lemon

1½ tablespoons chopped fresh dill

1½ tablespoons thinly sliced fresh chives

Smoked salt (optional, but highly recommended)

A silky bowl of mashed potatoes has its place, but this recipe is all about the crunch factor. Getting a potato crispy on the outside doesn't have to mean it's dry and mealy on the inside—I want the best of both worlds, so I cook potatoes in boiling water until ultrasoft, then smash them flat and crisp them up in a hot oven. Smashing the potatoes but leaving them mostly intact creates lots of craggy edges (in the spring, baby potatoes are the perfect size for this), and after roasting, those crunchy little bits give the dish great texture and lots of flavor! The dill, capers, and crème fraîche send this recipe over the top. It's the perfect side to just about anything, but I particularly love it with the Mustard Pan-Fried Fish with Carrot Top Verde Sauce on page 62.

1 Put the potatoes in a large pot and add water to cover. Bring to a boil over high heat, then season the water with a few heavy pinches of salt. (You want the water to taste like the ocean, kind of like you do when cooking pasta—potatoes are very bland and can use the salt.) Cook until the potatoes are fork-tender, about 25 minutes.

2 Preheat the oven to 400°F.

3 Drain the potatoes and transfer them to a large bowl. Add the olive oil and capers and toss to coat, then transfer the potatoes to a baking sheet. Use a potato masher or the back of a spatula to smash the potatoes flat against the pan. The flatter they are, the crispier they'll get, but don't overdo it—they should remain mostly intact. Spoon any capers and oil remaining in the bowl over the potatoes and season with pepper. Roast for 20 minutes, or until the edges of the potatoes are crispy and browned.

4 Meanwhile, in a small bowl, stir together the crème fraîche, garlic, lemon zest, lemon juice, and 1½ tablespoons water. Season with a pinch of salt and set aside.

5 Remove the potatoes from the oven and garnish with the dill, chives, and some smoked salt, if desired. Serve with a dollop of the garlicky crème fraîche.

Any Greens Colcannon

SERVES 4

2 pounds starchy potatoes, such as russet, peeled or not (cook's choice) and coarsely chopped

Coarse sea salt

½ cup (1 stick) unsalted butter

1 leek, halved lengthwise, thinly sliced into half-moons, and rinsed well to remove grit

Freshly ground black pepper

½ bunch kale or other greens (see headnote), leaves stemmed and chopped (about 1 cup)

Note: When you're adjusting the consistency with the reserved cooking liquid, keep in mind that if you're using the colcannon to top the shepherd's pie on page 78, it will dry and thicken a bit in the oven when the pie is baked.

No matter what season you're in, this recipe is a wonderful way to use greens. As they're gently sautéed in butter, the deep green leaves of kale, collards, or other greens you don't typically think of as tender soften into silky ribbons. I call for kale here, but you can swap it out for what you have—try Swiss chard, spinach, collards, or mustard greens, or, if you have a garden, practice root-to-stem cooking by using the greens or leaves of many varieties of vegetable, including carrot tops, broccoli leaves, radish greens, turnip greens, okra leaves, even the broad leaves that grow on the vine with green beans. Just remove any tough stems and chop the leaves as directed.

This dish is also a great way to explore the world of alliums, the plant family that includes pungent roots like onions and shoots like scallions and chives. In the spring, try wild ramp stems and leaves, or use spiraled garlic scapes. The combinations are endless!

1 Put the potatoes in a large pot and add water to cover. Bring to a boil over high heat. When the water comes to a boil, add a few pinches of salt and reduce the heat to maintain a simmer. Cook until the potatoes are very tender when pierced with a fork, about 10 to 15 minutes. Use a slotted spoon to remove the potatoes from the pot (do not discard the cooking liquid) and pass them through a potato ricer into a large bowl. (Alternatively, mash them with a potato masher.) Reserve about ½ cup of the cooking liquid and drain the rest. Wipe out the pot and set it on the stove over medium heat.

2 Drop 2 tablespoons of the butter into the hot pot and let it melt (I like to dice the butter first so it melts faster and more evenly, especially if I'm using it straight from the fridge). When the butter starts to foam and bubble, add the leek and stir to coat. Cook gently until the leek resembles soft, shiny ribbons and you can smell its delicate oniony aroma, about 4 minutes. Season with a sprinkle of salt and a pinch of pepper, then stir in the kale and let it cook down until it's ultrasoft, about 5 minutes more.

3 Remove from the heat and stir in the mashed potatoes and remaining 6 tablespoons butter. If the potatoes seem dry, pour in ¼ cup of the reserved potato cooking liquid and stir until incorporated (see Note). Taste and season with more salt and pepper as needed, then serve.

Schmaltzy Roasted Carrots, Celery, and Leeks

SERVES 4 GENEROUSLY

4 large carrots

3 leeks

6 celery stalks

2 tablespoons schmaltz (rendered chicken fat) or duck fat, melted

Coarse sea salt and freshly ground black pepper

6 sprigs thyme

2 sprigs rosemary

¼ cup chicken stock, homemade (see page 257), or store-bought, or water

Juice of ½ lemon (about 1 tablespoon)

This side dish was developed entirely from a desire to prevent food waste. I would buy carrots, celery, and leeks to use in stock, but I never seemed to use up the whole bunch, and eventually, they'd be forgotten, left to languish at the bottom of the crisper.

One evening, I found myself with some rendered duck fat from a gorgeous specklebelly goose I had shot in Arkansas. I had made stock earlier that week and was determined not to waste the extra vegetables, so I tossed them in a roasting pan, poured the rendered fat over them, and roasted them. It was such a simple side dish but turned out to be amazing—perfectly rich from both the fat and the deep flavors drawn out of the vegetables by the high heat of the oven.

This dish would be delicious as a side for roast chicken or sautéed fish. And while you can make it year-round, I particularly like it in the cooler months when the ingredients are truly in season—the celery will be crisp instead of fibrous and stringy, the carrots sweeter, and the leeks more flavorful.

1 Preheat the oven to 425°F.

2 To make sure the vegetables roast evenly, you'll need to slice them into pieces of roughly the same size: Cut the carrots in half crosswise (or where they begin to thicken toward the top), then slice the thicker top portions in half lengthwise (quarter them if they're really thick). Slice the leeks in half lengthwise and rinse them under cool water, fanning the layers a bit to remove any grit but keeping them intact. Pat dry. Cut the celery stalks in half crosswise.

3 Place all the vegetables in a large (at least 9 by 13-inch) roasting pan or baking dish. Pour the melted fat all over the vegetables, being sure to coat the bottom and sides of the pan. Sprinkle with a few generous pinches each of salt and pepper. Scatter the thyme and rosemary sprigs over the top and pour the stock and lemon juice into the bottom of the pan. Roast the vegetables, giving them a stir once or twice, for 45 minutes to 1 hour, until their edges are browned and caramelized; the carrots should be very soft.

4 Remove the vegetables from the oven and serve warm.

Strawberry and Red Wine Shortcakes with Vanilla Whipped Cream

SERVES 6

Strawberry and Red Wine Jam

2 cups coarsely chopped strawberries (1 pint)

¼ cup granulated sugar

¼ cup dry red wine

1 tablespoon cornstarch

Vanilla Whipped Cream and Macerated Strawberries

2 cups cold heavy cream

½ teaspoon pure vanilla extract

2 tablespoons confectioners' sugar, plus more as needed

1 pint strawberries, sliced

1 tablespoon granulated sugar

When I visited White Oak Pastures, a regenerative farm in Georgia, for an episode of *Wild + Whole: Sourced*, it was April, and the strawberry fields were popping! I asked Will Harris, the farm's founder, which ingredient produced on the farm he wished people would eat more of. His answer? Fat.

Cooking with animal fats like lard appeals to me because it means less of the animal is going to waste, but it also just tastes great. You can buy rendered lard in jars, but it's more economical to buy pork fat in bulk and render it yourself (see page 261). In this recipe, you can use bear, wild hog, or duck fat instead, as long as it was rendered over low heat and is pure white when chilled (avoid beef tallow, as the flavor is a little too "meaty"). In a pinch, European-style butter will work.

I developed this recipe to pay homage to the beautiful berries that were coming into season during my visit to White Oak Pastures, and to incorporate lard from the farm's pigs. Leaf lard is a dream to bake with—I've made biscuits with butter many times, but once I switched to lard, there was no turning back. Lard makes the biscuits in this recipe slightly crumbly in just the right way, and its savory quality keeps desserts from being overly sweet. Do yourself a favor and indulge in a few of these while strawberries are at their peak!

1 **Make the jam:** In a small saucepan, combine the strawberries, granulated sugar, and wine. Bring to a simmer over medium-high heat, then reduce the heat to low. Gently mash the strawberries and cook for about 5 minutes, until the berries are broken up into large chunks and the liquid in the pan is saucy.

2 In a small bowl, stir together the cornstarch and 1 tablespoon water, then pour the mixture into the pan and stir to incorporate. Cook for a minute or two to thicken, then remove from the heat. Transfer the jam to a jar or other airtight container. Let cool completely before using or storing; it will thicken as it cools. (The jam can be made a couple days in advance and stored in the refrigerator.)

3 **Make the whipped cream and strawberries:** In a large bowl, whisk the cream, vanilla, and confectioners' sugar until it holds soft peaks. Add more sugar to taste, if desired. Set aside. (If you won't be using

recipe and ingredients continued

Biscuits

5 tablespoons rendered lard

2 cups all-purpose flour, plus more for dusting

3 tablespoons granulated sugar

4 teaspoons baking powder

½ teaspoon baking soda

½ teaspoon kosher salt

½ cup cold heavy cream, plus more for brushing

½ cup cold whole milk

Confectioners' sugar, for dusting

Strawberry flowers, for garnish (optional)

it immediately, store in an airtight container in the refrigerator for up to 1 day.)

4 In a large bowl, stir together the strawberries and granulated sugar. Set aside to macerate for at least 30 minutes, or transfer to an airtight container and refrigerate for up to 24 hours before using.

5 **Make the biscuits:** Preheat the oven to 450°F. Line a baking sheet with parchment paper or a silicone baking mat. Place the lard in a small bowl and freeze it for 15 to 20 minutes while the oven is heating.

6 In a large bowl, whisk together the flour, granulated sugar, baking powder, baking soda, and salt. Scrape the chilled lard into the bowl and use a fork or pastry cutter to cut it into the flour mixture until it forms small, pebble-size pieces, then use your fingers to roll the fat and flour together until the mixture has the consistency of coarse sand. Pour in the cream and milk and stir just a handful of times, until the dough comes together in a shaggy ball.

7 Turn the dough out onto a flour-dusted surface and form it into a mound. Dust the top with a little flour and use your fingers to very gently pat it out to about 1 inch thick. It doesn't need to be a smooth layer—the dough should remain lumpy and barely hold together. Use a bench scraper to fold the dough in half from right to left, then pat it out again, resisting the urge to make it pretty—the secret to tall and fluffy biscuits is not overworking the dough! Fold it in half again from the bottom up. Repeat this process once more, folding from left to right, then from the top down (this creates layers in the biscuits).

8 Pat the dough out to a thickness of 1 to 1½ inches, then use a biscuit cutter to cut out 6 tall shortcakes. Place them on the prepared baking sheet, arranging them close together so they're touching; this will help them rise. Brush the tops with a little cream. Bake for 12 to 14 minutes, until the biscuits are cooked through and their tops are golden. Remove from the oven and let cool on the pan.

9 To assemble the shortcakes, cut each biscuit in half horizontally. Layer the bottom half with some of the strawberry jam, a spoonful of the macerated strawberries, and finally some whipped cream, then finish with the top half of the biscuit to make a sandwich. Dust with confectioners' sugar, garnish with fresh strawberry flowers, if you feel so inclined, and serve.

Balsamic Dewberry Hand Pies

MAKES 18 TO 20 HAND PIES

Balsamic Dewberry Compote

2 heaping cups (12 ounces) fresh or frozen dewberries, blackberries, or raspberries

6 tablespoons granulated sugar

2 tablespoons balsamic vinegar

1½ tablespoons cornstarch

Hand Pies

2 large eggs

1 tablespoon whole milk

1 recipe All-Purpose Pie Dough (page 260)

All-purpose flour, for dusting

Superfine sugar, for sprinkling

Between Easter and Mother's Day, you'll find me out at Travis's family's ranch, picking wildflowers and wild dewberries. Dewberries are very similar to blackberries in looks and taste, and you'll find them sprawling low to the ground across sunny fields or growing like weeds along roadsides. As they mature, the small green berries turn red, and eventually take on a dark purple hue. The best berries are plump, with skin that's lost its shininess—and their juice will stain your fingers!

Dewberries are versatile, but my favorite place to use them is in this jam-like compote. I use it to fill these hand pies and to top Sweet Corn Ice Cream (page 143), stir it into a bowl of granola and yogurt, or spread it inside a biscuit. What makes this compote special is the surprising addition of balsamic vinegar, which gives it a sweet and sour flavor that reminds me of Italian agrodolce. It's a perfect complement to the rich, almost savory pie dough.

1 Preheat the oven to 425°F with racks in the upper and lower thirds. Line two baking sheets with parchment paper or silicone baking mats.

2 **Make the compote:** In a small saucepan, combine the berries, granulated sugar, and vinegar and stir well, but resist the urge to smash the berries; the heat will break them down naturally as they cook. Cook over medium heat, stirring occasionally and reducing the heat if needed to ensure that nothing sticks or burns in the bottom of the pot, for 5 to 8 minutes, until the sugar caramelizes and the liquid coats the back of a spoon.

3 In a small bowl, stir together the cornstarch and 3 tablespoons water to make a smooth slurry, then gently stir it into the berry mixture, mixing well to incorporate. Cook for 1 minute more, then remove from the heat and let cool. The mixture should thicken to a jam-like consistency. At this point, the compote can be used immediately to fill the hand pies or stored in an airtight container in the refrigerator for up to a week to use as you like.

4 **Make the hand pies:** In a small bowl, beat the eggs and milk to create an egg wash. Set aside.

5 Pull one disk of the pie dough from the fridge. On a flour-dusted surface, roll out the dough into a round about ⅛ inch thick. Use a large (5-inch) round cookie cutter or the rim of a red wine glass to cut out rounds of dough. Gather the scraps and form them into a ball; if the dough starts sticking, chill it for 15 minutes, then roll out and cut more rounds of dough. Repeat with the second ball of dough. You should have 18 to 20 rounds of dough total.

6 Spoon about 1 tablespoon of the compote (don't overdo it!) into the center of each dough round, leaving the edge uncovered. Brush the bottom edge of the dough with egg wash, then fold it up to meet the top edge and form a half-moon. Press the edges together to seal and push out air, much like you would if you were making ravioli, then use a fork to crimp the rounded edge of the half-moon. With a sharp knife, cut a small slit in the top of each hand pie to vent steam. Brush the top with egg wash, then sprinkle with superfine sugar. Place the hand pie on one of the prepared baking sheets and repeat with the remaining dough and filling.

7 Bake for 15 to 18 minutes, until the tops are golden brown. Serve warm.

Summer

Abundance, Sunshine, Salt Water

FOR MANY PEOPLE, MYSELF INCLUDED, SUMMER *represents abundance in the garden. You might be jealous to hear that my growing season begins early here in South Texas, while many parts of the country are still shaking off spring's chill. In April, you'll find me leaning over squash plants, watching bees move from flower to flower, and harvesting my first round of vegetables—tender green beans.*

Tomatoes, the culinary darlings of summer, are sort of divas. They're heavy feeders and need more attention and care than other plants. Pinching suckers, pruning lower leaves, supporting with trellises, killing hornworms—it's all part of your investment. But once you taste your first bite of that homegrown tomato, be it a wedge of Green Zebra tucked into a zesty panzanella or a slice of Cherokee Purple on top of a BLT, you realize it's worth the effort.

When I'm not in the garden, you'll find me hiking around the Pineywoods of East Texas looking for chanterelles. These special mushrooms begin to fruit as the weather warms and the rains begin, usually in June. Their freshness fades within days of picking, and if they aren't eaten right away, their texture degrades and they become flavorless. I'm always preserving foods, so this immediacy is hard for me. I think it's nature's way of nudging me to embrace the chanterelles' short life span by enjoying them in a beautiful meal. Their perishability forces me to live in the present moment, not plan ahead.

As the season progresses, the days get longer and hotter—*much* hotter. To find relief, Travis and I head south to the Gulf Coast, where we turn our faces into the salty ocean breeze as we fish the shallow bay waters. Most of my time is spent sitting on a platform at the bow of our boat, scanning the water for copper-colored redfish, while Travis stands on an even taller platform and poles us around (it's kind of like a gondola ride, but a little less romantic). We keep a net on the boat, because we never know when we might float across a whopper of a blue crab, a perfect way to round out our sea-to-table meal. ◆

Summer Ingredients

PRODUCE (GENERALLY)

Alliums: garlic, garlic scapes, onion

Berries

Cowpeas

Cucumbers

Edible flowers

Eggplant

Figs

Green beans

Herbs: perennials (chives, rosemary, thyme, oregano, sage); warm-season annuals (basil, mint, lavender)

Melons

Okra

Peppers

Potatoes

Shelling beans

Squash (and squash blossoms)

Stone fruits

Sweet corn

Tomatoes

NORTHERN US

Beets

Brassicas: broccoli, cabbage, cauliflower

Carrots

Herbs: cool-season annuals (dill, cutting celery, cilantro, parsley, tarragon, sorrel)

FORAGED FOODS

Wild berries: huckleberry, elderberry, raspberry, blackberry, mulberry, service berry

Mushrooms: chanterelle, chicken of the woods, porcini, lion's mane, lobster

Nopales (cactus paddles)

Prickly pear

Purslane

WILD GAME AND FISH

Exotic (non-native) game animals: axis deer, nilgai, wild hog

Crustaceans: crab, lobster, shrimp

Freshwater fish: white bass, northern pike, walleye, trout, catfish

Saltwater fish (inshore and deepwater): redfish, salmon, snapper, striped bass, mahi-mahi, rockfish, halibut

Ceviche with Watermelon

SERVES 6 TO 8 AS A STARTER,
OR 4 AS A MAIN COURSE

1 pound skinless firm-fleshed saltwater fish fillets (see Note), cut into ½- to 1-inch pieces

½ small red onion, thinly sliced into half-moons

1½ cups fresh lime juice (from about 12 limes), plus more as needed

1 cup finely diced seedless watermelon

1 cup sliced cherry tomatoes

1 small jalapeño, finely diced

1 large Hass avocado, diced

3 tablespoons minced fresh cilantro

Coarse sea salt

Tortilla chips or plantain chips, for serving

Note: When choosing fish for this recipe, be sure to pick the best quality fresh or flash-frozen fish possible. Because I live near the Gulf Coast, I make this recipe with red drum (redfish) often (after it's been frozen for at least 30 days, since it's being served raw), but any firm-fleshed saltwater fish, such as snapper, mahi-mahi, halibut, rockfish, tuna, or wahoo, will work. You can also use peeled cooked shrimp.

Those of you who live in the South know how the heat of summer can feel unbearable. My remedy? This unconventional ceviche, influenced by the foods of the region. I use saltwater fish (or cooked shrimp) and hit up my favorite roadside stand in Hempstead, Texas, a small town where the sandy-loam soil produces some of the best watermelons in the country. The fruit adds just enough sweetness to counterbalance the acidity of the lime-soaked fish and onions. Serve it cold as a refreshing appetizer, especially on a hot day, or make it a main course with some warm tortillas and rice.

1 Place the fish and onion in a large nonreactive bowl and pour in the lime juice. Cover and refrigerate for at least 30 minutes and up to 4 hours, stirring occasionally to ensure all the fish is evenly covered in the lime juice. The acid in the citrus will cure the fish, essentially cooking it.

2 Drain off and discard the lime juice. Add the watermelon, tomatoes, jalapeño, avocado, cilantro, and a couple pinches of salt to the bowl with the fish and stir to combine. Serve immediately with chips or crackers.

Black Bean, Corn, and Tongue Empanadas with Cilantro-Lime Crema

MAKES SIXTEEN TO EIGHTEEN
6-INCH EMPANADAS

Cilantro-Lime Crema

1 cup Mexican crema or sour cream

Zest and juice of 1½ limes

½ jalapeño, chopped

½ bunch cilantro, chopped

1 garlic clove, peeled

Filling

2 or 3 deer tongues; 1 elk, nilgai, or pig tongue; or ½ cow's tongue

Beef tallow or neutral oil, such as avocado or grapeseed

1 teaspoon smoked salt

¼ teaspoon freshly ground black pepper

½ teaspoon dried oregano

¼ teaspoon ground cumin

½ cup finely diced red onion

1 serrano pepper, minced

Kernels from 1 ear corn, or ½ (14-ounce) can corn kernels, drained

Tongue is a rich and fatty piece of meat but eating an odd cut like this can be a mental challenge for some. I tell people who are new to cooking with tongue to prepare it as a starter. It's much easier to try something if you're just getting a taste, instead of making a whole meal out of it.

Small bites are also a great way to stretch something you've only got a little bit of. I love lengua (tongue) tacos, but no matter how delicious deer tongues are, there's no denying that you're investing a good chunk of time to slow-cook and peel them, only to end up with enough meat for a couple of tacos. I enjoy the process, especially when I have a beverage in hand and some good tunes playing, and pairing the tongue with black beans, sweet corn, and lots of cheese to fill empanadas ensures everyone gets a taste.

1 **Make the crema:** Combine all the crema ingredients in a small food processor and pulse until smooth. Transfer to an airtight container and refrigerate until ready to serve. (It will keep for up to 1 week.)

2 **Cook the tongues for the filling:** Using a vegetable brush, scrub the tongues clean under cool running water. Place them in a large pot and add enough water to cover, then bring to a boil over high heat. Reduce the heat to its lowest setting and simmer for 4 to 6 hours, until the tongues are very tender when pricked with a fork. Transfer to a cutting board and set aside until just cool enough to handle—the tongues are easiest to peel while they're still quite warm.

3 Use a knife or your fingers to peel away the skin covering the tongues. The skin can turn rubbery, and it's not always easy to remove, so practice patience. After peeling, you may notice some bumps on the surface of the meat—these are taste buds (they're perfectly safe to eat, but you can use a knife to shave them off if you find them unappealing). Coarsely chop the meat into ½-inch pieces or finely shred it. You should have 1 to 1½ cups of meat. (The tongues can be cooked a day in advance and stored in an airtight container in the refrigerator until needed.)

recipe and ingredients continued

2 garlic cloves, minced

Juice of 1 lime

½ cup canned black beans, drained and rinsed

1½ cups shredded queso Oaxaca or Monterey Jack cheese

2 large eggs, beaten, for egg wash

1 recipe Empanada Dough (page 260; see Notes)

All-purpose flour, for dusting

Notes: You can cook, peel, and chop the tongue and make the empanada dough and cilantro-lime crema several hours or up to a day in advance. Store everything in separate airtight containers in the fridge.

Don't have tongue? Any cooked shredded or ground meat will work just fine in its place—you'll need 1 to 1½ cups.

In a pinch, you can substitute All-Purpose Pie Dough (page 260) for the empanada dough, or use about 2 packages of thawed frozen puff pastry dough.

4 **Finish the filling:** Heat about 1 tablespoon tallow in a medium skillet over high heat. When the tallow is hot, add the meat and cook, undisturbed, for 1 to 2 minutes, until browned on the bottom, then use a metal spatula to flip the meat and cook for a couple of minutes more, until crispy and browned like fried carnitas. Season with the smoked salt, black pepper, oregano, and cumin. Transfer to a large bowl, being sure to scrape the browned bits from the bottom of the pan into the bowl as well; set aside.

5 Reduce the heat to low and heat a couple teaspoons of tallow in the skillet. Add the onion and cook until soft and translucent. Add the serrano, corn, and garlic and gently sauté for 3 to 5 minutes, until soft. Pour in the lime juice and let it lift all the delicious browned bits from the bottom of the pan. Remove from the heat and transfer the vegetables to the bowl with the meat. Let cool completely, then stir in the beans and cheese.

6 **Assemble the empanadas:** Preheat the oven to 400°F. Line a baking sheet with parchment paper.

7 Pull one ball of the empanada dough from the fridge and place it on a flour-dusted surface. Dust the dough lightly with flour, then roll it out about ⅛ inch thick. Using a 5- to 6-inch round cutter (or a bowl, red wine glass, or martini glass), cut rounds of dough. Add two small spoonfuls of the filling to the center of each dough round (don't overfill them), leaving ½ to 1 inch uncovered around the edge. Fold the dough in half to form a half-moon and press the edges to seal, kind of like you would if making ravioli. Crimp the edge with a fork or roll it to seal. If your hands get sticky, pause a moment and wash them. Take time and enjoy the process—turn some music on and relax!

8 Transfer the empanadas to the prepared baking sheet and brush the tops generously with the egg wash. Bake for 25 to 28 minutes, until the tops are golden brown.

9 Serve warm with the cilantro-lime crema. Or let cool, freeze on a baking sheet until solid, then store in an airtight bag in the freezer. Defrost them and reheat in a 375°F oven for 10 minutes, or until the insides are hot.

Raw Oysters with Cucumber Mignonette

MAKES 12 OYSTERS

1 tablespoon minced shallot

1 tablespoon minced seedless cucumber

Juice of 2 lemons

12 raw oysters, ice-cold

Oysters are an iconic symbol of the Texas coast, where Travis and I spend a lot of time fishing. And although we sometimes curse the oyster reefs for scratching up the bottom of our boat, they're integral to the coast's shallow bay systems, providing habitat for other wildlife and plants, filtering the water, and preventing erosion. Our reefs have been hit hard by natural disasters in recent years and were overharvested by unsustainable practices, forcing the state to suspend commercial oyster fishing on public waters. The great news is that Texas is actively working to rebuild its damaged reefs, and we've integrated oyster mariculture (shellfish farming in the ocean), a very sustainable practice with a positive impact on our coastal waters.

Don't worry about the old advice to eat oysters only in months that end in *r*. This is partly a holdover from the era before refrigerated transport, when oysters would spoil quickly in the heat, and partly because wild oysters spawn in warmer weather, making them skinny and unappetizing. You can eat plump (and properly refrigerated!) farm-raised oysters year-round, and during the summer, this simple cucumber mignonette makes a refreshing companion.

1 In a small bowl, combine the shallot, cucumber, and lemon juice to make the mignonette.

2 Rinse the oysters under cool running water. If they're muddy, you can use a brush to scrub the outside. To shuck, nestle an oyster the flat-side up (or bowl-side down so you can collect the juices inside) in a towel, with the hinged end poking out and facing away from you. Gently push the tip of an oyster knife into the hinge by rocking the knife from side to side. Once you have some leverage, give it a good twist and pop the hinge. Continue to twist with the broad side of the oyster knife to pry the shell fully open all the way around, being careful not to spill the precious juices inside! Lift off the top of the shell and you're done. If you're a slow shucker like me, place the oysters on a tray of ice as you finish them to keep them cold as you work.

3 Spoon a very small amount of the mignonette onto each oyster (just a splash with a few pieces of minced shallot or cucumber will do!) and serve immediately.

Purple Hull Pea and Yogurt Dip

MAKES 2½ CUPS

2 cups fresh or frozen purple hull peas or other cowpeas, such as black-eyed peas or lady cream peas (see Note)

Coarse sea salt

1 head garlic

¼ cup extra-virgin olive oil, plus more for drizzling

½ cup plain yogurt

2 tablespoons fresh lemon juice (from 1 lemon)

1 teaspoon ground cumin

Freshly ground black pepper

Cucumber Relish (page 128), for serving

Grilled or toasted naan or pita chips, for serving

Note: Purple hull peas are cowpeas, a type of legume more similar to a bean than an English green pea, and any other cowpea will work in this recipe (you could even substitute butter beans or chickpeas, in a pinch). Fresh or frozen cowpeas work best because they cook faster and yield a smoother consistency. If you're cooking with dried cowpeas, soak them overnight before using them and increase the cook time to 1 hour, or until the peas are tender.

Saving seeds is a way to pay homage to the cultures and communities that grew and harvested vegetables before us. It's also a wonderful way to build new relationships and connect to others. One summer, I was given a jar of purple hull peas by my Arkansan friend Misty Newcomb. They were second-generation seeds, grown from some peas that had been passed down in her family. After moving to the extremely hot and dry climate of South Texas, I decided to plant Misty's peas in my newly built garden. While other vegetables suffered under the intense sun, the purple hull peas thrived! This cool and refreshing dip is an out-of-the-box way to serve them, and it's perfect for summer.

1 Preheat the oven to 375°F.

2 Place the peas in a wide pot and add water to cover. Bring to a boil over high heat, then reduce the heat to maintain a simmer. Season the water generously with salt (as if you're cooking pasta) and cook for about 30 minutes, until the peas are very tender when smashed with a fork.

3 While the peas cook, place a whole head of garlic on a square of aluminum foil and drizzle with olive oil. Wrap the foil around the garlic to enclose it completely, then roast for 30 minutes to 1 hour, until the garlic cloves are soft and golden brown. Remove from the oven and set aside until it's cool to the touch. Unwrap the garlic, cut off the root end, and squeeze the cloves out of their papery skins into a small bowl.

4 When the peas have finished cooking, drain them and rinse well with cold water, then transfer to a blender or food processor. Add the roasted garlic, yogurt, lemon juice, olive oil, cumin, and 2 tablespoons water. Puree until smooth. Taste and season with salt and pepper.

5 Scrape the dip into a serving bowl. Drizzle with more olive oil and serve topped with the cucumber relish and naan chips on the side.

Crab Toast with Old Bay Vinaigrette

SERVES 6 TO 8 AS A STARTER,
OR 2 AS A MAIN COURSE

Old Bay Vinaigrette

½ cup plus 2 tablespoons extra-virgin olive oil

¼ cup lemon juice (from 1 to 2 lemons)

2 garlic cloves, minced

2 teaspoons minced fresh parsley

2 teaspoons Old Bay seasoning

Toasts

1 loaf ciabatta or French baguette, sliced ½ inch thick

Olive oil

Old Bay seasoning

2 large avocados, thinly sliced or mashed

3 medium heirloom tomatoes, thinly sliced into half-moons

1 pound lump crabmeat

Handful of microgreens (see page 167)

One summer, I got to hang out in Connecticut with *Bon Appétit* chef Brad Leone, catching and eating blue crabs. In his words, "There are two types of people in this world: those who eat the crabmeat as they pick it, and those who save the meat till the end." Unlike Brad, I fall into the latter category, preferring to do the hard work up front, then enjoy all the sweet and succulent crabmeat in one glorious bite. If you've ever gone to the trouble of picking crabs yourself, you know how much work it is and how that makes you appreciate the meat a whole lot more. It's a fun chore that you can do while sitting around with friends and family and drinking an ice-cold beer, relaxing during the dog days of summer. But catching enough crabs to turn into a big meal isn't always a guarantee, so I'm not opposed to shelling out some cash to buy picked lump crabmeat for this starter.

This recipe is as simple as it gets, but the Old Bay dressing spooned over the top is out of this world. This makes a great one- or two-bite appetizer for a group, but Travis and I like to enjoy it as a big meal for just the two of us.

1 Preheat the broiler.

2 **Make the vinaigrette:** In a 1-pint jar, combine all the ingredients for the vinaigrette, cover, and shake until emulsified. (Alternatively, whisk together all the ingredients in a medium bowl.)

3 Lightly brush each slice of bread with olive oil and season with a dash of Old Bay. Arrange them on a baking sheet and broil for 2 to 3 minutes, until golden brown. Remove from the oven.

4 Spread a thin layer of avocado over each slice of toast, then top each with a slice of tomato. Add a generous amount of crabmeat, in proportion to the size of the toast, followed by a pinch of microgreens. Drizzle with a spoonful or two of the vinaigrette and serve immediately. Store the remaining vinaigrette in the refrigerator for up to 3 days to use as a salad dressing.

Blackened Fish with Sweet Corn and Roasted Poblano Grits

SERVES 4

Blackened Fish

4 (½- to 1-inch-thick) mild white-fleshed fish fillets, such as redfish, snapper, catfish, walleye, or rockfish (see Notes)

Ancho Chile Seasoning (page 254)

Sweet Corn and Roasted Poblano Grits

2 ears sweet corn, husked

1 tablespoon unsalted butter

½ medium yellow onion, finely diced

2 garlic cloves, minced

2 poblano peppers, roasted, peeled, and diced (see Notes)

1 cup stone-ground yellow grits (not instant)

1½ teaspoons coarse sea salt, plus more as needed

¼ cup crumbled feta cheese

Freshly ground black pepper

Red drum, also known as redfish, is one of the most iconic fishes found along the southern coast of the US, from North Carolina all the way down to the lower Laguna Madre in Texas. Today they're a symbol of our healthy and thriving estuaries, but a few decades ago, a trend driven by legendary Louisianan chef Paul Prudhomme sent their numbers plummeting. In the 1980s, they were one of the most popular items on menus across the country, thanks to Chef Prudhomme's signature blackened redfish. Soon after the dish was introduced, the commercial industry began to drastically overharvest the fish. With the help of conservationists, strict regulations were set on the fishery so that future generations will be able to enjoy both the deliciousness of a blackened redfish and the abundance of these incredible fish in our oceans.

It's hard to improve upon Chef Prudhomme's creation, so I let it be an inspiration for this dish, turning the Cajun seafood classic into a sweet-and-spicy fish 'n' grits meal. You can blame it on my roots, but I always find a way to infuse Tex-Mex into everything I cook, and cumin, oregano, and ancho—my version of the holy trinity—are woven into a spice blend that coats the flaky white-fleshed fish before it's blackened. The stone-ground yellow grits, which I source locally from Barton Springs Mill in Dripping Springs, Texas, are amplified with grated sweet corn and roasted poblanos. It's as comforting as it is filling and one of my favorite ways to pair Gulf Coast redfish with end-of-summer ingredients.

1 **Start the fish:** Remove the fish from the refrigerator at least 30 minutes before cooking and pat it dry.

2 **Make the grits:** Using the large holes on a box grater, grate the corn kernels from the cobs into a large bowl (this ensures the juices don't get all over the countertop).

3 Heat a 2-quart saucepan over medium-high heat. Add the butter and let it melt. When it begins foaming, add the onion and cook, stirring occasionally, for 4 to 6 minutes, until soft and golden brown. Add the garlic and cook for 1 minute to release its aroma. Stir in the poblanos, grated corn, grits, salt, and 3 cups water. Bring to a simmer,

To Finish

3 tablespoons unsalted butter

Neutral oil, such as avocado or grapeseed

2 scallions, thinly sliced

Handful of cilantro leaves

Lime wedges

Notes: In some states, like Louisiana, you can buy wild-caught redfish, but in Texas, only farmed redfish are legal to sell commercially. "Puppy" drum (young black drum) and sheepshead are great substitutes from the Gulf Coast.

To roast the poblanos, follow the instructions for roasting and peeling the bell pepper on page 137, then dice the flesh.

then reduce the heat to the lowest setting and cook for 20 minutes, until thickened. In the last few minutes of cooking, stir in the feta, taste, and season with additional salt and some black pepper.

4 **Meanwhile, finish the fish:** Just before cooking, generously season both sides of the fish with the spice blend until fully coated, shaking off any excess.

5 Turn your vent fan on high and maybe crack a window! Heat a wide cast-iron or stainless-steel skillet over high heat. Before the pan starts smoking, pour in roughly 1½ teaspoons oil, add ½ tablespoon of the butter, and swirl to coat the pan. When the butter starts foaming, lay 2 fish fillets down in the pan, being sure to leave space between them. Cook, undisturbed, until the fish is about 75 percent cooked through (check the sides of the fish—if the flesh is opaque about three-quarters of the way, it's ready to go) and has developed a dark brown crust, 2 to 4 minutes. Using a fish spatula, very carefully flip the fish and drop a tablespoon of the butter into the pan. The pan should be very hot and the butter should melt instantly. Tilt the pan so the butter pools along one side and use a spoon to baste the tops of the fillets with the butter until the fish is cooked through and flakes easily with a fork, 1 to 2 minutes more. Using the fish spatula, immediately transfer the fillets to a plate lined with paper towels to absorb excess oil; don't overcook them.

6 Wipe any burnt seasoning out of the pan, then repeat to cook the remaining 2 fillets. If needed, reduce the heat to medium-high so that this batch of fish doesn't burn before it's cooked through.

7 Spoon the grits onto four plates (or ideally into wide pasta bowls) and top each with a fish fillet. Garnish with the scallions, fresh cilantro, and a squeeze of lime juice and serve immediately.

Broiled Salmon with Miso-Peach Jam and Crispy Fried Rice

SERVES 4

Salmon

½ cup peach jam

¼ cup plus 2 tablespoons white miso paste

2 tablespoons soy sauce

4 (6- to 8-ounce) skinless salmon fillets

Crispy Fried Rice

1 tablespoon neutral oil or butter

1 teaspoon toasted sesame oil

4 cups cooked white rice (you can use leftover rice)

3 scallions, thinly sliced

1 tablespoon soy sauce

Neutral oil, for greasing

Shichimi togarashi (optional)

Toasted sesame seeds, for garnish

Fresh cilantro, for garnish

I've always loved spending time in the kitchen, but after I moved from the city to the country, where there are only a few restaurant options, I was cooking three meals a day for Travis and myself, nearly every day, and it started to feel like a chore. To keep my relationship with my kitchen intact, I scaled back on making elaborate meals and instead looked for quick recipes like this one.

Any type of salmon will work here, but I prefer a fattier variety like king salmon or coho. The miso-peach jam doubles as a marinade and a sauce for the fish. I like to serve this with a side salad or some quickly stir-fried shaved napa cabbage or bok choy to complete the meal.

1 **Marinate the salmon:** In a small bowl, stir together the jam, miso, and soy sauce. Transfer half the marinade to a separate small bowl and set aside. Brush a generous amount of the remaining marinade over the salmon and let stand at room temperature for at least 45 minutes or up to 12 hours. (Cover and refrigerate if it's marinating for longer than 1½ hours; pull the salmon from the fridge 45 minutes before cooking to bring it to room temperature.)

2 **Meanwhile, make the fried rice:** Heat a wide skillet or sauté pan over medium-high heat. Add the neutral oil and the sesame oil to the hot pan. When the oil is hot, add the rice and scallions and use a spatula to flatten the rice into an even layer. It should sizzle but not sputter oil. Cook, undisturbed, until the bottom turns golden, 3 to 4 minutes, then stir well and cook for a few minutes more. Add the soy sauce and stir to incorporate. Remove from the heat and set aside.

3 Preheat the broiler to high. Line a baking sheet with aluminum foil and generously oil it so the fish doesn't stick.

4 Place the salmon on the prepared pan and sprinkle with shichimi togarashi (if using). Broil for 8 to 10 minutes (a 1½-inch-thick piece of salmon will take 8 minutes to cook to medium-rare; thinner fillets will cook faster,) until the tops of the fillets caramelize.

5 Add about 1 tablespoon water to the reserved miso-peach marinade to thin it to a sauce consistency. Divide the rice among four plates and top each with a salmon fillet. Garnish with sesame seeds and cilantro and serve immediately, with the sauce alongside.

Venison Fajitas with Grilled Peppers and Onions

SERVES 4 TO 6

Citrus Marinade

⅓ cup fresh lime juice
(from 2 to 3 limes)

⅓ cup fresh orange juice

2 tablespoons soy sauce

½ bunch cilantro

1 teaspoon ground cumin

½ teaspoon cayenne pepper

4 garlic cloves

½ cup neutral oil, such as avocado
or grapeseed

Fajitas

1 inside (top) round from a deer
(1 to 2 pounds; see Faking Flank
Steak with Venison, page 113)

1 tablespoon brown sugar

Coarse sea salt

2 bell peppers, sliced into
matchsticks

2 jalapeños, sliced into thin
matchsticks

1 yellow onion, thinly sliced

Beef tallow or neutral oil, such as
avocado or grapeseed

12 (6-inch) corn or flour tortillas,
warmed

My roots are in Texas, and this is hands down my favorite dish from my home state. I judge every Tex-Mex restaurant by how well they make beef fajitas, and I've spent a lot of time trying to perfect them at home. Fajitas originated back in the 1930s on the ranchlands of West and South Texas when Mexican vaqueros (cowboys) received "throwaway" cuts of beef as pay. Those cuts included the skirt and flank steaks, which you should use if you're making this recipe with beef, moose, nilgai, or elk. When you're making fajitas with deer or antelope, the skirt and flank are awfully small, but the inside (or top) round in the hindquarter—a thick and very tender cut with a long grain line—works really well instead.

Part of the fun of eating fajitas is having a smorgasbord of sides and condiments to pile on top of the delicious meat. This recipe includes a step for sautéing onions and peppers in a cast-iron skillet, but feel free to build on those with the other toppings I've suggested. And be sure to have plenty of tortillas and cervezas on hand!

1 **Make the marinade:** In a food processor, combine all the ingredients for the marinade and pulse until emulsified. Measure out ¼ cup of the marinade and set it aside.

2 **Make the fajitas:** Using a sharp knife, slice crosswise through the middle of the venison roast (almost like you're butterflying it) to create two thinner rectangular pieces. Use the smooth side of a meat mallet to pound the meat evenly to about ½ inch thick. Place the venison in a large container or resealable bag and pour in the marinade. Marinate in the refrigerator for 6 to 12 hours, turning the meat or massaging the bag every few hours to distribute the marinade.

3 About 30 minutes before you plan to grill, remove the meat from the marinade, letting as much liquid drip back into the container or bag as possible (discard the marinade). Pat the meat as dry as you can with paper towels, then sprinkle each side with the brown sugar and some salt. Set aside to come to room temperature.

4 Prepare a wood-fired grill (or use charcoal with some wood chips added for smoky flavor) and heat to medium-high.

Faking Flank Steak with Venison

My favorite cut of venison for fajitas is the tender, buttery inside round (or top round) from a deer or antelope. This thick rectangular roast can be found on the inward-facing side of the hindquarter, just above the shank (see the illustration on page 45). It has a long grain line and can be sliced crosswise through the middle, then pounded flat to an even ½-inch thickness with a meat mallet, giving you two wide, rectangular pieces of meat similar to beef flank steak. These are perfect for flash searing and slicing across the grain and work well in any recipe that calls for beef flank or skirt steak. The inside round from larger game animals like moose, nilgai, and elk will also work, but the meat will be considerably thicker. For these animals, I would use the flank or brisket instead. You'll have to trim the thin layer of silver skin that encapsulates the muscle, but all you need are a little patience and a very sharp knife!

Optional Toppings

Pico de gallo

Guacamole

Sour cream

Shredded cheese

Charro beans

Spanish rice

Lime wedges

5 In a large bowl, toss the bell peppers, jalapeños, and onion with the reserved ¼ cup marinade until well coated.

6 Set a large cast-iron skillet or griddle on the grill and let it get hot. Add the vegetables to the skillet, close the lid, and cook, stirring occasionally, for about 15 minutes, until the onion and peppers are soft and beginning to char and caramelize on the outside. Transfer the vegetables to a dish (leave the skillet on the grill!) and keep warm.

7 Stoke the fire and get the grill burning really hot. Add about 1 tablespoon beef tallow to the skillet and let it melt. Lay the venison in the pan and sear for 2 to 3 minutes on each side, until medium-rare (the exact timing will depend on the thickness of the meat); use tongs or a meat thermometer to check for doneness (see the temperature chart on page 164). Transfer to a cutting board to rest for 8 to 10 minutes before slicing.

8 Thinly slice the meat across the grain at a 45-degree angle and serve in warm tortillas with the peppers and onions, any toppings you like, and cerveza. ¡Salud!

Thai-Inspired Wild Hog Lettuce Cups

SERVES 4

Vinaigrette

3 tablespoons fresh lime juice (from 1½ limes)

2 tablespoons honey

1 tablespoon fish sauce

1 tablespoon chile paste, such as sambal oelek

¼ cup neutral oil, such as avocado or grapeseed

Salad

2 tablespoons uncooked glutinous (sticky) rice or crushed roasted, unsalted peanuts

Lard or neutral oil, such as avocado or grapeseed

1 pound ground wild hog, pork, turkey, or venison

Coarse sea salt

3 small shallots, finely diced

3 Fresno chiles (or bird's-eye chiles for more heat), minced

3 garlic cloves, minced

1 tablespoon minced fresh ginger

½ cup mixed fresh herbs, such as cilantro, Thai basil, and/or mint, chopped

2 heads Boston or iceberg lettuce, leaves separated

1 cucumber, thinly sliced into half-moons

This Thai-inspired meat salad served in lettuce cups is one of the first recipes I cooked with wild game, and it's been in my rotation for many years. I've made it more times than I can count with all manner of ground game. Incorporating several seasonal ingredients like cucumbers and tomatoes helps me stretch the meat, and those vegetables also make this a healthy, well-rounded meal. During the cooler seasons, I serve this with dried chiles instead of fresh, and substitute radishes and julienned carrots for the cucumber and tomato; you can skip the basil and mint, in that case, and just use cilantro for the garnish.

1 **Make the vinaigrette:** In a jar, combine the lime juice, honey, fish sauce, chile paste, and oil. Cover and shake vigorously to emulsify. Set aside.

2 **Make the salad:** In a dry sauté pan, toast the uncooked glutinous rice over medium-high heat, stirring often so it doesn't burn, for 2 to 3 minutes, until lightly golden in color. Don't let it burn. Transfer the rice to a spice grinder and pulse until it's broken down to a coarse, granular consistency. Set aside. (Skip this step if using peanuts.)

3 Heat a large skillet over medium-high heat. Add enough lard to lightly coat the bottom of the pan. When the fat slides across the pan quickly like water and starts to shimmer (but not smoke), add the ground hog and pat it into an even layer over the bottom of the pan. Cook, undisturbed, for a few minutes or until the meat lifts freely from the pan without sticking and you can see and smell the bottom starting to caramelize and brown. Flip the meat, break it apart, and cook for 3 to 5 minutes more, until the meat is cooked through. Transfer to a large bowl and season with a couple pinches of salt.

4 Add a bit more lard or oil to the pan, if needed, and then add the shallots, chiles, garlic, ginger, and a pinch of salt. Cook, stirring occasionally, for 3 to 4 minutes, until the vegetables have softened. Be careful not to stick your face directly over the pan—the fumes from the chiles will make you cough! Add the vegetables to the bowl with the ground hog and stir to combine. Add about ¼ cup of the vinaigrette and the toasted rice (or peanuts) and stir until fully incorporated. Set the filling aside to rest and cool for 10 to 15 minutes.

2 cups cherry tomatoes, quartered

2 cups cooked glutinous (sticky) rice or jasmine rice

Lime wedges, for serving (optional)

Note: Glutinous rice, despite its name, doesn't contain any gluten. (The word itself just means "gummy.") When toasted and ground, it adds a nutty flavor, and the starch that makes the rice sticky when cooked thickens the juices in the dish.

5 Just before serving, stir the fresh herbs into the filling. Taste and season with salt if needed. Scoop the filling into the lettuce cups and serve with the cucumber, tomatoes, and cooked rice, drizzled with more vinaigrette or a squeeze of lime juice, if desired.

Chicago-Inspired Venison Sausages with Sweet-and-Spicy Pickled Zucchini Relish

SERVES 8
(MAKES ABOUT 4 CUPS RELISH)

Pickled Zucchini Relish

1 pound zucchini (about 3 small or 2 large), finely diced

½ cup finely diced red bell pepper

½ cup finely diced sweet onion

2 jalapeños, minced

1 tablespoon kosher salt

1 cup apple cider vinegar (5% acidity)

½ cup white wine vinegar (5% to 7% acidity)

1 cup sugar

1½ teaspoons mustard seeds

1½ teaspoons celery seeds

¼ teaspoon red pepper flakes

I was never much of a hot dog person until I took a vacation to Chicago and tried one of the city's signature dogs. It blew my mind. It was piled with so many fresh and pickled toppings—"dragged through the garden," as locals say—that I instantly wanted to make my own version at home.

This recipe is a wonderful compromise between the things I want to eat at the height of summer (*all* the veggies from the garden) and what Travis wants to eat (just a damn hot dog). It allows me to indulge in sliced fresh heirloom tomatoes and to turn my excess zucchini into an amazing relish (which is also excellent served with the Smoked Hocks and Butter Beans on page 220). Travis gets his hot dog and a full belly. It's a win-win for everyone.

A true Chicago-style dog starts with an all-beef frankfurter, but since these are very challenging to make at home, I took the salty, smoky flavors I love in a Chicago dog and applied them to a fresh venison sausage instead. While these sausages are easier to make in a home kitchen than an all-beef frank, they're still a labor of love, so I only break out all my sausage-making equipment once a year. If you don't have the time or tools to make these from scratch, shell out a few extra bucks at your local butcher shop to get good-quality sausages. Trust me, they're worth it!

1 **Make the relish:** In a large bowl, combine the zucchini, bell pepper, onion, and jalapeños, then stir in the salt. Let stand for 30 minutes, then drain the vegetable mixture in a colander.

2 In a 2-quart saucepan, combine both vinegars, the sugar, mustard seeds, celery seeds, and red pepper flakes. Bring to a simmer over medium-high heat, stirring to dissolve the sugar, then add the strained vegetable mixture. Simmer for 8 to 10 minutes, until the vegetables are tender but not mushy. Divide the relish among clean ½-pint jars and let cool, then screw on the lids. (The relish will keep in the refrigerator for a few months.)

3 Preheat the oven to 350°F.

recipe and ingredients continued

8 brioche hot dog buns

3 tablespoons poppy seeds

8 Fresh Venison Sausage with Garlic (page 251) or beef frankfurters

Yellow mustard

3 tomatoes, sliced into wedges

½ cup diced sweet onion

8 dill pickle spears

Sport peppers or peperoncini

Celery salt

4 Place the buns on a large piece of aluminum foil. Ever so lightly brush the tops with a little bit of water, then sprinkle with the poppy seeds. Crimp the edges of the foil together to enclose the buns and bake for 5 minutes, until the buns have softened just a little bit (but not so much that they'll turn to mush when you try to eat the hot dog). Remove from the foil and let cool while you cook the sausages.

5 Prepare a charcoal or gas grill for medium-high heat and set up a zone for indirect heat (or have a grill grate raised higher above the heat source). Grill the sausages over direct heat until browned all the way around, 2 to 3 minutes on each side, then transfer them to the indirect heat zone and cook for another minute or two, until they register 160°F. Avoid overcooking. Set the sausages aside to rest while you get your toppings ready.

6 On each bun, spread some yellow mustard, then add a sausage. Top with some sliced tomato, some onion, a pickle spear, a spoonful of the zucchini relish, sport peppers, and a pinch of celery salt. Enjoy immediately.

Garlic-Honey Grilled Chicken with Herbes de Provence

SERVES 4

Garlic Honey

1 head garlic

2 cups raw, unpasteurized honey (preferably local)

Grilled Chicken

2 teaspoons coarse sea salt

½ teaspoon freshly ground black pepper

3 garlic cloves (from the garlic honey jar or fresh), minced

2 teaspoons herbes de Provence, very coarsely ground with a mortar and pestle

1 (3- to 5-pound) whole chicken

½ cup (1 stick) unsalted butter

Neutral oil, such as avocado or grapeseed

I think of this recipe as the outdoor counterpart of a classic crispy-skinned roast chicken—and it's nothing short of amazing. I absolutely adore herbes de Provence, a seasoning blend originally from the eponymous region in southeastern France. The flavors are simple, but the garlic-infused honey (yes—it's a must-try combination!) offers just a little something extra. Look for a local variety—the flavor is affected by the nectar the honeybees drink from the plants they pollinate, so honey from your area will have a unique flavor profile.

Infusing the honey and dry-brining the chicken (see page 66) requires some advance prep, but the actual cooking couldn't be easier! The result is unfussy yet still elegant enough to serve as a special meal for friends and family. The chicken is excellent with the blistered green beans and peppers on page 138; just skip the pesto and drizzle the vegetables with extra honey-butter and a squeeze of lemon juice instead.

1 **Make the garlic honey:** Separate all the garlic cloves, lightly smash them, and peel. Place them in a 1-pint jar and add the honey. The garlic cloves will likely float to the surface—that's okay. Put the lid on the jar, set it upside down on the counter, and let stand for 1 day.

2 The next day, flip the jar right-side up and crack open the lid so the gas inside can escape (it's fermenting!), then seal and set it upside down again. Let stand for 2 days more, flipping the jar each day (make sure the lid is tight first) so the garlic cloves are immersed in the honey and cracking the lid for a few moments to release gas. After the third day, the garlic honey is ready to use. (You won't need all of it for this recipe; store the leftover portion in the jar at room temperature. It will keep for several weeks and can be used in any savory recipe that calls for honey.)

3 **Make the chicken:** In a small bowl, combine the salt, pepper, garlic, and herbes de Provence. (This should be enough rub for a 5-pound bird, so if yours is smaller, you may not need all of it.)

4 Use poultry shears or heavy-duty scissors to cut the backbone out of the chicken, then use a meat cleaver or heavy knife to split the breastbone straight down the middle and cut the whole bird

continued

Pollinators Make the World Go Round

Honeybees get a lot of attention (because, well, honey!), but our native bees and other pollinators are critical to life on Earth. According to the Natural Resources Conservation Service (NRCS), "Three-fourths of the world's flowering plants and about 35 percent of the world's food crops depend on animal pollinators to reproduce. More than 3,500 species of native bees help increase crop yields. Some scientists estimate that one out of every three bites of food we eat exists because of animal pollinators like bees, butterflies and moths, birds and bats, and beetles and other insects." In return, pollinators (and wildlife) themselves rely on a diversity of native plants for their own survival.

Incorporating native plant species and wildflowers into your home landscaping is one of the most effective ways to support your local pollinator population and increase biodiversity—plus, they're beautiful to look at. (See pages 262–263 for more on how to turn your backyard into native habitat for wildlife, and why.)

in half. Place the chicken on a baking sheet and season it with the rub, gently lifting the skin and seasoning the meat as well. Refrigerate, uncovered, ideally for 12 hours but at least 1 hour before grilling, then pull the bird from the fridge and let it come to room temperature.

5   In a small saucepan, melt the butter over low heat. As soon as the butter starts to foam, stir in ½ cup of the garlic honey and remove from the heat so it doesn't caramelize. Pour half the garlic-honey butter into a small bowl and keep warm for serving. You'll use the other half to baste the chicken as it cooks.

6   Pat the bird really dry (the salt in the rub will draw out moisture) and then rub the outside of the skin with a drizzle of oil.

7   Prepare a charcoal or gas grill for medium to medium-high heat and set up two zones (one for direct heat, one for indirect; if using a propane grill, start with all the burners on). Start the chicken skin-side down over direct heat. Use tongs to press all around the outside of the meat to flatten the chicken and get as much contact as you can while it's doing its thing. Resist the urge to check it, flip it, or move it around—just leave it alone for 5 to 7 minutes, until the skin gets crispy and has beautiful char marks. Flip the chicken and move it to indirect heat (if you're using a propane grill, turn off the burners directly underneath the chicken). Immediately after flipping, baste the chicken with the garlic-honey butter, close the lid, and cook for 25 to 30 minutes, basting again with the garlic-honey butter halfway through. Try to maintain a temperature between 350° and 400°F inside the grill; if it's too hot, open the lid until the temperature goes down. In the last minute of cooking, baste the chicken again and then flip it one last time so that it's skin-side down and let the honey caramelize. The chicken is done when the internal temperature at the thickest part of the thigh reaches 165°F.

8   Transfer the chicken to a cutting board and let it rest for 10 minutes before carving. Serve with a drizzle of the reserved garlic-honey butter.

BLTT (Bacon, Lettuce, Tomato, and Tomato Jam)

SERVES 4

12 slices bacon, homemade (see page 125) or store-bought

8 heirloom tomato slices, preferably from Black Krim, Cherokee Purple, or Mortgage Lifter tomatoes

Coarse sea salt and freshly ground black pepper

½ cup mayonnaise, homemade (see page 249) or store-bought

1 garlic clove, grated

8 slices sourdough bread

½ cup Tomato Jam (recipe follows)

4 crisp green lettuce leaves

Guy Clark put it best when he sang, "Only two things that money can't buy, that's true love and homegrown tomatoes!" I immediately understood this after biting into my first homegrown tomato, but I really think his song is a tribute to the small farmers and growers who still value the simplicity of a seasonal tomato as opposed to the watery, commercialized hothouse variety you can buy in January. Even if you can't grow your own, it's absolutely worth your time and money to seek out local farmers planting heirloom varieties, because nothing compares to a perfectly ripe tomato in the middle of summer. You'd be hard-pressed to find a better way to eat them than in a sandwich with smoked bacon. The only way I've been able to top the near perfection of a BLT is by adding more tomatoes in the form of tomato jam!

1 Preheat the broiler to high.

2 In a large skillet, cook the bacon over medium-low heat until the fat has rendered and the bacon is crispy and light brown on the bottom, 4 to 5 minutes. Flip and cook until light brown on the second side, 4 to 5 minutes more. Transfer the bacon to a paper towel–lined tray to drain. Reserve the rendered fat in the pan.

3 Season the tomato slices with a sprinkle each of salt and pepper. (It's best to do this several minutes before eating.) In a small bowl, mix the mayonnaise with the garlic to make a quick aioli.

4 Arrange the bread on a baking sheet. Brush one side of each slice with some of the rendered bacon fat, then toast under the broiler until golden brown, 1 to 2 minutes per side. Remove from the broiler.

5 Generously swipe 4 slices of the sourdough toast with tomato jam. Pile the bacon, sliced tomatoes, and lettuce. Spread a generous swipe of aioli on the remaining slices of toast and close the sandwiches. Enjoy immediately, with a big smile on your face!

Tomato Jam

MAKES 2 CUPS

2 pounds cherry tomatoes, halved

1 cup sugar

3 tablespoons red wine vinegar

1 teaspoon coarse sea salt

¼ teaspoon ground allspice

I think of tomato jam as a fancier version of ketchup, one that's less sweet and actually tastes like tomato—and once you make it, you'll have a hard time going back to the squeeze bottle. It's amazing on a charcuterie board with cheese and crackers, slathered on a burger, or with this BLT. (This recipe is adapted from a basic tomato jam recipe provided by the National Center for Home Food Preservation.)[11]

Combine all the ingredients in a medium saucepan. Bring to a simmer over medium-high heat, then reduce the heat to maintain a gentle bubble. Cook, stirring every 10 to 15 minutes or so to make sure nothing is burning or sticking to the bottom, until the tomatoes reduce to a jam-like consistency, about 2 hours. Remove from the heat and transfer to a clean 1-pint jar. Let cool completely, then seal the jar and store in the refrigerator for up to 1 week or in the freezer for up to 1 year. Thaw frozen jam in the refrigerator and use within 1 week.

Homemade Smoked Bacon, Three Ways

One evening I peeked into my freezer and realized I didn't have enough meat to make it to fall's big-game hunting season. Luckily, invasive wild hogs run rampant here in Texas, and because they're considered exotic, we can hunt them year-round. My husband and I headed to our family ranch and built a C-trap (a corral that's effective for trapping a group of hogs instead of one at a time), and after a few failed attempts, we finally got the trip wire right and were rewarded with a few hogs. Typically, hogs have a thick layer of hide but very little fat or meat on their bellies—not enough to make bacon—so I was very happy to discover that one of the hogs we trapped was an extra-fatty sow. I cured the belly for a week, smoked it, and enjoyed it in the most succulent BLT ever (see page 122).

Wild hog belly is similar to domestic pork belly, but there are a few differences. Hog bellies are considerably smaller, typically have less fat, and have tougher connective tissue—but the flavor is phenomenal and more robust than domestic pork.

Since the meat in my diet is primarily lean wild game, I tend to crave bacon often, but getting a fatty hog for bacon is rare. Buying pasture-raised pork belly from a local farmer is my way of supporting the community and satisfying that urge. I like to smoke large batches of bacon and freeze them in smaller portions to use in recipes throughout the year. Here are a few of my favorite ways to cure and prepare it. The first is seasoned with an all-purpose blend, and the flavor will work in any recipe in this book that calls for bacon, such as Coq au Vin (page 174) or Smoked Hocks and Butter Beans (page 220).

Classic Smoked Bacon Cure

MAKES 5 POUNDS

¼ cup packed brown sugar

3 tablespoons coarse sea salt

2 teaspoons freshly ground black pepper

1 teaspoon Prague powder #1 (see Notes)

5 pounds pork belly, skin on, if possible (see Notes)

1 **Make the cure:** In a small bowl, stir together the brown sugar, salt, pepper, and Prague powder #1.

2 Coat the pork belly with the cure, rubbing it in thoroughly and making sure to get all sides covered. Place the pork belly in a large container with a lid or 2-gallon resealable plastic bags and cure in the fridge for 5 days for a thinner 1-inch-thick belly from a wild hog, or up to 7 days for a 2-inch-thick domestic pork belly. The salt will begin to draw juices out of the meat, causing it to pool up at the bottom of the container, so every day redistribute the liquid by massaging the meat so it's evenly coated.

3 Set a wire rack on a rimmed baking sheet. Remove the belly from the container and rinse it thoroughly with cold water. Pat dry and place it on the rack. Return the meat to the refrigerator and let stand, uncovered, for 12 to 24 hours more. (This dries the outside of the meat so the smoke will stick.)

4 Prepare a smoker using fruitwood or hickory and set the temperature to about 200°F.

5 Place the pork belly directly on the grates of the smoker, skin-side down, and smoke for 2 to 3 hours, depending on thickness, until the internal temperature registers between 150° and 160°F. Remove the pork from the smoker and let stand until cool enough to handle, then remove the skin, if there is any (reserve the skin for another use; see Notes).

6 You can use the bacon immediately, but it's easiest to slice after it's been refrigerated for several hours or overnight. Using an electric slicer or a sharp knife, slice the bacon to your desired thickness. It will keep for 3 to 4 weeks in the refrigerator, but you likely won't want to eat 5 pounds of bacon in that short amount of time. It's better to divide the bacon into 1-pound portions, vacuum seal each individually, and freeze them for up to 1 year. Pull one out and thaw it in the refrigerator before using.

Herbed Bacon

This flavorful bacon is perfect for soups or a pot of beans (see page 220). Follow the classic recipe, substituting granulated sugar for the brown sugar in the cure. After rinsing, rub with a mixture of ½ teaspoon dried rosemary, ½ teaspoon dried thyme, ½ teaspoon crushed fennel seeds, and 1 garlic clove, smashed to a pulp or grated. Smoke as directed opposite.

Sweet-and-Spicy Bacon

This is exactly as described. It's a great way to add a little extra oomph to your breakfast tacos, BLT, or next round of jalapeño poppers. Follow the classic recipe, but after rinsing, rub with an additional ¼ cup packed brown sugar mixed with ½ teaspoon cayenne pepper, then smoke as directed opposite.

Notes: If I'm using domestic pork belly and can get one with the skin on, I prefer to keep it on. (With wild game, I remove the skin to avoid having to blanch or burn the hair off the hide.) The skin helps keep the meat moist while smoking, and as an added bonus, you can save it to use as a flavoring ingredient. Chop it into pieces and freeze it, then drop a chunk or two into a simmering pot of soup or beans later in the year to impart its salty, smoky flavors.

Prague powder #1, also known as pink curing salt #1 or Insta Cure #1, is a mix of salt (sodium chloride) and sodium nitrite. (Why pink? It's dyed to make sure you don't get it mixed up with table salt.) The nitrites add a pink color to bacon and a specific flavor that I prefer, but what's more important, they make meat cooked at low temperatures safer to eat by preventing the growth of *Clostridium botulinum*, the bacteria that cause botulism.[12]

Lean wild hog bellies can dry out easily, so after 1½ to 2 hours in the smoker, I wrap them in foil, then smoke for 3 to 4 hours more. The smoky flavor won't be quite as intense, but the meat will be juicier.

Mushroom Shawarma with Cucumber Relish and Garlic Labneh Sauce

SERVES 4 TO 6

Garlic Labneh Sauce

1 cup labneh or plain full-fat Greek yogurt (see Notes)

2 garlic cloves, grated

Zest of 1 lemon

Shawarma–Marinated Mushrooms

2 pounds mushrooms, such as shiitake caps, cremini (baby bella), trumpet, chicken of the woods, or lion's mane

3 tablespoons minced red onion

3 garlic cloves, smashed and coarsely chopped

1½ teaspoons ground coriander

¾ teaspoon ground cumin

¾ teaspoon ground cinnamon

¾ teaspoon ground cardamom

¾ teaspoon kosher salt

⅛ teaspoon cayenne pepper

¼ cup fresh lemon juice (from 1 to 2 lemons)

When I crave vegetables for dinner, I always look to this Middle Eastern–inspired recipe. It's incredibly delicious and also filling enough to satisfy Travis's stomach. In his words, "I've never been so excited about eating a vegetarian meal in my life!"

Shawarma is a Middle Eastern dish of thinly sliced spiced meat served on flatbread or in a pita. Typically, the meat is sliced, seasoned, and stacked, then skewered on a spit, from which vendors shave slices to order. In this recipe, shawarma-spiced mushrooms are standing in for the meat (and we're forgoing the rotating spit!). You can use a variety of mushrooms, as long as the type you choose has some structural integrity. I'd stay away from delicate or thin-capped mushrooms like chanterelles and oysters. Tried-and-true portobello mushrooms and shiitake caps work, or you could venture into the world of wild mushrooms and use chicken of the woods or king trumpets. I've even tried this with shredded chunks of lion's mane—the ends turned so crispy and delicious!

1 **Make the labneh sauce:** In a small bowl, stir together the labneh, garlic, and lemon zest. Cover and refrigerate until ready to serve.

2 **Make the mushrooms:** Brush the mushrooms clean. If using shiitakes, remove the stems. If using king trumpet mushrooms, slice them crosswise into ½-inch-thick pieces so they look like scallops. If using lion's mane or chicken of the woods, cut or tear them into thick 2-inch chunks. Whichever mushrooms you're using, aim to make all the pieces the same thickness so they cook evenly (reserve any stems for making stock or, if they aren't too woody, for duxelles). Put the mushrooms in a large bowl.

3 In a small food processor or blender, combine the onion, garlic, coriander, cumin, cinnamon, cardamom, salt, cayenne, and lemon juice. Process until well combined, then slowly stream in the oil and process until emulsified.

4 Pour the marinade over the mushrooms. Mix thoroughly by hand, making sure the marinade gets up under the caps of all the mushrooms. Set aside to marinate for at least 1 hour or up to 4 hours. (If marinating for longer than a couple hours, cover and refrigerate.)

recipe and ingredients continued

¾ cup neutral oil, such as avocado or grapeseed, plus more for the grates

Cucumber Relish

2 cups finely diced seeded cucumber

6 tablespoons finely diced red onion

1½ tablespoons minced fresh parsley

1½ tablespoons minced fresh mint

2 tablespoons fresh lemon juice (from 1 lemon)

2 tablespoons extra-virgin olive oil

Kosher salt and freshly ground black pepper

To Serve

2 clumps of large cherry tomatoes on the vine (8 to 10 per clump) or small vine tomatoes

Neutral oil, such as avocado or grapeseed

Kosher salt and freshly ground black pepper

Flatbread and/or cooked basmati rice

Notes: You can use 4 teaspoons of a premade shawarma spice blend instead of the spices called for in the marinade.

If you're using yogurt for the sauce, you'll need to strain out some of its liquid so it doesn't dilute the sauce. Place the yogurt in a fine-mesh strainer set over a bowl and let stand in the fridge for 1 to 2 hours before using.

5 Meanwhile, make the relish: In a small bowl, stir together the cucumber, onion, parsley, mint, lemon juice, and olive oil. Season with salt and black pepper and set aside until ready to serve.

6 If your mushrooms are in the fridge, pull them out 30 minutes before you plan to grill. If using bamboo skewers, soak them in water for about 30 minutes before using so they don't burn.

7 To finish: Prepare a charcoal or gas grill for medium-high heat and oil the grates.

8 Divide the mushrooms evenly among four to six skewers, stacking them close together on the skewers, then lay them on the grill. Lightly coat the tomatoes with oil and season with salt and black pepper. If the tomatoes are attached to the vine, you can grill them in a clump, or cut larger vine tomatoes in half and place them on the grill, cut-side down. Close the lid and cook until the mushrooms are charred on one side, 3 to 4 minutes, then flip and cook on the second side for 3 to 4 minutes. By this time, the mushrooms should be tender, but keep turning the skewers until you get crispy charred bits all the way around, then remove from the grill and transfer to a platter. Grill the tomatoes for 5 to 8 minutes, until the skin gets wrinkly and the flesh is soft, but not so much that they fall apart! Remove from the grill and transfer to the platter with the skewers.

9 Serve the mushroom kebabs immediately with the relish, labneh sauce, grilled tomatoes, and flatbread.

Summer Panzanella with Marinated Chanterelles, Heirloom Tomatoes, and Apricots

SERVES 4

2 cups torn (1-inch pieces) sourdough bread (or use croutons)

Olive oil

Coarse sea salt and freshly ground black pepper

2 pounds mixed ripe tomatoes, coarsely chopped

2 apricots, or 1 peach, pitted and sliced into wedges

2 scallions, thinly sliced

8 to 10 fresh basil leaves, sliced into thin ribbons

¼ cup crumbled feta cheese

1 cup Marinated Chanterelles (recipe follows), marinade reserved for dressing

Finding my first chanterelle is an enduring memory for me. I was foraging in the quiet woods of Sam Houston National Forest, where chanterelles grow wild. It had rained the day before, and the dewy forest floor had come to life. To my surprise, it didn't take me long to spot one, as their vibrant yellow and orange colors stand out like ornaments strung along the ground. I identified it as a *Cantharellus cinnabarinus*, commonly known as a cinnabar chanterelle. I squeezed the stem between my fingers and watched it exude moisture. It smelled of humus, petrichor, and apricots—an aroma I've come to love so deeply that I want to turn it into a candle. Once home, I decided to pair the cinnabars with stone fruit, which were coming into season at the farmers' market. Just as Mother Nature would have it, the tomatoes in my garden were starting to ripen as well—a sign that these ingredients were made to be enjoyed together. They truly shine in this delicious summer bread salad.

The chanterelles are roasted and then marinated and can be used on their own as a condiment so good, you'll want to put it on everything. I use the mushroom marinade to dress the salad. If you can, use a blend of ripe tomatoes with a range of flavors. I love mixing deep, rich Black Krims with sweet cherry tomatoes.

1 Preheat the oven to 350°F.

2 Spread the bread pieces over a baking sheet and drizzle with olive oil. Season with salt and pepper, then toast in the oven for 10 to 12 minutes, until golden brown. Remove from the oven and let cool.

3 In a large bowl, combine the toasted bread, tomatoes, apricots, scallions, basil, and feta. Using a slotted spoon, scoop the chanterelles out of their jar, letting the excess marinade drain off, then add them to the salad and gently fold to combine. Season with salt and pepper. Shake the jar with the chanterelle marinade to emulsify, if needed, then use a couple of spoonfuls to dress the salad. Serve immediately.

continued

Marinated Chanterelles

MAKES 1½ PINTS

1 pound chanterelles, cleaned and dried (see Note)

¾ cup extra-virgin olive oil, plus about 3 tablespoons for drizzling

Coarse sea salt

¾ cup white wine vinegar

2 tablespoons sugar

3 garlic cloves, minced

2 teaspoons mixed chopped fresh oregano, rosemary, and thyme

Note: Rain will often kick dirt and debris underneath the chanterelles' wavy ridges, so you may need to soak them or rinse with cold water, then drain and dry them well. To dry large amounts of sturdier chanterelles (like the smooth and golden variety), spin them in a salad spinner. Cinnabars are very delicate, so I prefer to gently pat them with paper towels and let them air-dry in the refrigerator for several hours before cooking. Store them in a brown paper bag in the fridge if you're not using them right away. If you're using wild mushrooms and they're relatively clean, you can brush or wipe away any dirt with a cloth. If you're using cultivated mushrooms, just brush them clean with a slightly damp paper towel.

These marinated mushrooms are also delicious with bread and butter. If chanterelles aren't available, substitute another wild mushroom, such as porcini, hedgehog, or lobster mushrooms, or use a cultivated variety, such as shiitake or cremini (baby bella).

1 Preheat the oven to 400°F.

2 Tear or chop the mushrooms into even-size pieces, then spread them out over two baking sheets, leaving a little space between the mushrooms so the moisture they release can evaporate. Drizzle the mushrooms with enough olive oil to lightly coat (about 3 tablespoons) and season with salt. Roast for about 20 minutes, until the edges are crispy and golden in color, flipping the mushrooms halfway through. Divide the mushrooms evenly among three ½ pint jars and set aside.

3 Meanwhile, in a small saucepan, combine the vinegar, sugar, and 1 tablespoon salt. Bring to a boil over high heat, then add the remaining olive oil, garlic, and herbs and whisk to combine. Remove from the heat and pour the marinade over the mushrooms. Let cool completely, then seal the jars and refrigerate until chilled before using. The mushrooms will keep in the refrigerator for up to 5 days; shake the jar to re-emulsify the marinade before using.

Chargrilled Okra and Romesco

SERVES 6 GENEROUSLY

2 pounds small to medium okra pods

Coarse sea salt and freshly ground black pepper

Neutral oil, such as avocado or grapeseed

Aleppo pepper, for garnish (optional)

Romesco Sauce (recipe follows)

Okra is a favorite vegetable of the Prewett clan, and we love to both grow and eat it. My father-in-law shared his favorite okra variety with me—Green Velvet, known for its tender pods—and also his trick of laddering them on skewers so they cook evenly on the grill.

Okra doesn't deserve the bad rap it often gets as being woody or slimy and only palatable if fried. It can be tough, however, so choosing the right size pods is incredibly important. At my favorite farmstand in Hempstead, you'll find people crowded around the big wooden bins, sorting through piles of community-grown okra. The locals know that size matters, and you'll see them picking out the small to medium pods (3 to 4 inches long, roughly the width of your palm, is ideal), which are more tender. I save any overgrown ones for seeds or give them to my dog Zissou as a reward for keeping a careful watch over my garden.

Cooking the okra hot and fast, as I do here, ensures it won't be too gooey in the middle, and the light charring adds a nice layer of flavor. I like to dip the charred okra into a bowl of romesco, a smoky roasted pepper and tomato condiment that originated in Spain.

1 Soak twelve to fourteen wooden skewers in water for 30 minutes before grilling. Prepare a charcoal or gas grill for high heat (450° to 500°F).

2 Skewer the okra pods perpendicularly on two skewers to create a ladder-like effect, sliding them close together and leaving 2 to 3 inches exposed at the top and bottom of the skewers. Drizzle with enough oil to lightly coat, 1 to 2 tablespoons, and season generously with salt and black pepper.

3 Lay the skewers on the grill, close the lid, and grill the okra for 3 to 4 minutes. Flip, close the lid again, and grill for 3 to 4 minutes more, until you see good grill marks and parts of the okra begin to char. Remove from the grill and serve warm, with a sprinkle of Aleppo pepper, if desired, and the romesco sauce alongside for dipping.

continued

Romesco Sauce

MAKES 2 CUPS

3 medium vine tomatoes, quartered

⅓ cup extra-virgin olive oil, plus more for drizzling

Coarse sea salt and freshly ground black pepper

¼ medium-sized yellow onion

1 head garlic

2 red bell peppers

¼ cup fresh parsley leaves

2 tablespoons red wine vinegar or sherry vinegar

1 teaspoon smoked paprika

½ cup Fried Bread Crumbs (page 58; omit the paprika and salt) or panko bread crumbs

I make big batches of this romesco to freeze and serve later in the year with fish or potatoes. It's an excellent way to upscale a simple meal without extra effort.

1 Prepare a charcoal or gas grill for high heat (450° to 500°F) and set up two zones (one for direct heat, one for indirect).

2 Place the tomatoes on a large piece of aluminum foil, drizzle with olive oil, and season with salt and black pepper. Shape the foil into a shallow bowl so that, as the tomatoes roast, you capture those delicious juices! Place the head of garlic on a separate square of foil, drizzle with oil, and crimp the foil tightly closed. Rub the onion quarter with a little bit of oil and season with salt and black pepper.

3 Place the tomatoes and garlic on the grill over indirect heat and the onion quarter directly on the grill grates over direct heat. Grill until the onion is charred on both sides, about 2 minutes, then add it to the foil "bowl" with the tomatoes so it can steam and soften; cook over indirect heat until the vegetables are very tender and the skins slip off the tomatoes, about 15 minutes. Remove from the grill and set aside to cool. Grill the garlic until the cloves are tender, about 15 minutes, then remove from the grill and set aside to cool.

4 Grill the bell peppers over high direct heat, turning them with tongs every few minutes, until charred completely all the way around. (This makes them easier to peel.) Remove from the grill and set aside to cool.

5 When the peppers are cool to the touch, slice them open and pour the juices inside into a blender or food processor. Discard the stems and seeds. Peel off and discard the skin and add the flesh to the blender.

6 Cut off the root end of the roasted garlic and squeeze the soft cloves into the blender. Add the grilled tomatoes and onion, the parsley, vinegar, paprika, bread crumbs, and ¼ teaspoon salt and pulse until broken down into a coarse liquid.

7 You can enjoy the romesco immediately or store it in an airtight container in the refrigerator for up to 5 days. It also freezes really well for up to a year.

Blistered Green Beans, Shishitos, and Bell Peppers with Classic Pesto

SERVES 4 (MAKES 1 HEAPING CUP PESTO)

Pesto

¼ cup slivered almonds

1 garlic clove, smashed

2 cups tightly packed basil leaves

¼ cup grated Parmesan cheese

2 tablespoons fresh lemon juice (from 1 lemon)

½ cup extra-virgin olive oil, plus more as needed

¼ teaspoon kosher salt

Neutral oil, such as avocado or grapeseed

1 pound tender green beans, trimmed

1 red, orange, or yellow bell pepper, sliced into ¼-inch-wide strips

6 green or orange shishito peppers (see Note)

Coarse sea salt and freshly ground black pepper

I absolutely love growing green beans. When I first started gardening, I found it all very intimidating, and I worried that despite the time and money I'd invested in creating my raised beds, I'd end up with nothing to show for it. But when the stringless Contender bush beans I planted produced an abundant harvest, it made me feel like a master gardener, not the total novice I was. And it gave me the confidence to keep working at this new hobby of mine.

Green beans are one of the easiest vegetables to grow, and their roots fix nitrogen in the soil—plus, they taste delicious. This recipe is specifically made for those young beans that are good enough to eat raw, right off the vine. The hot-and-fast cooking application also works great with other summer garden veggies like bell peppers and shishitos. The bell peppers contribute sweetness, the shishitos lend their subtle heat, and both add beautiful color to the dish.

1 **Make the pesto:** In a food processor, combine the almonds, garlic, basil, Parmesan, and lemon juice. Pulse until well combined and broken down into a rough paste. With the motor running, slow stream in the olive oil, then add the salt and process until well combined. Scrape the pesto into a jar and pour a thin layer of olive oil over the top to prevent oxidation. Screw on the lid and store in the refrigerator until needed. (The pesto will keep for up to 4 days. After each use, make sure the surface is covered in a thin layer of oil.)

2 Heat a wide cast-iron skillet over medium-high heat, then add enough neutral oil to coat the bottom of the pan, 1½ teaspoons or so. Add the green beans, bell pepper, and shishitos and leave them alone to cook, undisturbed, for a few minutes. (This can get a little smoky, so make sure you have your vent fan on high!) Give the skillet a shake or flip the veggies around with tongs; the undersides should be blistered. Cook, stirring or flipping every so often, until the vegetables are blistered all the way around, then reduce the heat as needed to prevent burning and cook until the veggies are tender. The whole process should take 10 to 15 minutes total.

3 Remove from the heat, season with a couple pinches of sea salt and some black pepper and stir in ¼ cup of the pesto. Serve immediately.

Note: If you're not getting your shishitos from a farmers' market or growing them yourself, you may end up having to buy an 8-ounce bag, which will leave you with a bunch of extra peppers. These can be charred following the method above and served simply sprinkled with flaky sea salt or with pesto as a starter (warn your guests that shishitos are generally mild, but once in a while, you'll get a fiery one!), or try pickling them (see page 250).

Crispy Squash Blossom "Churros"

SERVES 4 TO 8

16 squash blossoms (see sidebar, page 142)

Neutral oil, such as avocado or grapeseed, for frying

½ cup turbinado sugar

1 teaspoon ground cinnamon

½ cup cornstarch

½ cup all-purpose flour

1 teaspoon baking powder

½ teaspoon coarse sea salt

1 cup sparkling water

2 teaspoons pure vanilla extract

I'm an average gardener at best, and every year I struggle to grow squash because of those pesky squash vine borers. My solution is to plant more, because even if I lose half my harvest to bugs, I'm still left with plenty of fruit. But to be completely honest, my real reason for growing that many squash plants is so that I have lots of blossoms—I love, love, *love* eating squash blossoms!

You'll find recipes from cultures around the world who share my sentiment, and while most are savory, the blossoms' delicate floral flavor actually makes them a wonderful dessert. They're fried to a crisp, which gives them an incredible texture, and after they've been rolled in cinnamon sugar, they remind me of a Spanish churro—just so simple, and so good.

1 Gently open each blossom and remove the stamen (if male) or pistil (if female) with long, narrow scissors or tweezers. Leave the stems attached so the blossoms are easier to handle as you're coating and frying them. Lay them on a tray or plate and let them air-dry in the refrigerator, uncovered, for a few hours before cooking.

2 Fill a deep skillet or wide pot with 1 to 2 inches of oil (it should be deep enough that when you add the blossoms, the oil covers them about halfway). Heat over medium-high heat to 350° to 375°F.

3 In a large bowl, stir together the sugar and cinnamon; set aside. In a separate medium bowl, combine the cornstarch, flour, baking powder, salt, sparkling water, and vanilla. Whisk until the batter is no longer lumpy.

4 Working in batches as needed, dip each blossom into the batter, swirling it around so it's fully coated. Let the excess batter drip off, then immediately transfer the blossom to the hot oil. Fry for 1 to 2 minutes on each side, until the batter forms a solid, crispy bubbled crust. (This "fritto misto" style of batter is very light and won't turn a deep golden brown.) Use a spider or skimmer to remove the blossoms from the oil, letting any excess drain back into the pot. Transfer the fried blossoms directly to the bowl of cinnamon sugar (don't blot these with paper towels) and toss until fully coated. Repeat to fry and coat the remaining blossoms. Enjoy immediately!

How to Harvest Squash Blossoms

Squash blossoms are one of summer's greatest gifts. You might be able to find them at the farmers' market (don't be afraid to ask vendors to save you some), but they're easy to harvest straight from summer or winter squash plants in your own garden.

If you're picking from your own garden, it's best to harvest blossoms early in the morning when the bud is open and before the afternoon heat wilts the flowers. Each plant grows both male and female flowers. The female flowers have a small bulb at the bottom that grows into the squash itself. With help from pollinators like bees, the pollen from the male flowers (which have long stalks attached directly to the stem of the plant) fertilizes the females, so pick no more than 75 percent of the male flowers at a time, since you'll need some for pollination.

Squash blossoms are very perishable, so it's best to eat them the same day you harvest them, but they can last a few days if stored properly; just spread them over a baking sheet lined with a slightly damp paper towel and keep them in the fridge.

Sweet Corn Ice Cream with Graham Cracker Crumbles

MAKES 1 QUART

3 ears sweet corn, husked

1 cup whole milk

¾ cup sugar

3 cups heavy cream

5 large egg yolks

1 tablespoon pure vanilla extract

8 whole graham crackers, crushed into crumbs, or Balsamic Dewberry Compote (page 92), for topping

Note: When stone fruits are in season, grill a few and slice into wedges to serve over top.

This is a custard-based ice cream, which means it has a rich, creamy texture. It's best made during the heat of summer when corn is at its finest, and it's my favorite dessert to bring to backyard BBQs because it's so unexpected and yet feels so appropriate for the season that it's hard to imagine going without it. It's excellent when paired with a good glass of bourbon. You could even serve it as my friend Ivy does, with a couple spoonfuls of bourbon on top to make a boozy ice-cream float. Another great way to serve it is with a dollop of the Balsamic Dewberry Compote.

The custard ice-cream base isn't difficult to make, but it does take a little bit of time, so be sure to plan accordingly. To help speed up the process, I grate the corn before adding it to the cream, a trick I learned from award-winning chef and restaurateur Kevin Gillespie—it infuses the cream with flavor much faster. Last but not least, don't forget to account for the chilling and churning time!

1 Using the large holes of a box grater, grate the corn kernels from the cobs into a large bowl; discard the cobs. Transfer the grated corn to a blender, add the milk and sugar, and pulse until the mixture reaches a coarse consistency.

2 Pour the corn mixture into a 3-quart saucepan and add the cream. Bring to a very gentle simmer (scalding temperature) over medium-low heat, then cook for 10 minutes to infuse the liquid with the corn's flavor. Remove from the heat.

3 Strain the mixture through a fine-mesh strainer, pressing on the solids with a spatula to extract as much liquid as possible. Return the corn-infused cream to the saucepan and bring to a gentle simmer over medium-low heat.

4 Meanwhile, beat the egg yolks in a small bowl until pale yellow and thick. While whisking continuously, carefully ladle in about 1 cup of the hot cream mixture to temper the eggs, then whisk to emulsify. Repeat with another cup of the cream, then, while whisking, pour the tempered egg mixture into the pot with the remaining cream. Cook over medium-low heat, stirring, until the custard thickens enough to

continued

coat the back of a spoon, 5 to 8 minutes. Be careful not to let it come to a boil. I like the custard to be so thick that when you lift the spoon out, the custard slowly falls back into the pot in a V shape as opposed to dripping straight down.

5 Fill a large bowl with ice and water. Place a slightly smaller bowl in the ice bath and set a clean fine-mesh strainer over the bowl. Remove the custard from the heat and pour it into the strainer to remove any solid particles of cooked egg. Stir in the vanilla and let cool. Press a sheet of plastic wrap directly against the surface of the custard to prevent a skin from forming and refrigerate for at least 4 hours and up to 24 hours before churning.

6 Pour the chilled custard into an ice-cream maker and churn according to the manufacturer's instructions. For soft ice cream, serve immediately, or transfer to an airtight container and freeze until hardened to your liking before serving. (The ice cream will keep for up to 6 months.)

7 Scoop some ice cream into individual bowls and top with the graham cracker crumbs or compote.

Fall

Game Season, Bird Dogs, Brown Butter

WHEN THE AUTUMNAL EQUINOX HITS, *I'm usually still sweating in the garden amid the swarms of butterflies that migrate through the heart of Texas this time of year. Just as the northern US experiences a true spring very late in the season, the South has to wait patiently for fall to come. Eventually, it does, and I watch the leaves change from green to vibrant orange before falling to the ground.*

Fall is game season for me, and most of my days are filled with travel and adventure as Travis and I hunt for the hard-earned meat that sustains us for months to come. The season kicks off early, in the days when summer slowly melds into fall and bull elk can be heard bugling in the mountains of the West. After we've exhausted ourselves on the rugged, intense terrain, we shift gears. My heart longs to be in the wide-open grasslands of the Midwest, where we quietly hike miles and miles until Zissou goes on point and the sudden flush of a bird's wings breaks the silence. As the days get shorter and winter creeps closer, rifle season opens up and the rut begins; in that short period of time, bucks throw all logic out the window in their search for does. It's an incredible moment to be outdoors and watch one of nature's greatest shows.

After we've filled our freezers, we celebrate by cooking, and the smell of butter browning or apple cider simmering on the stovetop fills my kitchen. This is my time for indulgence, and the calories I consume are my reward for the physical energy I put into harvesting the animals we hunted. ◆

Fall Ingredients

PRODUCE (GENERALLY)

Apples

Beets

Brassicas: broccoli, Brussels sprouts, cabbage, cauliflower

Carrots

Cranberries

Edible flowers

Figs

Ginger

Grapes

Greens: collards, Swiss chard, kale, spinach, broccoli and cauliflower leaves, mustard greens

Herbs: perennials (chives, rosemary, thyme, oregano, sage), cool-season annuals (dill, cutting celery, cilantro, parsley, tarragon, sorrel)

Lettuce

Pears

Persimmons

Pomegranates

Radishes

Storage vegetables: dried beans, peas, and corn; onions, garlic, potatoes

Sweet potatoes

Winter squash

SOUTHERN US

Cucumbers

Field peas

Green beans

Peppers

Squash (summer and winter)

Tomatoes

NORTHERN US

Celery

Chicory

Fennel

Kohlrabi

Leeks

Parsnips

Rutabaga

Turnip

FORAGED FOODS

Pawpaw

Persimmons

Tree nuts: acorns, pecans, hazelnuts, hickories, walnuts, etc.

Rose hips

Wild grapes

Wild mushrooms: chanterelles, porcini (and other boletes)

WILD GAME AND FISH

Venison: elk, deer, pronghorn, etc.

Upland game birds: pheasant, grouse, partridge, etc.

Black bear

Waterfowl: ducks, geese

Freshwater fish

Saltwater fish (inshore and deepwater)

Shellfish: clams, scallops, oysters, mussels, etc.

Butternut Squash Chutney with Blue Cheese and Crackers

MAKES ABOUT 4 CUPS CHUTNEY

Butternut Squash Chutney

1¼ cups apple cider

½ cup apple cider vinegar

1½ cups honey

¾ teaspoon ground cinnamon

¼ teaspoon ground ginger

⅛ teaspoon (or a heavy pinch) ground cloves

1 teaspoon coarse sea salt

2½ cups finely diced butternut squash

To Serve

Blue cheese wedge

Crackers

I love finding creative, out-of-the-box ways to use ingredients you might think of as savory in sweet applications, and vice versa. This extremely versatile butternut squash chutney is a great example, and infusing winter squash with apple cider and warm spices might make you reconsider the way you approach cooking with vegetables. The chutney works well in savory foods, such as with cheese and crackers for a charcuterie board, as it's presented here; with caramelized onions on top of baked Brie; or in the pork chop recipe on page 172. It's also delicious in sweet applications—I've spooned this chutney on top of pancakes and stuffed it into puff pastry for a mock apple pie—and the cinnamon syrup can be used as a substitute for honey in any baked recipe. This recipe makes a pretty big batch, but you'll find endless uses for it. During the summer, you can replace the squash with watermelon rind. Just peel off the tough green outer layer and use the light greenish-white portion of the rind.

1 **Make the chutney:** In a medium saucepan, combine the apple cider, cider vinegar, honey, cinnamon, ginger, cloves, and salt. Bring to a boil over high heat, stirring continuously to ensure the mixture is well blended, then add the squash. Reduce the heat and cook at a soft boil for 5 minutes, or until the squash is tender but still firm (it should be neither crunchy nor mushy). Remove from the heat and let stand for 15 minutes.

2 Drain the squash, reserving the cooking liquid, and divide it evenly between two 1-pint jars; set aside. Return the cooking liquid to the saucepan and bring to a boil over high heat. Boil for 5 to 8 minutes, until the liquid reduces and lightly coats the back of a spoon. You're aiming for a thin syrup consistency; it will continue to thicken as it cools. Remove from the heat.

3 Pour enough of the syrup into the jars to cover the squash. Let cool completely before serving or storing. The chutney will keep in an airtight container in the refrigerator for up to 1 month.

4 To serve, slice the blue cheese wedge into small pieces and serve with the chutney and crackers.

Venison Tartare with Parmesan and Horseradish Crème Fraîche

SERVES 4 TO 6 AS A STARTER, OR 2 AS A MAIN COURSE

Parmesan and Horseradish Crème Fraîche
(makes about ¾ cup)

½ cup crème fraîche

¼ cup grated Parmesan cheese

1 tablespoon thinly sliced fresh chives

1 tablespoon prepared horseradish

Coarse sea salt

Venison Tartare

1 (8- to 12-ounce) venison steak or roast (see Notes)

2 tablespoons extra-virgin olive oil

2 garlic cloves, minced or thinly sliced into even pieces

2 tablespoons minced shallot

2 tablespoons packed minced fresh parsley

1½ tablespoons capers, coarsely chopped

Parmesan and Horseradish Crème Fraîche (recipe follows)

Sliced sourdough bread, toasted

Microgreens, for garnish (optional)

I'm sure I say that every recipe is my favorite, but honestly, this is my favorite way to celebrate a successful hunt. It's what Travis requests for his birthday every year (we eat it as a main course with a side salad), and it's my go-to starter to serve a group of friends. With all the flavors of a traditional French beef tartare, this recipe is pretty evergreen, but it's fun to shake it up each season. In the summer, I love infusing it with Mediterranean flavors. Instead of capers, I use 2 tablespoons finely diced seedless cucumber and add a pinch of dried oregano. And instead of the crème fraîche and toast, I use toasted flatbread and labneh or plain 2% fat Greek yogurt. In the spring, swap out the shallots for ramps and serve the tartare on toasts with sautéed morels. In the winter, try finely diced kohlrabi or radishes instead of capers, and serve with the Creole Mustard Dressing on page 75.

1 **Make the crème fraîche:** In a small bowl, stir together the crème fraîche, Parmesan, chives, and horseradish until combined. Season with a couple pinches of salt. Transfer to an airtight container and refrigerate until ready to serve (it will keep for up to 5 days).

2 **Make the tartare:** If your venison is unfrozen, place it on a baking sheet and freeze for about 1 hour (this enables you to make cleaner cuts for pieces that are less likely to stick together; see Notes). If you're using meat that's been stored in the freezer, move it to the fridge the morning you plan to make the tartare; it should be just thawed enough when you're ready to dice it.

3 In a small skillet, heat the olive oil over medium-high heat. When the oil starts to shimmer, add the garlic. It should fry and lightly bubble when it hits the pan but shouldn't sputter and kick oil out; if it does, reduce the heat. Cook, giving the garlic a stir every now and then to make sure it's cooking evenly and not sticking, until golden in color, about 2 minutes. If you burn the garlic, you'll need to start over, so keep an eye on things and adjust the heat as needed. Use a slotted spoon to transfer the garlic to paper towels to drain, reserving the garlic-infused oil in the pan. Let the oil cool completely or chill it in the refrigerator for 15 to 30 minutes; it must be completely cool before it's mixed into the tartare.

recipe and ingredients continued

Grated Parmesan cheese,
for garnish

Lemon wedges

Flaky sea salt and freshly ground
black pepper

Jammy eggs (see page 58; optional)

4 Remove the venison from the freezer and use a sharp knife to finely dice it into ⅛- to ¼-inch cubes. Transfer the meat to a large bowl and gently fold in 2 teaspoons of the cooled garlic-infused oil, the toasted garlic, shallot, parsley, and capers.

5 To serve, swipe a dollop of the crème fraîche on a slice of toast, then spoon some of the venison tartare on top and garnish with some microgreens, if desired, and a little Parmesan. Squeeze a lemon wedge over the tartare, then season with a couple pinches each of flaky salt and pepper. Enjoy immediately, with some jammy eggs alongside, if you like!

Notes: You want the highest-quality meat for this recipe. For wild game, that means taking care of the animal by having good shot placement, field dressing in a clean manner, and cooling the meat quickly. During processing, after you've skinned the animal and removed the digestive tract, either clean your knife well or swap it out for a new one before cutting the meat away from the bone. Keep all dirt and hair off the meat and avoid chilling it in an ice-water cooler; you want it to stay cold and dry. If you're planning to freeze the meat to make this recipe later in the year, vacuum-seal it to prevent freezer burn and retain its quality.

Since the meat is diced so finely for this recipe, most cuts will work (even bottom round, which tends to be tougher). Choose a muscle with structural integrity and without any silver skin running through the middle. When I'm cutting steaks out of the backstrap, sirloin tip, heart, or flat-iron, I like to save the small, uneven scrap pieces for tartare.

Smoked Sage Venison Tenderloin with Brown Butter and Ultra-Creamy Mashed Potatoes

SERVES 2

2 whole venison tenderloins or 6- to 8-ounce steaks (see Notes)

8 fresh sage leaves

¼ teaspoon whole black peppercorns

1½ teaspoons smoked sea salt

1 pound russet or Yukon Gold potatoes, peeled and coarsely chopped

Coarse sea salt

4 tablespoons (½ stick) unsalted butter, cut into tablespoons, plus more if needed

Beef tallow or neutral oil, such as avocado or grapeseed

Cranberry sauce, for serving (optional)

The beautiful silver-green sagebrush that sweeps across the wide-open prairies of the Midwest is a native plant I've grown very fond of. From South Texas all the way up north into Canada, it's a symbol of our grasslands, which are home to a diverse array of wildlife and act as an important carbon sink. The heady yet softly sweet aroma of sagebrush is also nostalgic for me. It brings me back to evenings spent camping along the Little Missouri River, where we'd burn the leaves to keep insects at bay and enjoy their perfume. I also think of one Christmas morning, when we flushed a covey of bobwhite quail out of the brush while hunting on a patch of public land in South Texas. And I can't smell sagebrush without immediately returning to the day I took my first big game animal, a handsome pronghorn antelope buck, on the plains of Wyoming.

There are several varieties of sagebrush, and though some smell distinctly like Thanksgiving, it's actually a member of the sunflower family. Deer, elk, antelope, and grouse browse on the foliage or seeds of this native shrub, which imparts an earthy, grassy quality to their meat. This earthiness tends to be divisive; I think it's a beautiful flavor, one I like to highlight, not mask. Inspired by my experiences, I created an aromatic spice blend with smoked sea salt and garden sage to pay homage to the wild places and animals that I love so much.

1 At least 30 minutes and up to 1 hour before you plan to cook, remove the meat from the fridge to let it come to room temperature. If you're using a large tenderloin from an elk or nilgai, cut it in half, if needed, so that it fits in the skillet for searing.

2 Mince 2 of the sage leaves and place them in a small bowl; set the rest aside. Use a mortar and pestle to coarsely crush the peppercorns, then add them to the bowl with the minced sage. (If you don't have a mortar and pestle, pulse them briefly in a spice grinder or place them in a zip-top bag and smash them with a rolling pin.) Add the smoked salt and stir to combine. Set aside.

3 Place the potatoes in a large saucepan and pour in just enough water to cover. Add a few big pinches of coarse salt (roughly 1½ teaspoons) and bring to a boil over high heat. Reduce the heat to

continued

Notes: If you're using deer tenderloin, the recipe will serve two people. To serve four, you can use moose, nilgai, or elk tenderloin, 4 venison steaks, or 4 beef steaks. You'll also need to double the quantities of the other ingredients.

Though I call for tenderloins, you can use any steak for this recipe. Note that cooking times may vary depending on thickness. This recipe is also excellent with pheasant or grouse breasts in place of venison.

medium to maintain a simmer and cook until the potatoes are very tender when pierced with a fork, 15 to 20 minutes.

4 Put 2 tablespoons of the butter in a large bowl and set it nearby. Remove the saucepan from the heat and use a slotted spoon to scoop the potatoes into a food mill or potato ricer, reserving the starchy cooking water in the pot. Pass the potatoes through the food mill directly into the bowl with the butter. Using a spatula, fold about 2 tablespoons of the starchy water into the mashed potatoes to combine. Add another tablespoon of the starchy water, if needed, to reach a smooth and silky texture. Taste and season with more salt, if needed. Pour the water out of the saucepan, then return the potatoes to the pot, cover, and keep warm until ready to serve.

5 Heat a large cast-iron skillet over medium-high heat. Pat the meat very dry and season both sides with the sage seasoning. When the pan is hot, add enough tallow to lightly coat the bottom. Working in batches, if needed, lay the tenderloins in the pan, leaving a little space between them, and sear for 1 to 2 minutes on the first side, then flip and sear on the second side for 1 to 2 minutes more. Flip back to the first side and sear for 1 minute, then flip again and sear for a final minute (so each side has been seared twice). In that final minute, place the remaining 6 sage leaves over the meat and drop the remaining 2 tablespoons butter into the pan. Let the butter melt and foam, then tilt the pan and use a spoon to scoop up the melted butter and baste the sage and the top of meat. Do this a few times for each tenderloin, letting the hot butter fry the sage. After basting, use tongs to test the doneness of the meat (see Testing Steak for Doneness, page 44), or check it with a meat thermometer—you're aiming for medium-rare, about 130°F. The whole process may take 5 to 6 minutes for a deer tenderloin, or about 8 minutes for elk or nilgai. Transfer the meat to a cutting board to rest, uncovered, for 8 minutes. Pour the browned butter from the skillet into a small bowl so it doesn't burn. (If the butter seems burnt or tastes bitter, discard it and wipe out the pan; melt 2 tablespoons butter and toast it for a few minutes, until browned, then immediately remove it from the heat.)

6 Serve the venison drizzled with a spoonful of the browned butter, with the mashed potatoes and some cranberry sauce alongside, if desired.

Grilled Heart Skewers with a Red Wine and Wild Chile Glaze

SERVES 6 TO 8

Red Wine and Wild Chile Glaze

1 cup dry red wine (pinot noir or cabernet)

1 teaspoon dried chiltepins or chiles pequin, or 1 dried Thai bird's-eye chile or chile de árbol

¼ cup coarsely chopped red onion or shallot

¼ cup sugar

¼ cup red wine vinegar

Heart Skewers

Neutral oil, such as avocado or grapeseed

1 deer heart, or ½ elk, nilgai, or beef heart (see Note)

Coarse sea salt and freshly ground black pepper

Note: This recipe also works with duck or goose hearts. Use at least a dozen, and skewer them whole. They will only take a few minutes total to cook.

The idea of eating heart really freaks some people out, but the heart is a muscle just like any other cut of meat. The texture is a little denser, and it doesn't have long muscle fibers like the steaks and roasts you're used to eating, but it's incredibly tender! In this recipe, slices of heart are skewered and seared fast on a hot grill and basted with a sweet-and-spicy glaze that caramelizes under the heat. It's practically meat candy.

I use wild chiles called chiltepins, said to be the only chile native to North America, to make this glaze. I was first introduced to them by my in-laws, who always have a jar of pickled chiltepins in their refrigerator, gathered from the bushes growing wild on their property. Though the chiles are only the size of a peppercorn, they pack a serious punch—between 50,000 and 100,000 on the Scoville scale, same as a Thai chile! Wild chiltepins might be difficult to access, but you can readily find their domesticated cousin, chile pequin, in dried form.

---

1 **Make the glaze:** In a medium saucepan, combine the wine, dried chiles, and onion. Bring to a boil over high heat, then reduce the heat to medium-low and simmer for 5 minutes, or until the wine has reduced by half. Strain the reduction and set aside.

2 Rinse and dry the saucepan. Combine 2 tablespoons water and the sugar in the clean pan. Bring to a boil over high heat, stirring to dissolve the sugar, then cook until it reaches an amber color, about 3 minutes. Pour in the vinegar and the strained red wine reduction. It will immediately boil up, so be careful not to burn yourself! The sugar will initially seize up but will dissolve again as it cooks. Adjust the heat as needed to maintain a soft (not rolling) boil and cook, stirring occasionally, for 3 to 5 minutes, until the liquid thickens enough to coat the back of a spoon but will still drip off the spoon (aim for about 220°F on a candy thermometer). Keep in mind that it will harden as it cools. To check the consistency, place a small plate in the freezer for about 10 minutes, then spoon some of the liquid onto the plate. If it still has a liquid consistency, it hasn't cooked long enough. If it hardens into candy or caramel, it has cooked too

continued

How to Clean a Heart

When you buy a heart from the butcher, they've taken care of removing the pericardium, arteries, and atriums at the top, a task you'll have to handle yourself if you're butchering game at home. I was very intimidated the first time I had to clean a heart, so I found some videos online to get a better sense of what to do. Most of these made it look like a hack job, and the result was very unappealing. I strongly believe you eat with your eyes first, so presentation is really important—those hack jobs wouldn't fly in my book. Instead, I took a different tack and watched a video of surgeons dissecting a human heart. Morbid? Maybe—but I learned how to open a heart and cut it into two flat pieces that closely resemble steaks. Here's the method I use.

First, run lots of cold water through the heart and squeeze out any coagulated blood. Cut off the arteries and atriums (I give these to my dogs as a special treat!) and trim any hard white fat at the top. Look inside or use your fingers to feel where a wall of tissue (the septum) separates the heart into two chambers (or ventricles, if we're being technical). One chamber is essentially a big cone shape, almost like a bell pepper, and there's a smaller piece of meat wrapped around half of the left side that makes up the other chamber. Looking at the outside of the heart, you'll see a prominent artery (the coronary artery—I learned a lot in that video!) running from the top down through the middle before wrapping around to the back of the heart. This is the seam that divides the two chambers. Using a sharp knife, make an incision along the artery, following it down until the heart is separated into two pieces—the conical "bell pepper" and the thin outside piece that was attached to it. Next, cut the conical "bell pepper" piece straight down the middle to open it. It won't lie flat at first; you'll need to cut the numerous tiny tendons you see attached to the inside of the heart.

After cleaning off those tendons, I like to make some small slashes on the sides of the heart where it wants to curl up to help it lie flat.

You should now have two somewhat flat, rectangular pieces of meat. One is thin and small; the other is thicker and wider. You can sear each piece just as you would a steak (the thicker piece will cook in 4 to 6 minutes, the thinner one in 3 to 5 minutes), seasoning with a little bit of the Mushroom Rub on page 256 and adding a splash of bourbon and a pat of butter to make an incredibly easy sauce. Or you can thinly slice them into strips to thread on skewers for grilling as on page 158.

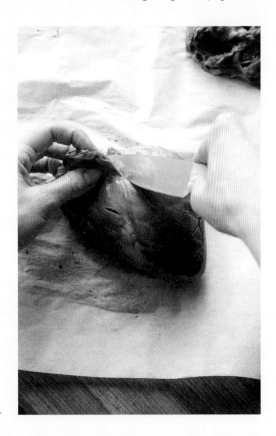

long; to fix it, add a couple tablespoons of water and boil until it dissolves, then check the consistency again. Transfer the glaze to a jar or airtight container and let cool. (It will keep in the refrigerator for several weeks.)

3 **Make the heart skewers:** If you're using wooden or bamboo skewers, soak them in water for 30 minutes to 1 hour before you plan to grill. Brush your grill grates with oil and heat the grill to very high heat.

4 Open up the heart (see page 159), wash it really well, and slice it into long, ¼-inch-wide pieces. Thread the strips of heart onto the skewers like a ribbon, slightly scrunching them together. Season the meat generously on both sides with salt and pepper and coat with a thin layer of oil. Set the skewers on the hot grill and cook until brown on the first side, 30 seconds to 1 minute. Flip the skewers, brush the tops with the glaze, and grill again for about 1 minute. Flip again and brush with the glaze; repeat this process a few times until the heart is cooked to medium-rare, 3 to 4 minutes total. The meat should still be pink in the middle.

5 Serve immediately.

Venison and Pumpkin Stew

Beef tallow, clarified butter, or neutral oil, such as avocado or grapeseed

2 to 2½ pounds venison, lamb, or beef stew meat

Coarse sea salt and freshly ground black pepper

2 tablespoons unsalted butter

1 large sweet onion, diced

3 medium parsnips, peeled and coarsely chopped

3 large carrots, coarsely chopped

¼ cup whiskey

6 cups venison stock or beef stock, homemade (see page 257) or store-bought

2 tablespoons pure maple syrup

1 (14-ounce) can pure pumpkin puree (see Note)

1 cinnamon stick

⅛ teaspoon ground allspice

3 or 4 sprigs thyme

Creamy Polenta (see page 232) or popovers (see page 208), for serving

Note: You can use 1½ to 2 cups of homemade pumpkin puree or mashed sweet potato in place of the canned pumpkin.

I'm not big on pumpkin spice lattes or any of the other fads that appear when September 1 rolls around, but if you're looking for a quintessential fall-inspired dish, this recipe is for you. (And the pumpkin, butter, maple syrup, and cinnamon might even scratch that PSL itch!) The pumpkin might sound unconventional, but it gives the stew a silkiness that feels decadent, especially for a dish that's so easy to make. I like to serve this stew with Creamy Polenta (page 232), but I particularly love it with the popovers on page 208 (if you go that route, make them with butter instead of tallow).

1 Heat a large Dutch oven or wide pot over high heat. Add enough tallow to lightly coat the bottom (about 1 tablespoon) and let it melt. Working in batches as needed, add the stew meat and cook, undisturbed, for a few minutes, until browned on the bottom. Give the meat a good stir and cook until browned all over, a few minutes more. Generously season with salt and pepper, then transfer the meat to a plate and set aside.

2 Reduce the heat under the pot to medium. Drop in the butter and let it melt, then add the onion and cook, stirring occasionally, for 4 to 6 minutes, until the onion begins to soften. Add the parsnips and carrots and cook for a few minutes more.

3 Carefully pour the bourbon (measure it out into a container first, don't pour it straight from the bottle!) into the pot and cook for a minute or two to burn off the alcohol. Pour the stock into the pan and stir, scraping up the browned bits from the bottom. Stir in the maple syrup, pumpkin, cinnamon stick, allspice, and thyme and return the venison to the pot. Reduce the heat to low, cover, and cook for 4 to 6 hours, until the meat is tender. (Alternatively, transfer everything from the pot to a slow cooker, cover, and cook on low for 4 to 6 hours; or cook in a pressure cooker at high pressure for 1½ to 2 hours.) About halfway through the cooking time, set the lid of the pot (or slow cooker) so it's partially covering the top to allow the liquid to reduce and thicken.

4 Taste and season with salt and pepper as needed. Serve hot, on top of the polenta or with popovers alongside.

Mushroom– Rubbed Roast Venison au Jus

SERVES 4 TO 6

1 elk, nilgai, moose, or buck sirloin tip, or 2 doe or antelope sirloin tips (see Note)

Mushroom Rub (page 256)

Beef tallow or neutral oil, such as avocado or grapeseed

3 cups unsalted venison stock or beef stock, homemade (see page 257) or low-sodium store-bought

4 garlic cloves, smashed and peeled

2 sprigs thyme

1 (¼-ounce) packet unflavored powdered gelatin (optional; see Level Up Your Store-Bought Stock, page 259)

1½ teaspoons Worcestershire sauce

¼ cup dry red wine

Note: The sirloin tip is a football-shaped muscle in a deer's hindquarter that serves a similar function as the quadriceps in your thigh. It sits above the kneecap and has to be carved off the femur. Technically, it's composed of three small muscles; don't try to separate these muscles to take out the two pieces of silver skin that divide them. This silver skin holds the roast together, and there's a good deal of fat and flavor worth saving between it and the meat. (But do go ahead and trim the silver skin on the outside!)

When I was learning how to process deer, I did it all by trial and error. I looked at a lot of butchering diagrams, but most of the muscles on a hindquarter were simply labeled as "roasts," and I wasn't sure what that meant exactly. Is it a noun, or a verb, or does it imply both? It's a vague term commonly used to describe a large cut of meat, and what makes it more confusing is that not all roasts should be cooked the same way—the Winter Pot Roast with Celery Root and Gremolata on page 231 is best braised, for example, but what if you want that rosy-red meat? I developed this recipe for anyone who wants to successfully "roast their roast" so it turns out similar to a juicy, meaty beef prime rib.

If you're concerned that you don't have the cooking chops to serve something like this, don't worry—this recipe is practically foolproof! Use a cut that's very tender and shaped in a way that ensures it will cook evenly. In fact, there are only two cuts I would use for this recipe: the inside round and the sirloin tip (see the diagram on page 45), which has fatty deposits on the inside that make it delicious. Then just pull out the roast when it hits the temperature called for in the recipe, and the meat will be perfect. If you've got leftovers, they're great sliced very thinly and served on sandwiches as either a French dip au jus, with Parmesan and Horseradish Crème Fraîche (page 152), or with Italian Dressing (page 76) and Bacon and Pickled Pepper Aioli (page 249).

1 Remove the meat from the refrigerator at least 30 minutes before cooking. Preheat the oven to 225°F on the convection setting (if you don't have convection, preheat to 250°F).

2 Trim off the thin layer of silver skin that covers the top and outside of the meat (don't try to break it down on the inside; see Note). Reserve the trimmings for making the jus. Use kitchen twine and truss the roast so that it will cook evenly (see Notes).

3 Heat a large skillet over very high heat, then add 1 to 2 tablespoons beef tallow. When the tallow is hot, generously rub the meat all over with mushroom rub and sear it until just golden brown on all sides, 3 to 4 minutes total. Transfer the meat to a baking sheet lined with a

continued

Notes: If you don't have venison, you can substitute a beef roast, or season other steak cuts, such as tenderloin or loin, with the mushroom rub and cook according to the instructions on page 46.

To give the roast an even shape, I typically just cut several 10- to 12-inch-long pieces of twine and wrap them around the meat at 1- to 2-inch intervals, tying them off with a square knot. (If you want to get fancy and truss it like the professionals do, there are lots of great videos online that demonstrate how!)

wire rack (set the skillet aside). Drizzle the top with some tallow and stick an oven-safe meat thermometer into the meat at its thickest point. Roast for 1 to 2 hours, depending on how thick the meat is (a doe's sirloin tip is a third the size of an elk's!), until the meat is 5 to 8 degrees from the desired final temperature (see chart below; carryover heat will continue cooking the meat as it rests).

4 Meanwhile, in a small saucepan, combine the reserved meat trimmings, stock, garlic, thyme, and gelatin (if using). Bring to a boil over high heat, then reduce the heat to maintain a gentle bubble. Simmer until the liquid has reduced to 1 cup, about 20 minutes. Strain and set aside.

5 When the meat has reached the desired temperature, remove it from the oven and transfer to a cutting board to rest. Set the skillet in which you browned the meat over medium-high heat. Pour in the Worcestershire, wine, and reduced stock and bring to a boil, stirring and scraping up the browned bits from the bottom of the skillet. Cook for 3 to 4 minutes to burn off the alcohol, then remove from the heat. Taste and season the jus with a few teaspoons of the mushroom rub, or to taste.

6 Slice the venison roast into ½- to 1-inch-thick slices or into very thin slices for French dip sandwiches. Serve with the hot jus.

Target Final Temperature

Rare: 125°F	Remove at 120°F
Medium-rare: 130°F	Remove at 125°F
Medium: 135°F	Remove at 130°F

Chile–Lime Roasted Winter Squash with Jicama Salad and Quinoa

SERVES 4

Honey–Lime Vinaigrette

¼ cup fresh lime juice (from 2 limes)

1 tablespoon honey

½ cup plus 2 tablespoons neutral oil, such as avocado or grapeseed

1 small garlic clove, grated or smashed to a pulp

Coarse sea salt

Roasted Winter Squash

2 to 2½ pounds winter squash, such as 1 large kabocha or 2 large acorn squash (see Notes)

Ancho Chile Seasoning (page 254)

Quinoa

1¾ cups Vegetable Stock (page 259) or water

1 cup uncooked quinoa

1 tablespoon neutral oil, such as avocado or grapeseed

Coarse sea salt

When I was thinking of how to show off winter squash and jicama, two of my favorite fall vegetables, I couldn't help but be inspired by their origins in Mexico and Central America. Winter squash, a New World food, played an important role in early American history, but the earliest squash likely originated in what is today Mexico during the Neolithic period, when humans were just starting to try their hand at agriculture. Together with beans and maize, it was among the first cultivated crops.

Jicama is a root vegetable native to Mexico that also grows in South and Central America and the southernmost regions of the US, and its origins can be traced back to roughly 3,000 BCE! Jicama can't tolerate cold weather, so it's typically harvested in the fall before the chance of first frost. The rough brown skin on the outside is easily peeled off to reveal the light-colored flesh underneath. Its texture is very much like an apple—crisp and juicy. But unlike an apple, jicama is almost flavorless, so it can act like a blank palette and soak up the flavors of whatever you dress it with. In this recipe, one of the most flavorful—and visually striking—vegetarian meals I've ever developed, I've chosen a sweet and tangy honey-lime vinaigrette that complements the chile-roasted squash and grassy quinoa beautifully.

1 Preheat the oven to 375°F. Line a baking sheet with parchment paper.

2 **Make the vinaigrette:** In a small bowl, whisk together the lime juice, honey, oil, and garlic until emulsified (or do what I've been doing lately: Combine everything in a jar and shake it really vigorously). Season with a couple pinches of salt and set aside. (The vinaigrette will keep in the refrigerator for up to 3 days.)

3 **Make the squash:** Using a very sharp, heavy knife, cut the squash into 3- to 4-inch-wide boats or cups. (If you're using an acorn squash, quarter it. If it's a kabocha, cut it in sixths. For a long, skinny delicata squash, cut it in half lengthwise. A large butternut squash can be halved lengthwise, then cut crosswise into thirds.) Use a spoon and scoop out the seeds and stringy flesh inside (save the seeds for roasting, if you like; see Notes).

recipe and ingredients continued

Jicama Salad

½ large red onion, thinly sliced

1 medium jicama (see Notes), peeled and cut into fine matchsticks

1½ cups fresh cilantro, chopped

¼ cup crumbled feta cheese

2 cups microgreens (a mix of spicy greens, or sunflower microgreens), alfalfa sprouts, or baby arugula

Notes: There are so many different kinds of winter squash; feel free to choose a variety you've yet to explore. The best I've ever tried in this recipe was an exceptionally soft heirloom red kabocha. Its vibrant orange color is not only beautiful, it's representative of the intensity of the squash's flavor. Acorn and Festival acorn, delicata, buttercup, butternut, and red kuri are also great choices.

If you can't find jicama, kohlrabi is a perfect substitute. It's a cruciferous vegetable that grows well in cooler weather, making it available from late summer to early fall in the northern part of US and during the winter months in the South. It has the exact same texture as jicama but with a slightly cabbagelike flavor. You could also substitute an apple or pear for the same textural crunch.

Kabocha squash seeds are very thick and chewy even after roasting, so I compost them instead.

4 Place the squash cut-side up on the prepared baking sheet. Using a pastry brush, generously coat the squash with some of the vinaigrette, then season generously with the chile seasoning; reserve the remaining seasoning and vinaigrette.

5 Roast the squash until the flesh is very tender when pricked with a fork, the edges begin to char and caramelize, and the squash is oozing delicious sugary liquid (you did line your pan, right!?). Depending on how you cut your squash, this could take between 45 minutes and 1 hour.

6 **Meanwhile, make the quinoa:** In a large (2- to 3-quart) saucepan, bring the stock to a boil over high heat. (I like to cook the quinoa in a bigger, wider pot because it allows the grains to spread out and makes the quinoa fluffier; narrower, taller pots create more steam and make the grains clump together.) Add the oil and several pinches of the remaining chile seasoning. Stir in the quinoa until combined, then reduce the heat to its lowest setting and cover. Cook for 15 minutes, or until the grains are soft and fluffy. Remove from the heat and take the lid off the pan to let the steam escape and allow the quinoa to cool. Taste, season with salt, and set aside.

7 **Start the jicama salad:** Place the onion in a small bowl and pour about ¼ cup of the remaining vinaigrette over the top. Use a fork to massage the vinaigrette in until the onion is fully coated. Let rest in the fridge for 15 to 30 minutes before serving—this will soften the texture and tame the pungency of the onion.

8 When the squash is tender, remove it from the oven and let cool slightly (it should still be warm—you just don't want to serve it piping hot with a cold salad on top).

9 In a large bowl, combine the jicama, cilantro, feta, and marinated onion (along with any vinaigrette in the bowl) and use tongs to gently toss them together. Spoon over more of the reserved vinaigrette until the flavor is to your liking. Add the microgreens at the very last moment before serving to keep them from getting soggy and wilting.

10 To serve, divide the squash pieces evenly among four plates, cut-side up, and layer a spoonful of quinoa on top of the squash. If desired, season with a little more vinaigrette (you'll want to drink the stuff, it's that good!) and then top with the jicama salad.

Wild Mushrooms with Seaweed Compound Butter

SERVES 4

Seaweed Butter

½ cup (1 stick) unsalted butter

2 tablespoons coarsely ground dried seaweed, such as sugar kelp, wakame, or nori (see Note)

2 scallions, white parts only, minced

2 garlic cloves, minced

1 teaspoon rice vinegar

Mushrooms

1 tablespoon neutral oil, such as avocado or grapeseed

1 teaspoon toasted sesame oil

1 pound wild mushrooms, torn into even pieces

2 tablespoons low-sodium soy sauce

2 scallions, green parts only, thinly sliced on an angle, for garnish

1 teaspoon sesame seeds, for garnish

Crushed dried seaweed flakes, for garnish

While I enjoy a good bowl of miso soup or wakame salad at Japanese restaurants, seaweed isn't something I cook with much at home. But when I started learning more about how sustainable and beneficial seaweed farming is for our oceans, I knew I needed to incorporate sea vegetables into my diet. There are many types of sea vegetables, and some are an acquired taste. My favorite varieties are sugar kelp, which has a slightly sweet marine flavor, and wakame, which is mild and nutty. This compound butter is great dropped into a pan of browned wild mushrooms with soy sauce and served with rice and a fried egg for lunch.

1 **Make the seaweed butter:** In a large skillet, melt the butter over medium-low heat. Add the seaweed, scallion whites, garlic, and vinegar. Cook, stirring occasionally, for a few minutes to allow the seaweed and aromatics to soften. Remove from the heat and transfer to a small glass container to cool, then refrigerate until set. Before using, stir the butter to re-emulsify the butterfat and milk solids.

2 **Cook the mushrooms:** Heat a wide skillet over medium-high heat. Add the neutral oil and sesame oil. When the oil is hot, add the mushrooms and spread them evenly over the bottom of the pan, trying to leave some space between them so they don't steam (work in batches, if needed). Cook, undisturbed, for 1½ minutes, then give them a stir and cook, stirring every minute or so, until golden brown and reduced in size, 4 to 5 minutes. Add 2 tablespoons of the seaweed butter, stir, and cook for 1 minute more, or until the mushrooms are tender and their edges are crispy. Pour in the soy sauce and cook, stirring and scraping up the browned bits from the bottom or the pan, until the liquid has evaporated. Remove from the heat.

3 Garnish with the scallion greens, sesame seeds, and seaweed flakes, then serve. The leftover seaweed butter will keep in an airtight container in the refrigerator for a couple of days or in the freezer for several months.

Note: You can buy dried seaweed already in flakes, or tear sheets or pieces of dried seaweed into large strips and pulse in a spice grinder until coarsely ground and flaky. Check out page 262 for some sustainably farmed seaweed sources.

Garlicky Meatballs with Spinach Orzo Pasta

SERVES 4

Meatballs

1 pound 80% lean ground venison, beef, lamb, wild hog, or pork

1 large egg, beaten

4 garlic cloves, minced

½ cup panko bread crumbs

2 tablespoons minced shallot

1 tablespoon minced fresh parsley

1¼ teaspoons coarse sea salt

½ to 1 teaspoon red pepper flakes (use the whole teaspoon if you like things spicy)

½ teaspoon dried oregano

¼ teaspoon freshly ground black pepper

Olive oil

Meatballs are a staple in my house, and I don't doubt they're a hit in your house as well. I make a variety of meatballs inspired by cuisines from around the world, but time and time again, I come back to this recipe because it's so versatile and delicious. I like to double (or even triple) the quantities and freeze the extra meatballs to use in other meals. In the summer, I stuff them inside warm pita bread with Greek yogurt and Cucumber Relish (page 128). In the winter, they're a fun addition to soups; I sometimes use them in place of the plain ground venison in the red pepper soup on page 215.

If you find yourself needing a break from the standard spaghetti and red sauce, this simple orzo pasta will be a hit. Try it in the spring with other greens or even asparagus substituted for the spinach.

1 **Make the meatballs:** Combine all the meatball ingredients (except for the olive oil) in a large bowl and mix thoroughly with a spatula until the mixture holds together when formed into a ball. Use an ice-cream scoop or your hands to roll the mixture into golf ball–size meatballs and set them aside on a baking sheet until ready to cook. (The meatballs can be formed up to 48 hours in advance and stored, covered, in the refrigerator; alternatively, freeze them on the baking sheet until solid, then transfer to an airtight container or vacuum-sealed bag and freeze for up to 6 months. Defrost overnight in the refrigerator and cook as directed.)

2 **Make the pasta:** Bring a large pot of water to a rolling boil over high heat. Season with a few big pinches of salt and add the orzo. Cook, stirring occasionally so the orzo doesn't stick, until tender and toothy, 15 to 20 minutes. Reserve 1 cup of the pasta water, then drain the orzo, rinse with cool water, and set aside.

3 Heat a very large skillet over medium-high heat. Add about 1 tablespoon olive oil to the skillet, enough to lightly coat the bottom. When the oil is shimmering, use tongs to set the meatballs in the pan one by one, leaving a little bit of space between each one. (Depending on the size of your pan, you may need to work in batches.) I like to do this in a clockwise direction, starting from the outside and swirling my way in to the center; the oil should sputter when you add the meatballs but not pop. By the time you add the last one, the first meatball should already be browned on the

Pasta

Coarse sea salt

2 cups orzo

1 tablespoon sun-dried tomato oil
(from the jar)

½ cup finely diced shallot

4 garlic cloves, minced

⅓ cup packed drained and sliced
sun-dried tomatoes

4 big handfuls of spinach

3 tablespoons red wine vinegar

½ cup grated Parmesan cheese

Red pepper flakes (optional)

bottom. Going in the same order you added them, flip the meatballs and cook until browned on the second side, about 2 minutes (if you've lost track of which one went in the pan first, just make sure they're browned on the bottom before you flip them). Reduce the heat to medium-low and give the pan a hard shake to roll the meatballs around. Cook, shaking the pan frequently to move the meatballs around, for 4 to 5 minutes more, until they're browned on all sides and cooked through. Keep warm until ready to serve.

4 Meanwhile, heat a large sauté pan (preferably with tall, slightly rounded sides) over medium-high heat. Pour in the sun-dried tomato oil and swirl it around the pan to coat. When the oil begins to shimmer, add the shallot and cook, stirring only once or twice, for 2 to 3 minutes, until soft. Add the garlic and cook for an additional minute, or until fragrant. Add the sun-dried tomatoes, spinach, and vinegar and gently toss to combine. Cook until the spinach starts to wilt, a minute or two. Add the cooked orzo, ½ cup of the reserved pasta water, and the Parmesan. Stir to combine. If it looks dry, stir in another ¼ cup of the pasta water. Taste and season with salt, then remove from the heat.

5 Serve the meatballs on top of the pasta, garnished with red pepper flakes, if desired.

Rosemary and Peppercorn Pork Chops with Butternut Squash Chutney

SERVES 4

4 (1½- to 2-inch-thick) bone-in pork chops

1 teaspoon whole black peppercorns

2 tablespoons coarse sea salt

4 teaspoons minced fresh rosemary

Neutral oil, such as avocado or grapeseed

4 tablespoons (½ stick) unsalted butter

½ cup finely diced sweet onion

2 garlic cloves, minced

1 cup unsalted pork stock or chicken stock, homemade (see page 257) or low-sodium store-bought

1 cup strained Butternut Squash Chutney (page 151; see Note), apple chutney, or applesauce

When I started buying domestic meat again as a way to support local farmers, I went for two things: cuts that the farmer had trouble selling (usually things like turkey wings or flank steak) and meat with a bunch of fat in it. After spending years eating lean game meat, I was craving a rich, juicy pork chop!

This recipe will remind you of the classic pairing of pork and apple, but as a twist on that theme, I opt for winter squash in the form of a chutney, which I stir into the pan juices to make a sweet and savory sauce. These chops are great served with some simply steamed green beans, roasted Brussels sprouts, or the Spinach and Buckwheat Salad on page 189.

1 Up to 48 hours before cooking, season the pork: Remove the pork chops from the fridge. Using a mortar and pestle, coarsely crush the peppercorns (alternatively, put them in a zip-top bag and crush them with a rolling pin or wine bottle). You're aiming for a more granular consistency than what you typically get from a pepper grinder. Transfer the peppercorns to a small bowl and stir in the salt and rosemary until well combined. Sprinkle the mixture generously over the pork chops on all sides. If you don't use it all, reserve what is left. Cover the pork and refrigerate until ready to cook.

2 Thirty minutes to 1 hour before you plan to cook, pull the pork chops from the fridge to let them come to room temp. Preheat the oven to 275°F.

3 Heat a wide ovenproof skillet over high heat, then add enough oil to coat the bottom of the pan in a thin layer. When the oil is hot, pat the meat very, very dry with paper towels (don't worry if you remove the seasoning in the process; you can add more later). Lay each pork chop in the pan, pressing down on it with your tongs or a spatula to ensure the surface of the meat is in full contact with the pan, and sear on the first side for 2 minutes, or until browned. Flip the meat, insert an oven-safe meat thermometer into the thickest part of one pork chop, and top each with about ½ tablespoon of the butter. Transfer to the oven and cook until the meat reaches 145°F. Remove from the oven and transfer the pork chops to a cutting board to rest.

Note: Use a slotted spoon to separate the chutney solids from the syrup before adding it to this recipe. You want to have just a little bit of syrup; be sure your chutney isn't drowning in it or your pan sauce will be far too sweet. In place of the winter squash chutney, any store-bought apple chutney, or even very finely diced fresh apple, will work; if using apple, be sure to add a pinch each of ground cinnamon and ground cloves for spice.

4 Return the pan to the stovetop over medium-high heat. Add the onion and cook, stirring occasionally, for 2 to 3 minutes, until soft and golden brown. Add the garlic and cook for another minute. Pour in the stock and bring the liquid to a boil, stirring and scraping up the browned bits from the bottom of the pan, then cook until the liquid has reduced by about half, about 4 minutes. Reduce the heat to medium-low and add the chutney and the remaining 2 tablespoons butter, shaking the pan and stirring to emulsify the sauce. Simmer the sauce for 2 to 3 minutes, until it thickens slightly. Taste and season as desired with the remaining rosemary-pepper blend.

5 Serve the pork chops with the warm chutney sauce and your choice of side.

Coq au Vin

SERVES 4 GENEROUSLY

2 whole pheasants, or 4 chicken legs (drumsticks and thighs; see Notes)

Kosher salt and freshly ground black pepper

Schmaltz (rendered chicken fat; see Notes) or neutral oil, such as avocado or grapeseed

½ medium onion, chopped

2 carrots, chopped

2 celery stalks, chopped

1 leek, sliced and rinsed well to remove any grit

6 garlic cloves, chopped

2 tablespoons tomato paste

2 tablespoons all-purpose flour, plus more if needed

2 cups full-bodied dry red wine, such as burgundy

2 cups chicken stock or pheasant stock, homemade (page 257) or store-bought, plus more if needed

3 or 4 sprigs rosemary and/or thyme

1 bay leaf

2 pints wild mushrooms or portobello mushrooms, coarsely chopped

1 cup frozen pearl onions, thawed and patted very dry

1 tablespoon red wine vinegar

2 tablespoons unsalted butter, melted (optional)

Minced fresh parsley, for garnish

This is the recipe I made with the very first pheasant I brought home from a hunt. It's a dish I'd made many times before with chicken, but it never tasted quite as incredible as it did that day. Perhaps it was the deep flavor of the meat, or maybe a combination of pride in my accomplishment and an overwhelming appreciation for what was on my plate. Whatever the case, it was an amazing meal, and now I make this special dish at least once a year to serve family and friends.

Coq au vin translates to "rooster in wine." Though it seems fancy, it's truly a hearty, rustic dish with peasant origins in the French countryside, where families who couldn't afford a tender young chicken would braise tough old birds in red wine to tenderize their meat. It's a perfect preparation for male pheasants, or "roosters," as we call them in the field.

Before cooking, be sure to read the recipe carefully all the way through. It requires a bit of time and a handful of steps, but don't let that intimidate you. Follow the instructions, and you'll be rewarded with a complex and richly flavored stew. Serve this with a starchy side like mashed potatoes or bread to soak up the sauce.

---

1 Cut each pheasant into serving pieces—breasts, thighs, wings, and drumsticks—and reserve the wings, carcass, and drumsticks for making stock (see Notes). Season the breasts and thighs with salt and pepper. Let stand on the counter, uncovered, for 1 hour, or refrigerate for a few hours or up to overnight, if time allows. (This acts like a dry brine and helps keep the meat juicy.)

2 Preheat the oven to 250°F.

3 Heat a large Dutch oven over medium-high heat. Add 2 tablespoons schmaltz to the pan and swirl to coat the bottom. Brown the pheasant pieces on both sides, working in batches as needed, then transfer to a plate.

4 Add another tablespoon of schmaltz to the pot, if needed, then add the chopped onion and cook for 3 to 4 minutes, until soft and golden in color. Stir in the carrots, celery, and leek and cook for an additional few minutes. Add the garlic and cook until fragrant, less than 1 minute.

continued

Notes: Like turkey, pheasant drumsticks have several tendons that turn hard when cooked. You can either use needle-nose pliers to pull the tendons out at the joint where it connects to the foot before cooking, or leave them, if you don't mind picking them out as you eat. Otherwise, just save the drumsticks along with the carcass and wings to use for stock.

If you're using chicken legs, separate the thighs and drumsticks at the joint before seasoning. After bringing the liquid in the pot to a simmer, return both the drumsticks and the thighs to the pot and braise in the oven for just 45 minutes to 1 hour total, until tender.

You can substitute ¼ cup chopped bacon (roughly ¼- by 1-inch pieces) for schmaltz or oil. I find I don't need the extra flavor of this addition when I make coq au vin with pheasant, but it's traditionally included when the dish is made with chicken. Cook the bacon in the Dutch oven over medium heat until crispy and brown, 5 to 8 minutes. Use a slotted spoon to transfer the bacon to a plate and set aside. Raise the heat under the pot to medium-high and use the rendered bacon fat to brown the pheasant or chicken pieces. Return the bacon to the pot after you've added the wine and stock.

5 Drop the tomato paste into the pot and mix. Sprinkle in the flour and stir to incorporate. Cook for 1 minute to lightly toast the flour. Pour in the wine and stock and stir, scraping up the browned bits from the bottom of the pot. Add the fresh herbs and bay leaf.

6 Bring the liquid to a simmer and return the pheasant thighs to the pot (reserve the breasts). Cover the pot with a lid and transfer to the oven. Braise the thighs for about 2 hours, then add the breasts to the pot and braise until all the meat is fork-tender, 1 to 1½ hours more. During the last 30 minutes of cooking, set the lid slightly ajar so the liquid can reduce.

7 Remove the pot from the oven and increase the oven temperature to 375°F. Spread the mushrooms and pearl onions over a large baking sheet and drizzle with a couple tablespoons of oil and the vinegar. Season with salt and pepper. Roast for about 20 minutes, until the mushrooms are golden brown and the onions are tender.

8 At this point, you can either add the roasted mushrooms and onions to the pot with the braised pheasant and enjoy it as a rustic stew or go for an elegant approach by creating a sauce with the braising liquid to serve with the pheasant and vegetables. To do the latter, remove the pheasant pieces from the pot, set aside on a plate, and keep warm. Strain the braising liquid and return it to the pot (discard the solids). Taste and season with salt and pepper, if needed. If the flavor is lackluster, bring the liquid to a boil and cook until reduced and thickened. If desired, stir together the melted butter and 1 tablespoon flour, then stir the mixture into the sauce to further thicken it.

9 To serve, arrange the pheasant pieces on a platter with the roasted mushrooms and onions alongside and drizzle with the sauce to finish. Sprinkle with the parsley and serve.

Garlic–Herb Roasted Pheasant with Grape and Shallot Pan Sauce

SERVES 4

2 whole pheasants, plucked (see Notes)

2 tablespoons Garlic and Herb Salt (page 256)

½ teaspoon baking powder

Neutral oil, such as avocado or grapeseed

2 tablespoons unsalted butter, at room temperature, plus more for basting

Sprigs of rosemary and/or thyme

6 to 8 small shallots, halved or quartered

1 large bunch of red or white seedless grapes

Coarse sea salt and freshly ground black pepper

1½ tablespoons red wine vinegar

¾ cup unsalted rich pheasant stock or chicken stock, homemade (see page 257) or low-sodium store-bought (see Notes)

¾ cup heavy cream

When Travis and I lived in North Dakota, our annual Thanksgiving tradition was to celebrate with a morning pheasant hunt. It was usually very cold, and most people were spending the holiday indoors, so we'd have the fields to ourselves. There'd be nothing in sight but the tall grass waving in the wind and our methodical bird dog working the field in a zigzag pattern until he zeroed in on a pheasant.

After the hunt, we'd return home, where I would have two pheasants from a previous hunt plucked, trussed, brined, and ready to roast in a hot oven. Each year, I'd experiment with a new method of roasting, always trying to get the juiciest, most tender meat and crispiest skin—no small feat, as wild birds can be very challenging. After years of practice, I've nailed the perfect recipe. I've adopted a reverse sear method, doing the majority of the cooking in a very low oven to keep the meat juicy and finishing with very high heat to brown the skin. You can roast the pheasant with the garlic and herb salt and serve it with gravy and all your favorite sides. But if you want to try something different, throw a handful of grapes and shallots into the roasting pan. They caramelize in the oven first and then get added to a creamy, savory pan sauce to spoon over the meat. This is one of the best recipes I've ever developed for pheasant and a wonderful way to honor such a beautiful bird.

1 A day before you plan to cook the pheasants, carefully loosen the skin; do this gently, as it's extremely delicate and tears easily. Divide the garlic and herb salt evenly between two bowls; add the baking powder to one bowl and set that aside. Spread the plain garlic-herb salt underneath the skin, rubbing it over the meat. Keep in mind that you won't be rinsing the pheasants to remove excess salt, so use only as much as you would typically use for seasoning (you won't need all of it). Apply the salt–baking powder mixture on the skin over the outside of the birds (again, you won't use it all). Set the birds on a baking sheet lined with a wire rack and place it in the refrigerator, rearranging things so they get plenty of airflow. Let stand in the fridge, uncovered, for 24 hours. Dry brining the pheasant this way not only makes the meat juicy, it also dries out the skin to help it brown better.

continued

Notes: For this recipe, you'll want a very rich stock. If you're using store-bought, see the sidebar on page 259 for tips on leveling up your stock.

Don't have a whole plucked pheasant? Make this recipe with skinless pheasant breasts, chicken breasts, or even pork chops: Season the meat with the garlic-herb mixture, cover (since it's skinless), and dry-brine in the fridge. When ready to cook, sear the meat on both sides in a hot skillet with oil until just barely cooked through, then drop in 1 tablespoon butter and baste the meat with the melted butter until it's finished. Transfer to a plate and set aside. Add the shallots to the pan, cut-side down, then add the grapes and all the liquids for the pan sauce and bring to a simmer. Gently cook until the shallots are tender and the sauce has thickened and reduced by at least half. If you're using thick pork chops or chicken breasts that haven't cooked all the way through after basting, you can add them to the pan sauce as it simmers to finish cooking. Serve the seared meat topped with the sauce.

2 The next day, remove the pheasants from the refrigerator 45 minutes to 1 hour before you plan to cook them. Preheat the oven on the convection setting to 225°F (or 250°F if your oven doesn't use convection). Lightly grease a roasting pan with oil.

3 Using a paper towel, pat the pheasants dry and dust off excess salt from the top. Rub the softened butter under the skin over the meat and then over the skin on the outside of the birds. Use kitchen twine to truss the legs and place a few sprigs of herbs inside the cavity of each birds.

4 Lightly coat the shallots and grapes with oil, then season them with salt and pepper. Place the shallots and grapes in the greased roasting pan and nestle the pheasants on top, using the grapes to support the birds so they sit breast-side up without rolling over. Place an oven-safe meat thermometer in the tenderloin (the breast meat closer to the bone; insert the thermometer vertically from the top of the bird downward) and transfer to the oven. Roast until the meat reaches 125°F.

5 Remove the roasting pan from the oven—but don't take the thermometer out of the pheasant!—and raise the oven temperature to 500°F convection (or as high as your oven will go if it doesn't have a convection setting). This may take 20 to 30 minutes, and you may notice the internal temperature of meat going down, but don't worry—it'll go back up in a hurry once it's back in the oven.

6 Baste the pheasants with more butter. When the oven reaches 500°F, return the pheasants to the oven and roast until the breast reaches 155°F. Remove from the oven and transfer the pheasants to a cutting board to rest.

7 Meanwhile, place the roasting pan on the stovetop over high heat. Add the vinegar, stock, and cream and bring to a boil, stirring and scraping up any browned bits from the bottom of the pan, then reduce the heat to maintain a simmer. Cook until the mixture has reduced by half, about 5 minutes, then remove from the heat. Taste the pan sauce and season with salt and pepper as needed.

8 Carve each pheasant into serving pieces. Serve with the pan sauce drizzled over the top and the roasted grapes and shallots alongside.

How to Pluck Wild Birds

Dry-plucking wild birds such as ducks, quail, and tender geese like specklebellies by hand is my preferred method. It's tedious work—you have to be patient, pull the skin taut, and pluck only a few down feathers at a time, pulling them out in a quick upward motion. Larger pinfeathers sometimes need to be pulled one by one. Grabbing and yanking large clumps of feathers is sure to rip the skin. Refrigerating the birds for 24 hours before plucking tightens the skin, which helps prevent tearing.

When it comes to pheasants, our dear friend Rhett Hall showed me a *much* easier way to take all the feathers off: scalding the bird in hot water. It takes very little time, and the feathers come off with little to no effort, resulting in a much prettier presentation. This method works best with freshly harvested birds. (Just note that it makes a mess, so it's best done outside with a portable burner, if you have one.) You'll need a thermometer to measure the temperature of the water and a pot big enough to submerge the whole bird; have a timer or stopwatch ready, too.

Fill the pot with water and heat it to about 150°F. Grab the bird by its feet and dip it into the water headfirst until it's submerged up to its feet. Keep the bird submerged for 50 seconds, vigorously swirling it around to make sure the whole thing—including the spaces between the thighs, breasts, and wings—makes contact with the water. When the timer goes off, pull it out and let the water drip back into the pot. As soon as the bird is cool enough to handle, hold it over a trash bag and gently pull off the feathers. You'll be amazed at how they just slip right off! If the feathers don't come off easily, swirl it around in the hot water for another 10 to 15 seconds, then try again.

Browned Butter Scallops with Pecan Dukkah and Pickled Raisins

SERVES 4

1½ pounds large dry scallops (4 or 5 per person)

Coarse sea salt

½ cup golden raisins

½ cup champagne vinegar or white wine vinegar

¼ cup honey

Neutral oil, such as avocado or grapeseed

1 small shallot, thinly sliced (about ⅓ cup)

½ cup (1 stick) salted butter, cubed

Pecan Dukkah (recipe follows)

Torn baby cilantro leaves, for garnish

Freshly ground black pepper

As summer slips into fall, the roadside stands transition away from peaches and into pecans, a staple ingredient in southern cuisine. Every October, I head to our family ranch to pick and crack pecans. Some of the trees on the property are very old native trees; others were planted many years ago by Travis's grandparents, who unfortunately passed away before I got the chance to meet and thank them. But every time I cook with those pecans, I think about what I hope to pass on one day, and how important it is to nurture and protect our landscape for future generations.

Like oysters, farmed scallops are not only very sustainable, they're available throughout most of the year, making this an evergreen recipe. In the fall and winter months, I like to pair them with oven-roasted winter squash, sweet potatoes, or carrots; in the spring, I opt for asparagus.

1 At least an hour before you're ready to cook the scallops, season them generously with salt on both sides. Place the scallops on a paper towel–lined baking sheet and cover with another layer of paper towels to soak up excess moisture. Transfer the pan to the refrigerator.

2 Place the raisins in a small bowl. Pour the vinegar into a small pot and season with a couple pinches of salt. Bring to a boil over high heat, then add the honey and stir until it has dissolved. Pour the hot vinegar mixture over the raisins and set aside to soak for at least 1 hour. (The raisins can be pickled several days in advance and stored in the pickling liquid in an airtight container in the refrigerator.)

3 Remove the scallops from the refrigerator at least 30 minutes prior to cooking and pat them very dry with a fresh paper towel, if needed. Lightly coat the bottom of a large skillet with a thin layer of oil and set over high heat. When the oil is shimmering, use tongs to place each scallop in the pan, leaving room between them (work in batches, if needed). Cook until the bottoms develop a golden-brown crust, about 3 minutes. You'll notice the opacity and texture changing on the sides of the scallops; they should be three-quarters of the way done. Flip and cook for 1 to 2 minutes on the second side, then transfer the scallops to a plate and set aside.

continued

4 Reduce the heat to low and let the pan cool for a couple of minutes, especially if it's smoking. Meanwhile, drain the raisins, reserving the soaking liquid, and set both aside.

5 Add the butter to the skillet and swirl it around in the pan to melt and foam. When the milk solids have separated from the butterfat and begun to toast, add the shallots. They will softly fry in the hot butter. Cook, stirring occasionally to separate the shallot rings, for a minute or two, until the butter turns golden in color. If at any point the butter burns, you'll need to start over, so stay attentive and lower the heat if needed. Remove from the heat and stir in the raisins.

6 Serve the scallops with a spoonful of the browned butter, making sure to grab some of the raisins and shallots. Spoon a few drops of the reserved raisin pickling liquid across the top for a hit of acidity, if you like, then sprinkle the top of each scallop with some of the pecan dukkah. Season with salt and pepper, garnish with cilantro, and serve.

Pecan Dukkah

MAKES 1 HEAPING CUP

¾ cup pecan halves

1 tablespoon fennel seeds

1 teaspoon cumin seeds

1 teaspoon coriander seeds

2 tablespoons benne (sesame) seeds

1½ teaspoons coarse sea salt

½ teaspoon brown sugar

⅛ teaspoon cayenne pepper

1 Preheat the oven to 375°F. Spread the pecans evenly over a large baking sheet and toast in the oven for 12 minutes, flipping once halfway through. Remove from the oven and let cool.

2 Meanwhile, heat a small skillet over medium-high heat. Add the fennel, cumin, and coriander seeds and toast, shaking the pan for even distribution and so that nothing burns, until the seeds are fragrant and starting to pop, about 1 minute. Transfer the toasted seeds to a mortar and pound them with the pestle to crush the spices to a coarse consistency. Transfer to a small bowl.

3 In the same skillet, toast the benne seeds over medium-high heat, shaking the pan or stirring frequently, for about 1 minute, until they turn light golden in color. Transfer them to the bowl with the crushed spices.

4 Coarsely chop the pecans by hand or pulse in a food processor until the nuts have a coarse, granular consistency. Add them to the bowl with the spices and benne seeds. Add the salt, sugar, and cayenne and stir until well blended. Store the dukkah in an airtight, container at room temperature for up to a few months.

Grilled Redfish on the Half Shell with Harissa and Ember– Roasted Sweet Potatoes

SERVES 4

2 large redfish or striped bass fillets, with skin and scales

Neutral oil, such as avocado or grapeseed

Coarse sea salt and freshly ground black pepper

¼ cup harissa paste, store-bought or homemade (recipe follows)

4 sweet potatoes

1 cup plain full-fat Greek yogurt or kefir

Every fall, the redfish run is one of the greatest phenomena taking place on the Texas coast. In the bay, you'll not only see fish schooling up, but also flocks of migratory birds that have made their way south and, like us, are looking for fish to eat. Their presence gives us clues to where the fish are, making this a unique time to sight-cast for these fish.

We catch redfish in a wide range of sizes, and although you can keep any fish within the slot length, we've found that a 24- to 25-inch fish is the sweet spot. It serves four people perfectly (not too much, not too little), and the thickness of the meat is fairly consistent, which means it grills perfectly "on the half shell," with the skin and scales still attached to the fillet. Redfish scales are incredibly tough and armorlike, and on the grill, they act like a buffer for the heat, making the flesh cook gently and evenly. The best part? There's no need to flip the fish. I just season the tops with salt and pepper and baste with a spicy harissa sauce. It's such a simple, primitive method for cooking fish that I like to take the same approach to the sides. The sweet potatoes are cooked directly on the coals, allowing their skin to blacken and char just like the redfish, while their bright orange flesh turns soft and the starches convert to sugar. With the harissa, it's the perfect balance of sweet and spicy.

1 Remove the fish from the refrigerator 30 minutes to 1 hour before grilling. Pat the fillets very dry with paper towels, then coat both sides of each fillet (especially the skin and scales) with a little oil. Season the flesh side with salt and pepper, then rub about 1 tablespoon of the harissa paste over the flesh of each fillet—a little goes a long way!

2 Prepare a grill by burning a big pile of charcoal or wood down to a white-hot coal bed. Place the sweet potatoes directly on top of the coals on one side of the fire (no need to season or oil them first, as you won't eat the skin). Cook the potatoes until soft when tested with a toothpick, 30 to 40 minutes, rotating them a quarter turn using tongs every 10 minutes for even cooking. Remove from the grill and keep warm.

3 While the potatoes cook, place a grill grate 8 to 12 inches above the coals. Lay the fillets on the grate, skin-side down, and cover with the grill lid or tent with foil. Cook the fish, without flipping the fillets, for 20 to 25 minutes, depending on the thickness of the fish, until the flesh flakes easily with a fork. If you notice the scales turning black while the flesh of the fish is still raw, the heat is too high. Raise the grill grate higher above the coals, if possible, or use a shovel and spread the coals out to disperse the heat. Remove the fish from the grill using a large spatula.

4 Spoon the yogurt into a bowl and swirl in 1 to 2 tablespoons of the harissa. Divide the grilled fish among four plates (the flesh should slide right off the skin). Dust the ashes off the potatoes, then cut them open lengthwise with a knife to reveal the flesh. Serve the fish and sweet potatoes with the harissa yogurt alongside.

Harissa Paste

MAKES 1 CUP

4 ounces dried chiles (see Note), stemmed and seeded

Boiling water

1 teaspoon coriander seeds

½ teaspoon cumin seeds

1 teaspoon caraway seeds

4 garlic cloves, minced

2 teaspoons white or red wine vinegar

2 teaspoons coarse sea salt

¼ cup extra-virgin olive oil

Note: For very spicy harissa, use 2 ounces chiles de árbol and 2 ounces guajillo chiles; for mild, use 4 ounces guajillo chiles.

1 Place the chiles in a large heatproof bowl and add boiling water to cover. Cover the bowl and let stand until the chiles are soft, 30 minutes to 1 hour.

2 Meanwhile, heat a small dry skillet over high heat. Add the coriander, cumin, and caraway seeds and toast for 15 to 30 seconds, until fragrant. Transfer the toasted spices to a spice grinder and pulse until coarsely ground.

3 Drain the chiles (reserve the soaking liquid for cooking grains or adding to stew, if you like) and place them in a small food processor. Add the toasted spices, garlic, vinegar, salt, and olive oil and puree until smooth. You'll still have some tiny visible pieces of chile skin; use a little elbow grease and a wide spatula to pass the harissa through a fine-mesh sieve to make it silky smooth. Store in an airtight container in the fridge for up to 4 days or in the freezer for up to 1 year.

Greek-Style Broccoli and Feta Pie

MAKES ONE 9-INCH PIE;
SERVES 6

2 medium heads broccoli

2 tablespoons extra-virgin olive oil, plus more as needed

1 small yellow onion, diced

1 leek, halved lengthwise, thinly sliced into thin half-moons, and rinsed well to remove any grit

4 garlic cloves, minced

2 cups chopped broccoli leaves, collard greens, or kale leaves

½ teaspoon dried oregano

2 teaspoons coarse sea salt

Freshly ground black pepper

5 sheets thick (#10) phyllo dough

2 large eggs, beaten

1 cup crumbled feta cheese

¼ cup chopped fresh parsley

¼ cup chopped fresh dill

Zest of 1 lemon

Broccoli is one of my favorite vegetables to grow in the cooler seasons because you can get so much more out of the plant than just the crown. Almost the entire thing is edible, including the leaves and stem. Since I grow a few broccoli plants at once, I needed to find a way to utilize as much of it as possible, and this pie fits the bill. Inspired by a Greek spanakopita, the recipe swaps out the spinach for broccoli but keeps the all the delicious fresh herbs and feta cheese. And instead of packing it all into a rectangular baking dish, I assemble it in a pie plate and cover the top with phyllo. I like it as a side dish for garlicky venison meatballs (see page 170), which I sometimes eat with tzatziki, and it's also great with roast chicken.

1 Preheat the oven to 375°F.

2 Separate the broccoli stems and crowns. Finely chop the crowns into small florets. Using a vegetable peeler, peel off the woody exterior of the stems and grate them on the medium holes of a box grater. You should have about 5 cups loosely packed florets and grated stems.

3 In a wide skillet, heat the oil over medium-high heat until it begins to shimmer and the pan is hot. Add the onion and cook, stirring occasionally, until soft and light golden in color, 4 to 5 minutes. Stir in the leeks and cook for a few minutes, until soft, then add the garlic and cook for another minute.

4 Add the broccoli, broccoli leaves, oregano, salt, and a few cranks of pepper. Cook, stirring every couple of minutes, until the broccoli is tender but retains a snappy texture, about 5 minutes. If the mixture seems watery, drain it in a fine-mesh sieve to remove excess moisture (don't force the liquid out), then transfer everything to a large bowl and set aside to cool.

5 While the broccoli is cooling, lightly oil a 9-inch pie dish or shallow springform pan (alternatively, line a baking sheet with parchment paper to make a free-form galette).

6 Tear 4 sheets of the phyllo dough in half (reserving the last sheet for topping). Place one piece in the bottom of the pie dish, letting the excess hang over the sides, then use a pastry brush dipped in

oil to lightly brush the top of the phyllo. Repeat this process with the remaining phyllo, rotating each so the dough covers the pie dish evenly.

7 Stir the eggs, feta, parsley, dill, and lemon zest into the bowl with the broccoli and mix until it's well combined. Pour the broccoli mixture into the pie dish, then fold the overhanging dough over the top outer edge of the filling, making sure it is very wrinkled. Tear the remaining phyllo sheet into large pieces, lightly crunching it up small in your hand and spreading it across the top of the pie, kind of how you would lightly stuff tissue paper inside of a gift bag, being sure to cover any exposed broccoli pieces. Brush the top with a light coat of olive oil.

8 Bake for 45 minutes, until the top is golden brown and crispy. Remove and let cool for about 5 minutes, then serve immediately. Leftovers can be stored in an airtight container in the refrigerator, but the dough won't be quite as crispy as it is hot out of the oven.

Spinach and Buckwheat Salad

SERVES 4

Red Wine Vinaigrette

1 cup walnut oil or warm rendered duck fat (see page 261)

6 tablespoons red wine vinegar

2 teaspoons Dijon mustard

¼ cup finely diced shallot

1½ tablespoons honey

Pinch of coarse sea salt

Salad

2 cups toasted buckwheat groats (kasha)

3 cups water or vegetable stock, homemade (see page 259) or store-bought

Coarse sea salt

6 cups (or large handfuls) baby spinach (one 5-ounce clamshell)

½ cup crumbled blue cheese

1 apple or pear, cored and diced

Buckwheat is one of my favorite grains to work with because it's packed with nutrients and gluten-free. But, in fact, it isn't truly even a grain—it's a pseudocereal, similar to quinoa. It makes a healthy and well-rounded side dish that's great for busy weeknights. The buckwheat has a toasted, nutty flavor that's echoed by the walnut oil in the vinaigrette. Sometimes I toss the grains with the spinach while they're still warm to ever so slightly wilt the greens, but if you prefer a cold salad, you can let the buckwheat cool, toss it with some of the vinaigrette, and store it in the fridge for up to a few days before adding the spinach. It can be served alongside practically any protein, like the roasted chicken or pheasant on page 177. If you're feeling adventurous, substitute rendered duck fat for the walnut oil in the dressing and serve the salad warm, alongside the seared duck breast from the Boozy Duck à l'Orange on page 217. It also works as an easy meatless lunch with jammy eggs (see page 58).

1 **Make the vinaigrette:** In a large jar, combine all the vinaigrette ingredients. Cover and shake vigorously to emulsify. (The dressing can be made up to 3 days in advance and stored in the refrigerator. If using duck fat, gently warm it over low heat to liquefy it before using.)

2 **Make the salad:** Place the buckwheat in a fine-mesh strainer and rinse thoroughly with cool water, then drain. In a large (2- to 3-quart) saucepan, combine the water and a few pinches of salt. Bring to a boil over high heat, then stir in the buckwheat. Reduce the heat to low, cover, and cook for 13 to 15 minutes. Remove the lid and check to see if all the liquid has been absorbed; if not, continue cooking until it has. Remove from the heat and fluff the buckwheat with a fork, then let it cool for a few minutes.

3 Transfer the buckwheat to a large bowl and toss with ¼ cup of the vinaigrette. Add the spinach, blue cheese, and apple and gently toss to combine. Dress with additional vinaigrette to your liking, season with salt, and serve.

Homesick Enchiladas

SERVES 4 TO 6

Filling

Beef tallow or neutral oil, such as avocado or grapeseed

1 pound 80% lean ground beef, venison, or lamb

1 teaspoon coarse sea salt

¼ teaspoon freshly ground black pepper

¼ teaspoon ground cumin

¼ teaspoon dried oregano

½ medium yellow onion, diced

3 garlic cloves, minced

Chili Gravy

¼ cup neutral oil, such as avocado or grapeseed, or beef tallow, as needed

¼ cup all-purpose flour

2 teaspoons grated yellow onion, or 1 teaspoon dried granulated onion

2 teaspoons grated garlic, or 1 teaspoon dried granulated garlic

2 cups venison stock or chicken stock, homemade (see page 257) or store-bought

1½ tablespoons tomato paste

1 teaspoon ground cumin

1 teaspoon dried oregano

1 teaspoon coarse sea salt

I grew up eating at hole-in-the-wall Tex-Mex restaurants, the kind of eclectic establishments where mariachi bands played every Friday night, the booths were separated by Mexican blankets for privacy, and each meal was finished with a bite of sugary pecan pralines. Every time I went, I ordered the cheesy beef enchiladas. It's such a nostalgic meal that any time I think of it, I immediately smell chiles and imagine being stuffed to the brim.

I started making these enchiladas whenever I felt homesick while I lived in North Dakota, far, far away from the Mexican border. I wanted to make them the way I remembered, so it's important to clarify that this recipe is not for traditional Mexican enchiladas; instead, it represents humble old-school Tex-Mex culture. These are topped with chili gravy, a cross between a brown gravy and a traditional Mexican red chile sauce, influenced by northern Mexico. It's a staple in Tex-Mex cuisine. Though these enchiladas are traditionally made with nothing but cheese and sometimes ground beef, I often make them with venison—either way, they're my homage to one of my favorite meals from childhood.

1 Preheat the oven to 400°F.

2 **Make the filling:** Heat a large sauté pan over medium-high heat. Add enough oil to thinly coat the bottom of the pan, then add the ground meat. Cook, undisturbed, for a few minutes, or until the bottom is browned, then flip the meat and break it up with a spatula. Cook, stirring occasionally, until browned and fully cooked through, 3 to 4 minutes more. Season with the salt, pepper, cumin, and oregano. Transfer to a large bowl.

3 Drizzle a bit more oil into the pan, if it looks dry, then add the onions and cook until soft and golden in color. Add the garlic and cook for 1 minute, then transfer to the bowl with the meat and mix to combine.

4 **Make the chili gravy:** Return the pan to the stovetop and give it a minute to cool off, if needed. There shouldn't be much oil in the pan—if there is, pour it into a measuring cup and add more oil as needed to reach ¼ cup. Pour the oil into the pan and heat over

recipe and ingredients continued

½ teaspoon freshly ground black pepper

2½ tablespoons ground ancho or red chile powder

To Assemble

Neutral oil, such as avocado or grapeseed

12 to 14 (6-inch) corn tortillas

6 ounces cheddar cheese, grated

6 ounces Monterey Jack cheese, grated

Charro beans and Spanish rice, for serving

medium heat until warm. While whisking continuously, sprinkle in the flour, then whisk until the mixture is smooth and there are no lumps of flour. Cook for a few minutes more, until the roux is lightly golden in color. Stir in the onion and garlic and cook briefly, just until fragrant.

5 While whisking continuously, slowly pour in the stock (all that whisking keeps the gravy smooth). Add the tomato paste, cumin, oregano, salt, pepper, and chili powder; the chili powder will immediately thicken the gravy. Remove from the heat. The gravy will thicken slightly as it cools and will thicken further as the enchiladas bake; add a splash of water to thin it to the desired consistency, if needed.

6 **Assemble the enchiladas:** Line a tray with paper towels. Heat a clean sauté pan or cast-iron skillet over high heat. Add ½ teaspoon oil and heat until the oil starts to sputter. Use tongs to lay a tortilla in the pan and fry for 15 seconds, then flip and fry the opposite side for 15 seconds. The tortilla should bubble as it fries, but remain soft and pliable. Transfer to the paper towels to drain and repeat with the remaining tortillas, adding more oil to the pan as needed between each.

7 Lightly grease a 9 by 13-inch casserole dish or 12-inch cast-iron pan with oil. Spread a large spoonful of the chili gravy in a thin layer over the bottom of the dish. Place a small spoonful of the chili gravy on a tortilla and scoop some of the filling over it. Top with a little grated cheddar and Monterey Jack and roll up the tortilla like a cigar. Place the rolled tortilla seam-side down in the dish and repeat until you have filled the casserole dish. Pour the remaining gravy over the rolled tortillas; there should be enough to generously coat them. (If you have any leftover filling, you can stir it into the gravy before topping the tortillas.)

8 Evenly sprinkle the top with the remaining cheese and cover with aluminum foil. Bake the enchiladas for 15 minutes, then remove the foil and bake for 5 minutes more, or until the cheese is bubbling. Serve immediately, with beans and rice alongside.

Chocolate–Porcini Pots de Crème with Hazelnut Whipped Cream

MAKES 6

Chocolate–Porcini Custard

½ cup whole milk

½ ounce (14 grams) dried porcini mushrooms, finely chopped

Pinch of coarse sea salt

5 large egg yolks

3 tablespoons granulated sugar

2 cups heavy cream

6 ounces bittersweet chocolate (60% to 70% cacao), chopped

1 tablespoon hazelnut liqueur, or 1½ teaspoons pure vanilla extract

Hazelnut Whipped Cream

1 cup heavy cream

1 tablespoon hazelnut liqueur

1 tablespoon confectioners' sugar

Shaved chocolate, for garnish (optional)

This dessert is everything you want from a perfect pot de crème and more: thick, silky smooth, and decadent. Chocolate and mushroom might sound like a weird combination, and frankly you might need an open mind to be willing to try it, but once you do, you'll be surprised how great the pairing is. That's because both chocolate and mushrooms share earthy aromatic compounds that not only make them compatible, but can intensify the flavor, making it seem even more chocolaty without being overly sweet! Trust me, you won't necessarily taste the mushroom flavor in this dessert, but you'll know there's something extra there you can't put your finger on, and without it, it's just not the same.

1 In a large saucepan, combine the milk, porcini, and a pinch of salt. Heat over medium-low heat just until bubbles form around the edges of the pan—do not allow the milk to boil—then remove from the heat and cover with a lid. Let stand for 30 minutes to infuse the milk with the flavor of the porcini.

2 Preheat the oven to 325°F.

3 In a medium bowl, whisk together the egg yolks and granulated sugar until smooth. Set aside.

4 Strain the infused milk through a fine-mesh strainer, lightly pressing on the solids with a spatula—but not so much that you're forcing pureed mushroom through—then return it to the saucepan (discard the solids and give the strainer a quick rinse, as you'll use it again). Add the cream and bring the mixture to a simmer over medium-high heat, then turn off the heat, add the chocolate, and stir until fully melted and combined.

5 While whisking continuously, use a ladle to slowly pour about ½ cup of the hot cream mixture into the eggs, then whisk until combined. Repeat with about ½ cup more of the hot cream mixture, then whisk the contents of the bowl into the saucepan with the remaining cream until the custard is well blended. Strain the custard to give it a silky texture and ensure that there are no bits of cooked egg, then stir in the hazelnut liqueur.

continued

6 Divide the custard evenly among six 4-ounce ramekins. Place the ramekins in a baking dish or a roasting pan and pour water into the pan to come about halfway up the sides of the ramekins. Cover with aluminum foil and poke several holes in the foil to release steam. Bake for 45 minutes, or until the custard is set; it will wobble in the middle if shaken, but the edges shouldn't move. Remove from the oven and carefully transfer the ramekins from the water bath to a wire rack to cool. You can serve the pots de crème warm, but they're best when covered and refrigerated for a few hours to thicken the custard (they will keep in the fridge for up to 1 week).

7 **Meanwhile, make the whipped cream:** In a large bowl using a whisk or handheld mixer, whisk the cream, hazelnut liqueur, and confectioners' sugar until it holds soft peaks. (If you're not serving it immediately, the whipped cream can be stored in an airtight container in the refrigerator for a few days.)

8 Serve the pots de crème warm or chilled, topped with the whipped cream and shaved chocolate, if desired.

Bourbon Butternut Squash Pie

MAKES ONE 9-INCH PIE

Neutral oil, such as avocado or grapeseed

1 large butternut squash, halved and seeded (see Note)

5 tablespoons salted butter

2 large eggs

2 large egg yolks

¾ cup heavy cream

3 tablespoons bourbon

¾ cup packed light brown sugar

1 teaspoon pure vanilla extract

½ teaspoon coarse sea salt

2 teaspoons ground cinnamon

⅛ teaspoon ground cloves

Freshly grated nutmeg

½ recipe Pie Dough (page 260)

All-purpose flour, for dusting

Vanilla Whipped Cream (page 89)

Note: You can substitute 15 ounces of canned pure pumpkin puree for the roasted squash; add an extra teaspoon or two of sugar if you have a sweet tooth.

I was never much of a bourbon drinker, so I didn't cook with it much—until I had the opportunity to do a barrel pick at Buffalo Trace Distillery. I'll never forget the incredible oak wood smell of the warehouse where the barrels are aged. Bourbon is made with varying amounts of corn, barley, and rye, and each adds its own distinct notes; in the barrels I tried, I picked up vanilla, caramel, wood, spice, and even nutty flavors.

I hadn't thought of bourbon as a drink with such complexity, and when I got home, I wanted to make a bourbon-spiked seasonal pie that captured and amplified some of those flavors. In my first few tries, I thought it needed a stronger bourbon flavor, but adding more just made the pie too acidic. Instead, it was better to use just enough to add an undertone that carried throughout the pie and let the brown butter and warm spices enhance the bourbon's flavors. It's not a dessert that screams "bourbon!" but without it, the pie would taste flat. Serve a slice with a dollop of whipped cream and a glass of your favorite bourbon.

1 Preheat the oven to 400°F. Line a baking sheet with parchment paper.

2 Lightly oil the squash halves and place them cut-side down on the prepared baking sheet. Roast for 50 minutes, or until soft. Flip and cook for 15 minutes more to let the flesh of the squash dry out a little. It should be very soft but not watery (you're looking for the consistency of canned pumpkin). Remove from the oven and set aside until cool enough to handle; reduce the oven temperature to 375°F.

3 Use a spoon to scoop the flesh into a bowl, then measure 1¾ cups of the flesh (that's roughly half of a large butternut squash) into a high-powered blender. (Reserve the remaining squash to eat as a savory side.)

4 Meanwhile, place the butter in a pot or skillet over medium heat. Swirl the pan around continuously as the milk solids begin to toast and turn golden in color. As soon as it turns light brown, remove it from the heat, keeping in mind that the residual heat will continue to cook the butter. (If you burn the butter, you'll need to toss it out and start over.) If you need to, pour it into a bowl set over a larger bowl of ice to rapidly cool it.

5 Add the warm browned butter to the blender with the squash and puree until silky smooth. The mixture may be pretty warm; let it cool for a few minutes, if necessary, while you mix the remaining ingredients.

6 In a large bowl, whisk together the eggs, egg yolks, cream, bourbon, brown sugar, vanilla, salt, cinnamon, and cloves. Add a generous grating of nutmeg (about 10 seconds of grating a whole nutmeg). Add the squash puree and mix until smooth.

7 Pull the pie dough from the fridge. On a flour-dusted surface, roll out the dough into a round large enough to fit a 9-inch pie dish. Transfer the dough to the pie dish, letting it gently sink into the corners and fall over the sides. Use kitchen scissors to trim the overhanging dough, then crimp the edges; wrap the excess dough in plastic wrap and return it to the fridge. Prick the bottom and sides of the dough with a fork. Line the dough with a piece of parchment paper, then fill the bottom with pie weights or dried beans. Bake the pie shell for 15 minutes, then remove it from the oven and remove the pie weights and parchment paper. Return the pie shell to the oven and bake for 5 minutes more, then remove from the oven. Reduce the oven temperature to 350°F, cracking the oven open to speed things up (and warming up the cold house in the process).

8 Pour the filling into the pie shell and carefully wrap the edges of the shell with a pie shield or aluminum foil to keep them from getting too brown. Bake for 60 to 70 minutes, until the filling is set and a toothpick inserted into the center comes out clean; a slight wobble when you shake the pie is okay, but the filling shouldn't shake like Jell-O. Remove from the oven and let cool completely.

9 Meanwhile, line a baking sheet with parchment paper. On a flour-dusted surface, roll out the reserved scraps of pie dough and cut out your desired shapes with a cookie cutter. Transfer to the lined baking sheet and bake for 15 to 18 minutes, until the dough is cooked through and lightly golden in color.

10 Serve the pie topped with the cutouts and a dollop of whipped cream.

Every Meal Has a Story to Tell

When I say every meal has a story to tell, I mean something like this one.

I've been fortunate to hunt alongside my husband, Travis, for many years, but one autumn, I decided I wanted to go it alone. I hatched a plan to drive from Texas to the North Dakota Badlands for five days of sharptail grouse hunting and camping with Zissou, my incredible Deutsch Drahthaar, as my only companion. There's so much to learn when you're forced to make decisions all by yourself, and I also wanted to experience the bond between bird dog and handler, the unspoken language of trust Zissou and I developed as we learned to work together. My friends and family didn't quite understand the allure of my "vacation" plans, and my dad in particular was concerned about me being alone, but I was determined. Zissou and I piled into the car and hit the road.

Sharptail grouse are incredibly resilient native upland game birds with dark red meat that's utterly delicious when cooked like duck. They live in wholly undeveloped landscapes under incredibly harsh conditions (I still wonder how anything survives when it's –30°F); these are extremely wild birds, and if you're hunting grouse, you really have to work for it. I knew I'd be hiking long, windy miles across the badlands, and that the calories I burned would far exceed what I'd gain if the hunt was successful.

Cold and wind and long miles aside, I started the trip excited, but three days in, I hadn't seen a bird within shotgun range. To make matters worse, the temperature had dropped into the teens and a heavy snow was falling. I was born with a hard-ass attitude, and I like to think I've got a little grit, but that night I felt utterly defeated.

After dinner—rabbit and potato soup (see page 229) I'd brought from home, reheated and eaten straight out of the Jetboil—I got ready for bed, placing my water bottle and contacts case in my sleeping bag with me so they wouldn't freeze overnight. Zissou laid down next to me, shaking uncontrollably. That got me wondering what it would feel like to lose my nose to frostbite or, worse, freeze to death. I unzipped my sleeping bag and pulled him in to keep us both warm. I was questioning my life choices, but there was nothing to be done at that point. I just needed to sleep. With Zissou as the little spoon, his head next to mine on the pillow, I drifted off.

Perhaps it was the sun beaming down, or maybe it was Zissou's tail wagging a hundred miles per hour in our sleeping bag, his energy and excitement contagious, but I woke up the next day feeling reinvigorated. We set out to hunt again, and after hiking about five miles, the moment I'd been waiting for finally happened—Zissou locked up on point. We found birds tucked into a grove of buffalo berry shrubs, eating the tart red fruit. In the blink of an eye, a covey flushed. Without hesitation, I shouldered my gun, shot, and watched a bird fold. It was one of those scenes where everything plays out exactly as you hope, and I couldn't have been happier.

I walked away from that memorable hunt with an unbreakable bond with my dog and hard-earned meat. Back at home, I seared the grouse breast in a skillet. Out on the badlands, I'd had the presence of mind to grab a handful of the buffalo berries the birds had been eating, and I added those to the pan to make a sauce. Spooned over the grouse, the acidity of the fruit was a perfect complement to the robust flavor of the meat.

What I loved most about those five cold days was getting a true sense of the wild. Amid that seemingly untouched expanse of grasslands, I felt small, knowing it had existed almost just as I was seeing it for thousands of years. It was a humbling experience.

In uncomfortable situations out in the wild, like that grouse hunt, it's easy to ask myself, *Why am I doing this?* But without these experiences, I wouldn't have the same appreciation or understanding of how the natural world and the

This story is a reminder of why I hunt in the first place—it's the ultimate act of eating with full understanding of everything at stake, and it enables me to feel a connection to my food and, ultimately, to the world we live in. This is eating consciously: looking at the ingredients on your plate and asking, *What's your story?*

food we eat are interconnected, knowledge that gives context and meaning to everything I eat—knowledge that gives every meal a story.

The meal I cooked with that sharptail told the story of what it took to bring it home. It's the story of an underappreciated game bird that, like many other native species of wildlife and pollinators, relies on that prairie habitat to survive. It's the story of how these once vast grasslands became the fastest disappearing ecosystem in the United States, losing 53 million acres—two-thirds of their expanse—to agriculture and development in the past decade alone.[13] It's the story of how our food system has damaged one of our greatest carbon sinks and turned microbe- and nutrient-rich soil into lifeless dirt.

This story is a reminder of why I hunt in the first place—it's the ultimate act of eating with full understanding of everything at stake, and it enables me to feel a connection to my food and, ultimately, to the world we live in. This is eating consciously: looking at the ingredients on your plate and asking, *What's your story?*

Pan-Seared Sharptail Grouse with Raspberry Sauce

SERVES 4

4 sharptail or sage grouse breasts, 4 small duck or goose breasts, or 4 mule deer or antelope steaks (see headnote)

½ teaspoon whole black peppercorns

2 teaspoons coarse sea salt

1 teaspoon minced fresh rosemary

Neutral oil, such as avocado or grapeseed

½ cup salted chicken stock, homemade (see page 257) or store-bought

1 tablespoon red wine vinegar

1 teaspoon honey

¼ cup frozen raspberries, thawed, juices reserved (see Note)

1 tablespoon salted butter

Note: I've substituted raspberries for the buffalo berries I used in the meal that inspired this dish, but if you live in an area where buffalo berries are accessible, use them!

There are many native grouse species in the US, but when it comes to cooking, they shouldn't all be treated the same. Sharptails and sage grouse have dark red breast meat and should be cooked similarly to wild duck and are best served medium-rare to preserve the flavor and color of their meat (which turns an unappealing gray if you cook it all the way through).

1 Remove the grouse from the refrigerator at least 30 minutes and up to 1 hour before cooking. Using a mortar and pestle, coarsely crush the peppercorns. Add the salt and rosemary and mix well. Just before cooking, season both sides of the grouse generously with the rosemary mixture, reserving a bit to season the pan sauce.

2 Heat a large stainless-steel skillet over medium-high heat. Coat the bottom of the pan in a thin layer of oil. When it begins to shimmer add the grouse (skin-side down, if plucked), using tongs to press each breast against the pan to get full contact. Cook, undisturbed, until browned on the bottom, 1 to 2 minutes, then flip. Cook until browned on the second side, another minute or two, then flip again and cook for about 30 seconds. Check the meat for doneness—pull it when it reaches medium-rare, about 130°F. (Sage grouse breasts will take a couple minutes longer to cook; if using duck, see page 218 for cooking times.) Transfer to a cutting board to rest.

3 Pour the stock, vinegar, and honey into the same pan and bring to a boil over high heat, stirring and scraping up the browned bits from the bottom. Boil for 3 to 4 minutes, until reduced by about half. Reduce the heat to medium-low and add the raspberries (and their juices) and the butter. Shake the pan vigorously to emulsify the butter into the sauce. Cook gently for about 2 minutes more, until the sauce has thickened. Taste and season with some of the reserved rosemary seasoning. (This might not seem like a lot of sauce, but trust me—a little goes a long way!)

4 Serve the grouse immediately with the sauce spooned over top.

Winter

Migration, Wood Fires, Frost

WE TEND TO THINK OF WINTER LANDSCAPES *as still and quiet, but if you spend enough time outside, you know the earth is still very much alive. Wild native truffles are fruiting underground in the Pacific Northwest; walleye are swimming happily under several feet of ice; cottontails are zig-zagging from brush pile to brush pile despite the freezing temperatures. Wildlife never ceases to amaze me with their resiliency.*

One of my favorite signs of winter's arrival is the great waterfowl migration. Ducks and geese are among my favorite game animals to eat, and I've spent many hours in the truck with Travis, scouting fields to find where the birds roost and feed. Before dawn, we set up decoys and lie silently in a blind, moving nothing but our eyes as hundreds of geese weave through the sky above us, cupping their wings to land and making so much noise that I can feel it in my chest. It's an incredible experience. We don't get to do this often, so when I bring home a duck or a goose, I always make the most of it in the kitchen. There are few things I love more than a beautifully seared duck breast or an incredible confit made with underappreciated goose legs.

In my garden, the window for growing cold-weather crops is relatively short, and I always hope to harvest as much as I can before a hard frost hits. Sometimes I luck out; other times I'm reminded of an important lesson—you can't control the weather. When the plants in my vegetable and flower beds die, I give a little sigh of relief, knowing I can let go of the need to keep the landscaping perfectly groomed. I leave the dead brown foliage standing; it might look unsightly for a while, but it benefits the insects and birds that visit my yard. The flora that makes my garden vibrant and colorful will come back in its own time. Spring is just around the corner—and before I know it, the cycle of the year starts all over again. ◆

Winter Ingredients

PRODUCE (GENERAL)

Beets

Carrots

Celery root

Chicories: endive, escarole, frisée, radicchio

Citrus

Edible flowers: pansy, snapdragon, sweet alyssum

Fennel

Herbs: perennials (chives, rosemary, thyme, oregano, sage)

Kohlrabi

Leeks

Lettuce

Parsnips

Preserved vegetables

Rutabagas

Storage vegetables: dried beans, peas, and corn; onions, garlic, potatoes, winter squash

Turnips

SOUTHERN US

Brassicas: broccoli, Brussels sprouts, cabbage, cauliflower, romanesco

Celery

Ginger

Herbs: cool-season annuals (dill, cutting celery, cilantro, parsley, tarragon, sorrel)

FORAGED FOODS

Oyster mushrooms

Truffles

WINTER GAME AND FISH

Venison: elk, deer, pronghorn, etc.

Upland game birds: pheasant, grouse, partridge, etc.

Small game: rabbit, squirrel

Waterfowl: geese, ducks

Freshwater fish (ice fishing)

Saltwater fish (inshore and deepwater)

Shellfish: clams, scallops, oysters, mussels, etc.

Popovers with Roasted Bone Marrow and Celery Leaf Gremolata

SERVES 6

Popovers

4 large eggs

1¼ cups skim milk

1 teaspoon coarse sea salt

½ teaspoon freshly ground white pepper

1¼ cups all-purpose flour

3 (6- to 8-inch) halved marrow bones, or 6 (3- to 4-inch-tall) cut femur bones

Neutral oil, such as avocado or grapeseed

Coarse sea salt and freshly ground black pepper

2 tablespoons tallow, lard, or oil

Lemon wedges, for serving

Celery Leaf Gremolata (page 232)

Flaky sea salt

Note: The popovers can be made in a 12-cup muffin tin; you might have a little extra batter left over and the popovers won't rise quite as high, but they'll still be delicious.

There's too much to love about this starter: the dramatically tall popovers that rise in the oven, the indulgent roasted bone marrow, the bright and flavorful gremolata. It's the perfect communal meal opener to share with friends during the holiday season. I've always loved to eat slowly, course by course, and part of the fun of this dish is letting each person spoon bone marrow into their own popover, knowing it's best enjoyed on the spot. As a cook, this immediate satisfaction allows me to relax, pour a drink, and savor the moment with my guests before turning my attention back to the kitchen to cook the main course.

This recipe is also satisfying for me because it uses ingredients—marrow bones and celery leaves, specifically—that might otherwise be discarded. You can use beef marrow bones, halved horizontally into canoes, but nilgai, elk, or moose femurs cut into 4-inch-tall pieces also work. And after you've eaten the marrow, save the bones to add to the pot the next time you make stock!

To get the most dramatic rise, be sure to let the popover batter rest for at least 30 minutes and up to 24 hours before baking, and don't overfill the wells of the pan. You'll be rewarded with popovers that balloon out of the pan like chefs' toques.

---

1 **Make the popover batter:** In a large bowl, whisk together the eggs, milk, salt, and white pepper until the egg yolks are no longer streaky. Add the flour and whisk until well blended; there should be no major lumps (some little lumps are okay). Set aside to rest for at least 30 minutes or cover and refrigerate for up to 24 hours before baking. Remove the batter from the fridge and let it come to room temperature before baking if it was chilled; stir briefly to recombine, if needed.

2 Preheat the oven to 425°F with racks in the upper and lower thirds. Make sure there's plenty of space above the lower rack for the popovers to rise. Set a 6-cup popover pan on a baking sheet and place it in the oven to preheat as well. Line a separate baking sheet with aluminum foil.

continued

3 Very lightly grease the bottom of the marrow bones with oil and place them on the foil-lined pan. Season the tops with a sprinkle of salt and some black pepper.

4 Carefully remove the popover pan from the oven (it should be smoking hot) and drop a heaping teaspoon of tallow into each well. The fat should immediately sizzle and bubble. Using a ladle, fill the wells halfway to three-quarters full of batter; avoid overfilling or the popovers won't rise as tall. Sprinkle the top of each with a pinch of flaky salt. Place the popovers on the lower oven rack and the marrow bones on the upper rack. Bake the popovers for 25 minutes, until they're lightly golden brown on top and have risen tall and puffed well over the rim of the pan. Bake the marrow bones for 15 to 20 minutes (pulling them out before the popovers are done); the marrow should be bubbling.

5 Remove the popovers from the oven. Use a toothpick to prick the top and bottom of each popover to release excess steam (this prevents deflating). They will eventually deflate some, but should mostly keep their height and structure.

6 To serve, squeeze some lemon wedges over the bone marrow and sprinkle the top with celery gremolata and some flaky salt. Tear open a popover, spoon some of the bone marrow and gremolata into the hollow center and enjoy!

Coffee-Cured Salmon with Truffles and Truffle-Infused Cream Cheese

SERVES 6

Truffle-Infused Dairy

1 (8-ounce) package cream cheese

¼ cup whole milk

1 Périgord or winter black truffle

Coffee-Cured Salmon

½ cup coarse sea salt

½ cup packed dark brown sugar

¼ cup freshly ground coffee beans

1 (2- to 3-pound) salmon fillet

¼ cup thinly sliced fresh chives

Lemon wedges and bagel crackers, for serving

My father-in-law always says, "Be careful what you introduce your taste buds to." It's a warning that once you try something incredibly good, you'll always crave it—for better or worse. That's how I feel about truffles.

One winter I had the opportunity to visit the Pacific Northwest to discover the incredible world of truffles. My trip started with a foraging foray with Alana McGee of the Truffle Hunting Dog Company; we found both the intensely pungent winter white truffle and the fruity Oregon black truffle. Their aromas were so strong, I could smell them as soon as Lolo, Alana's Lagotto Romagnolo, dug them from the ground. The next day, I went to Cartwright Truffière to learn about the mushroom's symbiotic relationship with trees and why they're so important to our forests. There, I got to try the cultivated Périgord truffle, which has a very nutty and slightly earthy smell.

Before that trip, my experience with truffles had been limited to truffle oil (which is often flavored with a chemical meant to taste like truffle, not the real thing!), and when I smelled and tasted a fresh truffle, I was surprised by how different it was. What amazes me about truffles is the way they can change or intensify the flavors of the foods they're paired with, allowing you to experience familiar ingredients in new ways. Here the truffle enhances the marine flavors of the salmon and brings out the nuttiness and fruitiness of the freshly ground coffee.

Truffle season begins right around the holidays, and truffles make a really cool gift. And because I think food is best shared with loved ones, I like to invite friends and family over for an extravagant Christmas brunch, featuring this coffee-cured salmon, truffle-infused cream cheese, and fresh shaved truffles.

1 **Infuse the dairy:** Open the foil wrapper to expose the cream cheese (or scoop it into a jar); pour the milk into a separate jar. Place the cream cheese and milk in a very large (1- to 2-gallon) jar or container (ideally glass) with a tight-fitting lid (leave the smaller jar uncovered). Wrap the truffle in a piece of paper towel to keep it from getting moldy and place it inside the large jar. Cover with the lid and place the jar in the fridge. Leave it to infuse for 3 to 4 days, wrapping the

continued

Truffle-Infused Everything

Truffles are expensive, so if you get your hands on one, make the most of it by stretching it into several dishes. A ripe truffle is pungent, and as soon as it emerges from the ground, it begins releasing its aroma. If you put that fresh truffle in a container with other ingredients, they'll draw in that aroma. Fatty ingredients work best; try infusing a stick of butter (still wrapped in its paper), an open jar of heavy cream, eggs, cheese, nuts, salmon, shortbread cookies, or an avocado—amazingly, the truffle's aromas will even penetrate the skin of the avocado, the eggshells, and the butter wrapper. Keep in mind that strong-smelling ingredients will also impart their aromas to other ingredients in the same container, so they're best infused separately. And after you've infused your ingredients, the truffle itself can be grated or shaved over whatever you like.

truffle in a fresh piece of paper towel each day. Lift the lid and give it a sniff—the smell of the truffle will infuse everything in the jar.

2 **Cure the salmon:** In a medium bowl, combine the salt, sugar, and ground coffee. Generously rub the mixture over the salmon to coat all sides; you might not use it all and can reserve some for sprinkling on top before serving. Place the fish in a vacuum bag and vacuum seal it (this presses the coffee mixture into the fish so it cures faster, a method I learned from chef Kevin Gillespie). Transfer to the fridge to cure for 6 hours for a thin (½-inch-thick) fillet, about 12 hours for a 1-inch-thick fillet, or about 24 hours for a 2-inch-thick fillet.

3 Rinse the salmon with cold water to remove any excess cure and pat it very dry with paper towels. (The salmon is best eaten the day it's finished curing, but can be placed in an airtight container and stored in the refrigerator for up to 1 day.)

4 When ready to serve, in a medium bowl, stir together the infused cream cheese and milk and the juice from a small lemon wedge until well blended. Grate half the truffle from the jar into the mixture using a Microplane or fine grater and stir to combine.

5 Very thinly slice the fish across the grain at a 45-degree angle. Spread the truffle-infused cream cheese on crackers, top with the sliced salmon, and sprinkle with the chives and a pinch of the reserved coffee rub. Using a truffle shaver, mandoline, or sharp knife, shave the remaining truffle half over the sliced salmon and serve.

Ground Venison and Red Pepper Soup

SERVES 4

Extra-virgin olive oil

1 pound 80% lean ground venison, lamb, or beef

1½ tablespoons smoked paprika

2 teaspoons crushed dried rosemary

Coarse sea salt and freshly ground black pepper

1 small yellow onion (the size of a baseball), diced

4 garlic cloves, minced

8 cups chicken stock or venison stock, homemade (see page 257) or store-bought, plus more if needed

1 (12-ounce) jar roasted red bell peppers, drained (liquid reserved) and cut into thin strips

1 cup Israeli couscous

2 cups kale leaves chopped, stems thinly sliced (crosswise)

This is a simple soup that I developed during the early days of the COVID-19 pandemic in 2020, when grocery shopping was extremely limited. I had Israeli couscous and jarred roasted bell peppers in the pantry, venison in my freezer, and hardy greens in my garden. If lockdown taught us anything, it's the importance of a well-stocked pantry, and today you won't find me without jars of stock, spices, and a variety of beans, grains, and pasta on hand.

I love this recipe because it's not only very flavorful, it's also very adaptable. You can replace the fresh kale with frozen spinach, for example, or swap out the couscous for canned chickpeas or great northern beans, brown rice, or diced potatoes (cooked beans won't absorb as much liquid as couscous or potato, so you may need only 6 cups of stock). The soup also reheats easily, so I'll often double the recipe and freeze half to take on hunting or camping trips or to keep on hand for busy weeknight dinners.

1 Heat a large pot or Dutch oven over medium-high heat. Add enough olive oil to coat the bottom of the pan in a thin layer. When the oil is shimmering, add the ground venison, working in batches as needed, and cook, breaking up the meat with a spoon as it cooks, until browned, 4 to 5 minutes. Season with the paprika, rosemary, and a couple pinches each of salt and black pepper. Stir to combine, then transfer to a bowl or plate and set aside.

2 Drizzle the pot with a bit more oil if it looks dry, then add the onion. Cook over medium-high heat, stirring occasionally, until golden in color and soft, 3 to 5 minutes. Stir in the garlic and cook for 1 minute, or until fragrant. Season with a pinch of salt.

3 Pour in the stock and stir, scraping up any browned bits from the bottom of the pot. Bring the liquid to a boil, then reduce the heat to maintain a gentle simmer. Return the venison to the pot and add the roasted peppers and the liquid from the jar and the couscous. Simmer for 20 to 25 minutes to cook the pasta and intensify the flavors.

4 Add the kale and simmer for 10 to 15 minutes more, until the kale is tender. Taste and season with salt and black pepper, if needed. Serve hot.

Creamy White Wine–Steamed Clams

**SERVES 4 AS A STARTER,
OR 2 AS A MAIN COURSE**

4 pounds littleneck, steamer, or Manila clams

2 tablespoons unsalted butter

1 small shallot, thinly sliced (about ⅓ cup)

4 garlic cloves, minced

1 cup dry white wine

2 tablespoons tomato paste

½ teaspoon fennel seeds, coarsely ground using a mortar and pestle or spice grinder

½ teaspoon dried thyme

Heavy pinch of saffron, crumbled between your fingers

½ cup heavy cream

1 tablespoon minced fresh parsley

Crusty bread, for serving

I've always enjoyed the hands-on aspect of eating bivalves—twisting the shells in half and using one side as a spoon to scoop the meat and delicious broth from the other. But I found a new appreciation for them during a visit to Connecticut one summer. After digging up some quahogs for dinner, the locals taught me that the secret to a delicious broth was preserving the liquid (or liquor) inside their shells. It's the same stuff, albeit fresher and better tasting, than the clam juice you buy in a bottle. Up to that point, I had always heard that bivalves needed to be soaked in cold water so they'd purge their grit, but in the process, they lose their natural juices and briny ocean flavor. Why hadn't I thought of saving that liquor before? Now, whenever I cook clams or other bivalves, I give them a quick scrub under cool water on the outside just before cooking. The small amount of grit inside their shells usually sinks right to the bottom of the pot (the broth is so delicious, it's practically drinkable, but avoid scooping up the last ¼ inch where the grit has collected). This dish is a comforting appetizer to share with friends and family, but I also like to serve it with a hearty salad, such as the winter brassica salad on page 239 or the snap pea and farro salad on page 75, as a meal for two.

1 As soon as you get home from the market, place the clams in a bowl and refrigerate them, uncovered, so they can breathe (don't submerge them in water). Just before cooking, gently rinse the clams under cold water and give the shells a quick scrub with a brush.

2 In a large pot or extra-wide braising pan (big enough to hold all the clams), melt the butter over medium heat. When it starts to foam, add the shallot and sauté for about 5 minutes, until soft and translucent but not browned. Add the garlic and cook for about 1 minute, then pour in the wine and stir, scraping up any browned bits from the bottom of the pot. Simmer for a few minutes to burn off the alcohol, then add the tomato paste, fennel, thyme, saffron, and cream and stir until well blended. Gently simmer for 2 to 3 minutes more, then add the clams and cover with a lid. Cook for 8 to 10 minutes, until the clams open; discard any that do not fully open. Remove from the heat.

3 Garnish with parsley and serve immediately, with crusty bread for soaking up the broth.

Boozy Duck à l'Orange with Spiced Parsnip Puree

SERVES 4

4 skin-on duck breasts (see Notes)

1 cup chicken stock or duck stock, homemade (see page 257) or store-bought

Wings and neck of 1 duck, roasted (optional)

1 medium shallot, sliced crosswise into rings

Spiced Parsnip Puree

1 pound parsnips, peeled and sliced into ½-inch-thick coins

¾ cup heavy cream

⅛ teaspoon ground cinnamon

⅛ teaspoon ground cloves

Coarse sea salt

2 tablespoons bourbon

1 tablespoon brown sugar

¼ cup fresh orange juice

1½ teaspoons unsalted butter

Zest of 1 orange

Sea salt, preferably flaky sea salt, for finishing

A perfectly cooked duck breast, with a juicy, medium-rare center and extra-crispy skin, is what I'd order for my last meal. It took me a while to figure out how to cook it just right because the birds I was using came from various regions, were of different ages, and had eaten diverse diets. These variables make wild ducks and geese beautifully unique and delicious, but add to the challenge of cooking them. Luckily, I've had a lot of practice. In our young and ambitious twenties, my husband and I were waterfowl-hunting fools. Equipped with a 15-foot enclosed trailer packed with decoys (that we also slept in), we hit the winter and spring seasons hard, and as a result, we were eating ducks and geese at least twice a week for an entire year! Today I hang my hat on this invaluable experience, and this recipe is a culmination of everything I learned.

This dish is a riff on the classic duck à l'orange. It's more savory than the original, and I love the addition of bourbon to the sauce—think of it like an old-fashioned! The sauce pairs so beautifully with the warm, wintery spiced parsnip, it would be a crime to replace the puree with anything else. While this recipe might sound intimidating, just know that one winter, I was able to pull it off in a tiny Airbnb kitchen with limited equipment. The instructions are very detailed, and if you follow them closely, the result will be delicious!

1 Remove the duck breasts from the refrigerator about an hour before cooking. Blot the skin with paper towels to remove as much moisture as possible. Using a sharp knife, score the skin and fat in a crosshatch pattern, being careful not to cut all the way through to the meat. (It helps to pull the skin taut with your fingers to be sure you're only slicing the skin and fat.) Set aside to come to room temperature.

2 Meanwhile, in a small saucepan, combine the stock, wings and neck (if using), and shallot. Bring to a soft boil over high heat, then cook until the liquid reduces to about ⅓ cup, for 5 to 10 minutes. Strain and set aside (discard the solids).

3 **Make the parsnip puree:** Put the parsnips in a large saucepan and cover with cold water. Bring to a boil over high heat, then reduce the heat to maintain a gentle simmer and cook until very tender when pierced with a fork, 15 to 20 minutes. Drain the parsnips, reserving

continued

Notes: This recipe works with both domestic and wild ducks. If you're using wild duck, I recommend plucked dabbling ducks, such as mallards, pintails, wood ducks, and wigeon. Small, tender geese such as specklebellies and snow geese are also great choices.

Cooking wild duck requires some intuition. Before you start, check the breasts to see how thick or thin the layer of fat beneath the skin is. Fat acts as a barrier to heat transfer in cooking, so if your duck breast has little to no fat, or is skinless, it will cook very fast, and you should treat more like a venison steak. If you start with a cold pan, you'll end up with overcooked meat, because there's no fat to insulate it. To remedy this, heat a drizzle of neutral oil (such as avocado or grapeseed) in a skillet over medium-high heat. Sear the breasts for 3 to 4 minutes on each side, until the meat hits between 128°F and 130°F.

The rendered duck fat can be saved and used in savory applications, such as roasting vegetables like Brussels sprouts or turnips, standing in for the walnut oil in the vinaigrette on page 189, or drizzling over popcorn.

about ¼ cup of the cooking liquid, and transfer to a high-powered blender or food processor. Add the cream, cinnamon, and cloves. Puree until the parsnips have the consistency of silky-smooth mashed potatoes; add 2 to 4 tablespoons of the reserved cooking liquid if needed. Taste and season with salt. Return the parsnip puree to the saucepan and keep warm until ready to serve.

4 If your ducks have a visible layer of fat underneath the skin, lay them skin-side down in a *cold* cast-iron pan. (For skinless ducks or ducks with very little visible fat, see the Notes.) Season the meat side with a pinch of salt and some pepper, then set over medium heat. As the pan heats up, you should hear the breast softly sputter and gurgle; if it's frying loudly, reduce the heat. As the breast cooks, it will contract and dome up in the center. Use a spatula to gently press down on the center or place a heavy baking dish on top so the skin gets full contact with the pan. Cook until the skin is brown and crispy, about 3 minutes for a duck breast or about 5 minutes for goose, flip the breast, and sear on the second side until the meat reaches between 128° and 130°F. If you don't have a meat thermometer, press into the breast with your tongs and feel for doneness like you would a steak (see page 44). The total cook time should be 5 to 6 minutes for a small wild duck breast, 6 to 7 minutes for a large wild duck breast, or 8 to 9 minutes for a wild goose breast or domestic duck breast. Transfer to a cutting board to rest. Pour 1 tablespoon of the rendered duck fat from the pan into the parsnip puree and stir to incorporate; pour the remaining fat into a jar and reserve for another use (see Notes).

5 While the pan is still warm, return it to medium heat, add the bourbon, and stir to scrape up the browned bits from the bottom. If you're using a gas stove, be aware that the pan will likely catch fire. Cook until the alcohol burns off, then add the sugar and orange juice. If the pan is not bubbling, increase the heat and bring the liquid to a soft boil, then cook until the sugars caramelize to a light brown color, 1 to 2 minutes. Add the reserved stock and cook for a few minutes more, until the sauce coats the back of a spoon. Finish with a pat of butter and swirl the pan to emulsify. Stir in the orange zest to finish.

6 Serve the duck breasts immediately on top of the parsnip puree with a spoonful of the boozy sauce. Be sure to season the tops of the duck breast with salt (flaky salt, if you have it!).

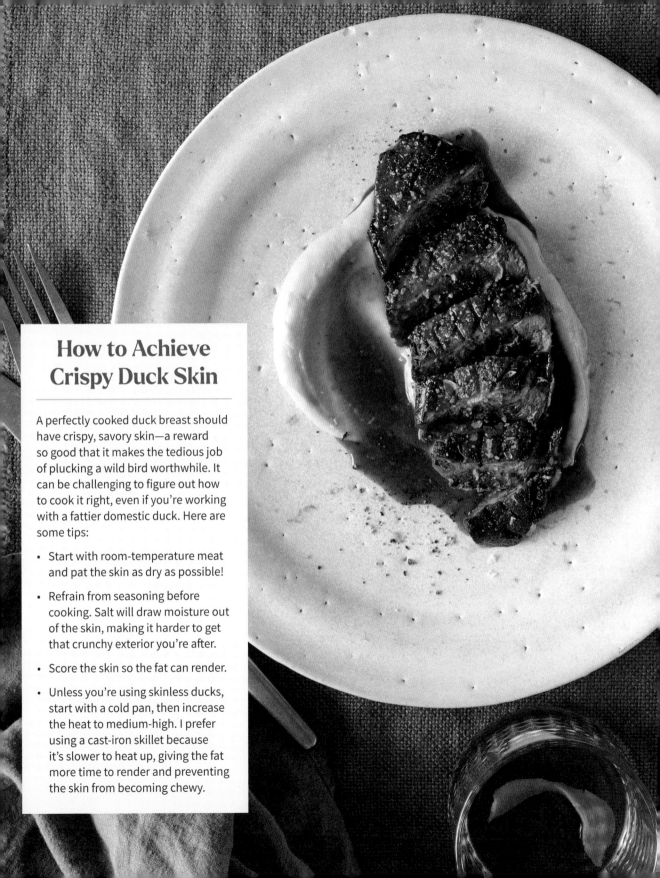

How to Achieve Crispy Duck Skin

A perfectly cooked duck breast should have crispy, savory skin—a reward so good that it makes the tedious job of plucking a wild bird worthwhile. It can be challenging to figure out how to cook it right, even if you're working with a fattier domestic duck. Here are some tips:

- Start with room-temperature meat and pat the skin as dry as possible!

- Refrain from seasoning before cooking. Salt will draw moisture out of the skin, making it harder to get that crunchy exterior you're after.

- Score the skin so the fat can render.

- Unless you're using skinless ducks, start with a cold pan, then increase the heat to medium-high. I prefer using a cast-iron skillet because it's slower to heat up, giving the fat more time to render and preventing the skin from becoming chewy.

Smoked Hocks and Butter Beans

SERVES 4 TO 6

2 smoked hog, venison, or pork hocks or shanks, or turkey drumsticks (about 1½ pounds total), store-bought or homemade (see DIY Smoked Shanks or Hocks, page 222)

1 pound dried butter beans (see Note)

Heaping ½ cup chopped bacon (¼- by 1-inch pieces), or about 4 slices extra-thick bacon, cut into ⅛- to ¼-inch-wide pieces

1 medium yellow onion, diced

Coarse sea salt and freshly ground black pepper

4 garlic cloves, minced

1 celery stalk, diced

1 large carrot, diced

8 cups unsalted hog stock or chicken stock, homemade (see page 257) or store-bought

½ teaspoon crushed dried rosemary

½ teaspoon dried thyme

1 bay leaf

Pickled Zucchini Relish (page 116) or chowchow, for serving

Note: If you're using domestic pork hocks, which take about half as long to tenderize, soak your beans overnight.

This stew is inspired by a smoked ham and cowpea dish my father-in-law makes every winter. It's a simple, classic southern recipe in which he simmers a smoked pork hock with lady cream peas and serves it with a spoonful of chowchow on top. This is my iteration of that meal. The smoked hocks act almost as a condiment, imparting smoky flavors but otherwise taking a back seat to the broth and the creamy butter beans that make up the bulk of the stew. Finishing each bowl with a spoonful of sweet-and-sour pickled veggies adds some zest.

1 Place the smoked hocks and butter beans in a large slow cooker.

2 Heat a large skillet over medium-low heat. Add the bacon and cook, stirring occasionally, until the fat has rendered and the bacon is crispy, about 10 minutes. Use a slotted spoon to transfer the bacon to a paper towel–lined plate to drain. Cover and set aside until ready to serve.

3 Increase the heat to medium-high and add the onion. Cook for 3 to 4 minutes, until soft and translucent, then season with a pinch each of salt and pepper. Add the garlic. Cook for an additional minute, then stir in the celery and carrot and season again. Cook for a few minutes until the vegetables begin to soften, and then pour a little bit of the stock into the pan to lift any browned bits from the bottom. Transfer everything into the slow cooker on top of the hocks and beans. Pour in the remaining stock and stir in the rosemary, thyme, and bay leaf. Cover and cook on low for about 5 hours, then give the pot a stir and set the lid ajar. Cook for 1 to 2 hours more, until the meat from the hocks is tender and slides right off the bone, the beans are buttery tender, and the liquid is no longer soupy. Use tongs to fish the hocks out and pull off the meat. Discard the bones and any bits of collagen that didn't break down and return the meat to the pot of beans. Season to taste.

4 To serve, spoon the stew into bowls and top with the bacon and some zucchini relish.

DIY Smoked Shanks or Hocks

MAKES 4 TO 6 HOCKS, OR 4
DRUMSTICKS

¾ cup packed brown sugar

¾ cup coarse sea salt

½ teaspoon Prague powder #1
(pink curing salt; optional)

10 cups ice water

4 wild hog or venison shanks,
whole or cut into hocks; 4 turkey
drumsticks; or 6 pork hocks

A hock is the section of the shank just below the kneecap, right where the heel (the meaty portion of the calf muscle) ends. Smoking them adds tons of flavor to dishes like collard greens and big pots of beans. Hocks are commonly sold in southern grocery stores (where you usually see only the meaty upper portion of the shank, still attached to the bone), but are very easy to make at home with wild hog or venison shanks, wild turkey drumsticks, or domestic pork. Keep in mind that the smoking process here is strictly to add flavor; the meat won't be tender enough to eat without additional cooking.

You can keep the shanks whole, but if they don't fit into a pot for cooking, you'll need to cut them down: First use C-clamps to secure the shanks to a worktable for safety. Use a sharp knife to cut across the meat, down to the bone. Then use a handsaw (made for bones) or a reciprocating saw to cut through the bone and separate the hock; reserve the end pieces of the shank for the stockpot. To cut shanks for osso buco, cut them crosswise into 1- to 2-inch-thick slices.

1 In a medium saucepan, combine the brown sugar, sea salt, curing salt, and 2 cups water. Bring to a boil over high heat, stirring until the sugar and salts have dissolved. Remove from the heat and transfer to a large stockpot or other large container. Stir in the ice water and let cool completely, then submerge the shanks in the liquid. Cover and refrigerate for 8 to 12 hours.

2 Drain the shanks and rinse under cool water. Pat dry and place on a baking sheet. Refrigerate, uncovered, for at least several hours or up to 1 day to dry further. (A dry surface absorbs smoke better.)

3 Heat a smoker to between 200° and 225°F, using apple or maple wood for a light, sweet smoke, or mesquite or oak for a heavier smoke. Smoke the shanks for 3 hours, flipping once halfway through. Remove from the smoker and use immediately or freeze for up to 2 years.

BBQ Confit Goose with Grilled Cabbage Wedges

SERVES 4

Goose Confit

8 wild goose legs, 16 wild duck legs, or 4 Moulard duck legs, skin-on or skinless (about 2½ pounds total)

Texas BBQ Rub (page 254)

Coarse sea salt and freshly ground black pepper

Neutral oil, such as avocado or grapeseed, or refined coconut oil

Grilled Cabbage Wedges

1 head green cabbage, cut into 1½- to 2-inch-thick wedges through the core

Coarse sea salt and freshly ground black pepper

Creole Mustard Dressing (page 75)

1 tablespoon thinly sliced fresh chives

To Serve (optional)

Pickles (see page 250)

Sweet Bourbon Cornbread (page 237)

BBQ sauce

Potato salad

Food-wise, one of the best things about the great state of Texas is our barbecue: We season light on the sugar and heavy on the black pepper, and we let oak wood infuse the meat with smoky flavors. When I lived in North Dakota, though, good barbecue was hard to find. Looking for the flavors of home without the twenty-hour drive, I tried smoking wild game many ways, but it always lacked the fat needed to stand up to long smoking times. As I was processing birds after a successful goose hunt one early winter, I noticed there was tons of fat around the tail and cavity opening, and a thought struck me: *What if I use a smoky BBQ rub as the curing mixture, slowly cook the legs in fat, and then finish them over a bed of hot wood coals?* I gave it a shot and was rewarded with incredibly tender meat that was both smoky and peppery. While I wouldn't consider it true Texas BBQ, it satisfied my cravings.

I always reserve goose and duck legs for confit because I truly think it's the best way to eat them, but anything that rich needs to be paired with something sweet and acidic. And since I'm taking the time to fire up the grill, I like to cook seasonal winter vegetables like cabbage. Instead of making a traditional coleslaw, I thickly slice the cabbage, give it a good char, and serve it like a wedge salad with a tangy mustard dressing and a side of Sweet Bourbon Cornbread (page 237).

1 **Make the goose confit:** Place the goose legs on a baking sheet or in a glass container with a lid. Generously apply the BBQ rub and a heavy pinch each of salt and pepper to the goose legs and coat both sides. Cover and refrigerate for 12 to 24 hours.

2 Remove the meat from the refrigerator and allow it to come to room temperature. Preheat the oven to 250°F.

3 Place the legs in a single layer in a large baking dish (you might have to puzzle piece them in to fit, or use two baking dishes). Pour in enough oil to cover them completely, then cover the baking dish with aluminum foil. Transfer to the oven and cook until the meat is very tender when pricked with a fork, but not so long that it slips off the bone or it will fall apart on the grill! Check periodically to make sure you don't cook it too long. Generally, this will take 4 to 5 hours for wild goose legs, or 3 to 4 hours for domestic duck, but the cooking

continued

time can vary greatly depending on the bird species—greater Canada geese are generally tougher than lesser Canada and snow geese—and also the age of the bird. (Geese can live up to 24 years, although most of the geese you'll shoot are within a few years old. Older birds are tougher and may take longer to cook.)

4 When the goose legs are done, use tongs to transfer them to a baking sheet, letting the excess confit oil drip back into the baking dish. Set the legs aside to cool completely while you prepare the grill; reserve the confit oil.

5 Prepare a grill by burning wood or charcoal down to a hot coal bed, then set up a direct heat zone by pushing the coals to one side. (Alternatively, prepare a gas grill for high heat and set up two zones, one for direct heat, one for indirect.) If using charcoal or gas, add a handful of oak or mesquite wood chips for smoke flavor.

6 **Grill the cabbage:** Season both sides of the cabbage with salt and pepper, then drizzle some of the confit oil across both sides of the cabbage. (The remaining confit oil can be stored in an airtight container at room temperature for several months and used to confit a second batch of goose legs.) Place the cabbage over direct heat, cover with a lid, and cook for about 3 minutes, until you see that the bottom edges are starting to char. Using a wide spatula, flip the cabbage, close the lid again, and cook on the opposite side for 3 more minutes. The cabbage should have plenty of char marks, but the texture will still be a little firm. Transfer the cabbage wedges to indirect heat, or place them on a higher grate raised away from direct heat, so they can continue to cook without burning for 3 to 5 minutes more, until softened. Remove from the grill.

7 Next you'll grill the confit goose legs over direct heat. Lay each leg skin-side down (if there's skin) and cook for 2 to 3 minutes on one side, then flip and cook on the opposite side for 2 to 3 minutes more. You should have nice grill marks, and if the skin is attached it should be crispy. Remove from the heat.

8 Drizzle the top of each grilled cabbage wedge with a spoonful of the Creole mustard dressing. Serve with the goose legs and any desired condiments and sides.

Beef Cheek, Red Wine, and Barley Stew

SERVES 4 TO 6

Beef tallow or neutral oil, such as avocado or grapeseed

1½ pounds trimmed beef cheeks, cut into 1- to 2-inch chunks (see Note)

Coarse sea salt and freshly ground black pepper

1 medium yellow onion, diced

4 garlic cloves, minced

4 large carrots, coarsely chopped

4 celery stalks, coarsely chopped

½ teaspoon crushed dried rosemary

½ teaspoon dried thyme

1 tablespoon tomato paste

2 cups dry red wine, such as zinfandel

6 cups beef stock, homemade (see page 257) or store-bought

2 bay leaves

¾ cup hulled barley

2 tablespoons minced fresh parsley, for garnish

This hearty stew is my idea of the perfect food to eat after a day outside in wet, cold weather. It's made with beef cheeks—and yes, that means literally the cheeks of a cow! Cows spend most of their lives chewing grass, so as you can imagine, the cheeks are a pretty tough cut. My appreciation for these odd muscles comes from a place of curiosity, but also from my experience with wild game. I learned early on how to cook with the whole animal, including the unloved muscles that are full of collagen. These tough cuts become succulent and tender when cooked for long periods. Unlike stew meat, which traditionally comes from a muscle with a long grain line, the cheek is made of tiny short muscle fibers; they become very soft when cooked, and turn the broth silky.

Beef cheeks aren't a common sight at the grocery store, but don't be afraid to contact a farmer or a butcher shop to request some. If you can't find cheeks, this recipe works with pretty much any type of tougher red meat. You can use 2 pounds of oxtails for a rich, gelatinous stew (keep some extra stock or water on hand to thin it if needed), or beef or venison stew meat, cut into 1- to 2-inch chunks before browning.

1 In a large Dutch oven or wide, heavy-bottomed pot, heat 1 tablespoon tallow over medium-high heat until it is hot. Working in batches, add some of the beef cheeks to the pot, leaving a little space between each piece. Cook, undisturbed, for 3 to 4 minutes, until brown on the bottom, then flip each piece or give it all a good stir and season with a few pinches each of salt and pepper. Cook for a couple minutes more, until browned on all sides, then transfer the meat to a plate and repeat to cook the remaining beef cheeks.

2 Add another tablespoon of tallow to the pan if it looks dry, then add the onion and cook, stirring occasionally, until soft and lightly golden in color, 3 to 4 minutes. Add the garlic and cook for 1 minute, then add the carrots and celery and give it all a good stir. Season with the rosemary, thyme, and a pinch each of salt and pepper. Cook for a few more minutes, then mix in the tomato paste and cook for a minute to lightly toast the paste. Pour in the wine and bring to a boil, stirring and scraping up the browned bits from the bottom of the pot, then cook for a couple minutes to burn off the alcohol. Pour in

Note: If you discover late in the game that your beef cheeks aren't trimmed, it's easy to trim them yourself—keep in mind that this could reduce the weight of the meat by up to 50 percent, in which case, just halve the other ingredients in the recipe.

the stock and add the bay leaves. Return the meat to the pot and stir to make sure everything is combined. Reduce the heat to its lowest setting (you only want to see the liquid bubble every so often, not maintain a full simmer) and cover the pot. Cook the stew for 3 hours, then stir in the barley. Cover, with the lid ajar, and cook, stirring often to release the starch from the barley (this adds a creamy texture to the soup), for 1 hour more, or until the meat is extremely tender.

3 Serve hot, garnished with the parsley.

Rabbit, Leek, and Root Vegetable Soup

SERVES 6

3 pounds whole rabbit
(3 cottontails, 1 snowshoe hare,
or 1 domestic fryer), cut into
6 pieces each (see Notes)

Neutral oil, such as avocado or
grapeseed

Coarse sea salt and freshly ground
white or black pepper

3 tablespoons unsalted butter

3 large leeks, halved lengthwise,
sliced into half-moons, and rinsed
well to remove any grit

3 celery stalks, sliced

4 garlic cloves, minced

3 tablespoons all-purpose flour

8 cups chicken stock, homemade
(see page 257) or store-bought

8 ounces turnips, peeled and sliced
into ¼-inch-thick wedges

1 pound small waxy potatoes,
sliced into ⅛-inch-thick rounds

½ teaspoon dill seeds

2 teaspoons mustard powder

2 bay leaves

2 cups heavy cream

The winters Travis and I lived through in North Dakota were pretty rough. It would have been easy to hibernate for a few months and never go outside, but we knew the key to our sanity was the outdoors. Every weekend, no matter how cold it got, we'd bundle up and take the dogs for a "walk," gun in hand. We'd seek out large open fields with broken-down barns, piles of brush, and shelter belts (long rows of trees planted by farmers to block wind and prevent erosion), knowing a cottontail was likely to pop out. Those cold and snowy Saturdays were synonymous with rabbit hunting, which meant that Sundays were dedicated to slowly simmering their meat in a creamy soup with leeks, potatoes, and root vegetables.

Rabbit could rival pork as "the other white meat." It tastes a lot like chicken or turkey, and the mild-flavored meat shreds apart easily after low-and-slow cooking. Rabbit is also one of the most sustainable meat animals; they require very little land and food, and they breed like, well, rabbits! If you can't get wild cottontails or snowshoe hare, you should absolutely seek out domestic rabbit from nearby farmers or FFA students. The only species I wouldn't use here is jackrabbit; its meat is dark red and would work better in a bolder dish, such as the Beef Cheek, Red Wine, and Barley Stew on page 226.

1 Remove the rabbit from the refrigerator at least 30 minutes before cooking and pat dry with a paper towel.

2 Heat a very large Dutch oven or other pot over medium-high heat. Add enough oil to lightly coat the bottom of the pot. Season the meat with salt and pepper on both sides. When the oil is hot, working in batches, brown the rabbit until golden in color on both sides. Add more oil as needed. Transfer to a plate and set aside.

3 Add the butter to the pot and let it melt, then add the leeks and celery. Season with a couple pinches each of salt and pepper, then cook, stirring occasionally, for 3 to 4 minutes, until soft. Add the garlic and cook for another minute, until fragrant. Sprinkle in the flour, stirring continuously to incorporate, then cook for a couple minutes, until the flour turns a light golden color. While stirring continuously, slowly pour in the stock, then stir until the liquid is well incorporated.

recipe and ingredients continued

To Serve

Crème fraîche or sour cream

¼ cup chopped fresh dill

¼ cup thinly sliced fresh chives

Crusty bread

Notes: In place of the rabbit, substitute poultry thighs, such as chicken, pheasant, ruffed grouse, spruce grouse, or dusky grouse. You can also use whole squirrels. Chicken thighs may take only 1 to 2 hours to cook; wild game will take 3 to 4 hours.

You'll want to use a whole rabbit because the bones add a lot of flavor to the soup. To divide it into serving portions, cut off the two hindquarters and the two front quarters, then cut the back in half (I use a meat cleaver for this). I typically cut out the ribs and back hips since their small bones are harder to fish out and don't hold a lot of meat; freeze them to add to the stockpot when you make chicken or pheasant stock.

4 Return the browned rabbit to the pot and add the turnips, potatoes, dill seeds, mustard powder, and bay leaves. Season with a pinch of salt and a good crack of pepper. Reduce the heat to its lowest setting and cover with the lid slightly ajar. The soup should barely simmer, bubbling only occasionally; it should not be boiling. Cook, stirring occasionally to make sure nothing sticks to the pot, until the meat is extremely tender, about 4 hours if using wild rabbit or about 2 hours for domestic rabbit. Use tongs to retrieve the rabbit pieces from the soup and place them on a baking sheet or large cutting board to cool.

5 Stir the cream into the soup and bring the liquid to a full simmer, raising the heat to medium-low, if needed. Cook for 15 minutes to reduce the cream a little, then taste and season with salt and pepper, if needed.

6 When the rabbit is cool enough to handle, use a fork to remove the meat from the bones and shred the meat. Return the meat to the pot.

7 Serve the soup topped with a small dollop of crème fraîche (which adds acidity and thickens the liquid) and garnished with a sprinkle of dill and chives. Enjoy immediately, with some crusty bread alongside.

Winter Pot Roast with Celery Root and Gremolata

SERVES 4 TO 6

Pot Roast

1 medium celery root (about 1 pound)

2½ pounds venison or beef neck, shoulder, osso buco, or oxtails (see Note)

Kosher salt and freshly ground black pepper

1 tablespoon beef tallow or neutral oil, such as avocado or grapeseed

1 yellow onion, chopped

1 leek, sliced and rinsed well to remove any grit

2 parsnips or carrots, peeled and coarsely chopped

1 celery stalk, coarsely chopped

4 garlic cloves, minced

3 tablespoons dry white wine

1 tablespoon fresh lemon juice

Several thyme and/or rosemary sprigs

6 cups chicken stock, homemade (see page 257) or store-bought

Note: If using beef instead of venison, choose a chuck roast or trimmed brisket. The only difference will be a shorter cook time, 2 to 3 hours.

If I were to give this recipe a different name, it would be "Not My Momma's Pot Roast." When I was growing up, it wasn't a meal I enjoyed; the meat was always dry and tough. As an adult, I made the shocking discovery that pot roast can, in fact, be truly delicious and knew I had to try my hand at the dish using venison. The result was tender, succulent, and flavorful—truly *not* my momma's pot roast. My favorite cut for this recipe is the neck, but you can definitely use osso buco or oxtail. The muscle fibers are interwoven with lots of silver skin, which is key to adding succulence and keeping the roast from drying out. And because I've burned out on the stereotypical tomato-paste-and-red-wine flavor profile that winter braises seem to favor, I've changed things up quite a bit. Wild game pot roasts can get dark and heavy fast, so I lighten the dish by using chicken stock, white wine, and winter vegetables like celery root to brighten the liquid and let the flavor of the meat stand out. I use a culinary herb in my garden called cutting celery (or leaf celery) for the gremolata, but you can use celery leaves or parsley instead.

1 **Make the pot roast:** Preheat the oven to 250°F.

2 Peel the celery root, then chop it into 1-inch pieces. Set aside.

3 Cut the venison into large (4- to 6-inch) chunks across the grain and season generously with salt and pepper. Heat the tallow in a Dutch oven over medium-high heat. When the oil is hot, add the meat, working in batches if needed, and cook until browned on both sides, 4 to 5 minutes total. Transfer the meat to a plate and set aside.

4 If the pan looks dry, add more oil, then add the onion and cook, stirring occasionally, until it starts to turn golden, 3 to 5 minutes. Add the leeks and cook, stirring occasionally, for a few additional minutes, until soft. Stir in the parsnips, celery, and celery root and cook for a few minutes more. Stir in the garlic and cook until the garlic is fragrant, less than 1 minute. Add the wine and lemon juice. Allow the alcohol to boil off, then stir, scraping up the browned bits from the bottom of the pot.

recipe and ingredients continued

Creamy Polenta

1½ cups whole milk

1 teaspoon kosher salt

½ teaspoon freshly ground white pepper

1 cup quick-cooking polenta

1 tablespoon unsalted butter

¼ cup shredded Parmesan cheese

Gremolata

2 tablespoons chopped cutting celery (see headnote), celery leaves, or fresh parsley leaves

1 teaspoon lemon zest

1 tablespoon grated Parmesan cheese

1 garlic clove, minced

5 Drop the herb sprigs into the pot. Return the chunks of venison to the pot and pour in enough stock to come about halfway up the sides of the meat (you may not need all the stock).

6 Cover the pot with a tight-fitting lid and place it in the oven. Braise for about 4 hours, until the meat is fork-tender. About three-quarters of the way through the cooking time, set the lid slightly ajar so the liquid can reduce and flip the meat if the top looks dried out. (If the liquid reduces too much, you can add a splash of stock to the pot.)

7 **Meanwhile, make the polenta:** Combine 1½ cups water, the milk, salt, and pepper in a 2-quart saucepan and bring to a soft boil over medium-high heat. Stir in the polenta and reduce the heat to low. Cook, stirring occasionally, for 5 to 10 minutes. Remove from the heat and stir in the butter and Parmesan. Let the polenta rest, uncovered, to thicken; serve hot.

8 **Make the gremolata:** In a small bowl, stir together the cutting celery, lemon zest, Parmesan, and garlic. Set aside until ready to serve.

9 Spoon the polenta onto serving plates. Top with the pot roast and vegetables, garnish with the gremolata, and serve.

Midwest Cioppino

SERVES 6

1½ pounds flaky white-fleshed fish fillets, such as redfish, cod, halibut, bass, swordfish, or walleye

Coarse sea salt and freshly ground black pepper

12 ounces hot Italian sausage, store-bought or homemade (see page 253)

1 medium yellow onion, diced

4 garlic cloves, minced

1 fennel bulb, bulb and stems thinly sliced, fronds reserved for garnish

2 cups white wine

2 (14-ounce) cans fire-roasted diced tomatoes, with their juices

4 cups seafood stock (see page 258)

¼ teaspoon dried oregano

Country or sourdough bread, for serving

Note: If you're using thinner fish, such as walleye or pike, the flesh will shred apart easily when it's cooked, so resist the urge to stir after you've dropped it into the soup and ladle it out very carefully to avoid shredding it. If you're using walleye, don't forget to add the cheeks!

I've only been ice fishing once, and it was without a doubt the coldest and most miserable day of my entire life! Travis and I had entered a popular ice fishing tournament on Devils Lake in North Dakota. The wind was blowing at more than 30 miles per hour, making the wind chill −35°F, and the rules of the tournament didn't allow ice houses or pop-up tents. The hole I was fishing kept freezing over, despite having a candle burning in a metal coffee can to drip ice melt into it. With snot frozen to my face, I had to break up the ice with an axe over and over again so I could get my line in. I only lasted for an hour and a half out there, and I never caught a single fish.

Needless to say, I haven't been ice fishing since, but I did gain a newfound respect for all the crazy souls who love it. I was also thankful that Travis didn't give up and continued to catch fish all winter long. One afternoon, he came home with a handful of walleye, and since I was craving a hot bowl of seafood stew instead of the typical fish fry, I used it to develop this variation of cioppino. In the Midwest, I certainly didn't have access to the variety of shellfish that cioppino recipes typically call for, so I applied the same philosophy to what I *could* get—walleye and hot Italian venison sausage. Now that I'm living in Texas, I make this stew using redfish from the Gulf Coast and sausage made with wild hog. I encourage you to use the seafood and meat you have access to and make this dish your own.

1 Remove the fish and sausage from the refrigerator at least 30 minutes before you plan to cook. Cut the fish into 6 serving pieces total and season both sides with salt and pepper.

2 Heat a very large saucepan or stockpot over medium-high heat. Add the sausage and cook, breaking up the meat with a spoon as it cooks, until browned and crispy on the outside, about 4 minutes. Transfer the sausage to a bowl and set aside.

3 If there is oil left in the pot, pour out all but 1 tablespoon. Add the onion and a couple pinches of salt. Cook, stirring occasionally, for 4 to 5 minutes, until soft and lightly golden in color. Stir in the garlic and fennel and cook for few minutes, until the fennel starts to soften. Pour in the wine and stir, scraping up any browned bits from the bottom of the pan. Cook for a couple minutes to allow the alcohol to burn off, then add the tomatoes and their juices, the stock, and the oregano. Bring to a simmer, then cook until the fennel is very tender, 10 to 15 minutes.

4 Reduce the heat to low and drop the fish into the pot. Gently poach the fish in the broth until the flesh is cooked through and gently flakes with a spoon, 3 to 8 minutes, depending on how thick the fish is (see Note). Keep the heat low to avoid overcooking the fish. Ladle into bowls and garnish with the fennel fronds. Serve warm, with sliced bread alongside.

Cauliflower Masala Soup

SERVES 4 TO 6

1 tablespoon unrefined coconut oil

1 medium yellow onion, diced

1 tablespoon minced fresh ginger

4 garlic cloves, minced

1 head cauliflower, florets coarsely chopped and stem diced

1 (28-ounce) can whole peeled tomatoes

1 tablespoon tomato paste

1 (14.5-ounce) can full-fat coconut milk (not coconut cream)

1 to 2 tablespoons garam masala, to taste (see headnote)

½ teaspoon sugar

Coarse sea salt

Yogurt, fresh cilantro, and warm naan, for serving

On cold days when I want a flavorful, creamy soup without heavy cream, this is what I turn to. Featuring a heavy dose of the Indian spice blend garam masala, coconut milk, and an entire head of cauliflower, it's a surprisingly filling soup. You can enjoy it two ways: with the big chunks of cauliflower left whole and served in the masala sauce over basmati rice, or pureed until ultrasmooth. I like this soup to be pretty bold flavor-wise. If you're new to using garam masala or prefer things less spiced, start with just 1 tablespoon and add more to taste at the end. Enjoy this as a light lunch or served as a side to roast chicken marinated in garlicky yogurt or the Mushroom Shawarma skewers on page 128.

1 In a very large saucepan or stockpot, melt the coconut oil over medium heat. Add the onion and cook, stirring frequently, for several minutes, until soft and translucent. Season with a couple pinches of salt, then stir in the ginger and garlic. Cook for another minute, then add the cauliflower. Cook, stirring occasionally, until it begins to soften and turn light brown in color, about 5 minutes. Season generously with several pinches of salt, then add the tomatoes, tomato paste, coconut milk, garam masala, and sugar. Stir well to incorporate and break up the tomatoes.

2 Cover with a tight-fitting lid and cook at a low boil for 15 minutes, or until the cauliflower is very, very soft. If you can hear it boiling vigorously, reduce the heat.

3 Remove the lid and use an immersion blender to blend the soup directly in the pot until smooth. (Alternatively, working in batches if needed, carefully transfer the soup to a high-powered standing blender, cover the lid with a dish towel, and blend until smooth.) Taste and season with salt; cauliflower is rather bland on its own, and you might need more than you think.

4 Ladle the soup into bowls and swirl a dollop of yogurt into each. Top with fresh cilantro and serve with warm naan alongside.

Sweet Bourbon Cornbread

SERVES 8 TO 10

1 cup stone-ground yellow cornmeal

1 cup all-purpose flour

2 teaspoons baking powder

½ teaspoon baking soda

1 teaspoon coarse sea salt, plus more for sprinkling

2 large eggs, beaten

½ cup (4 ounces) unsalted European-style butter, melted

¼ cup honey, plus more for drizzling

½ cup sugar

1 cup whole milk

3 tablespoons bourbon

My love of cooking with bourbon has led to some interesting discoveries about its potential as an ingredient. Case in point: this cornbread.

I developed this recipe for an event sponsored by a Kentucky bourbon company. In curating the menu, I needed to try to infuse the liquor into several dishes—and turns out, bourbon is an excellent stand-in for buttermilk in cornbread. It adds a similar amount of acidity but brings its own character to the table.

This cornbread is very sweet. In fact, I'd be comfortable serving it as a dessert with a drizzle of honey on top and some fresh sliced peaches in the summer or caramelized pears in the winter. It can also be served alongside savory dishes, like the Smoked Hocks and Butter Beans on page 220 and the BBQ Confit Goose with Grilled Cabbage Wedges on page 223.

1 Preheat the oven to 375°F. Place a 10- to 11-inch cast-iron skillet in the oven to preheat as well.

2 In a large bowl, combine the cornmeal, flour, baking powder, baking soda, and salt. In a separate large bowl, mix together the eggs, 7 tablespoons of the melted butter, the honey, sugar, milk, and bourbon. Fold the dry ingredients into the wet ingredients until just incorporated.

3 Remove the hot cast-iron pan from the oven and pour in the remaining 1 tablespoon melted butter. Swirl to coat the bottom of the pan, then pour in the cornbread batter. Season the top with a sprinkle of salt. Bake for about 45 minutes, give or take 5 minutes (depending on the size of your pan), until a toothpick inserted into the center comes out clean. About halfway or three-quarters of the way through cooking, cover the top with foil to prevent it from browning too much.

4 Serve warm, drizzled with honey.

Winter Brassica Salad with Pear, Parmesan, and Lemon-Dill Vinaigrette

SERVES 4

Lemon-Dill Vinaigrette

¼ cup fresh lemon juice
(from 1 to 2 lemons)

1 garlic clove, minced

2 tablespoons grated Parmesan
cheese

1 tablespoon chopped fresh dill,
plus more as needed

½ cup walnut oil or extra-virgin
olive oil

Coarse sea salt and freshly ground
black pepper

Cauliflower Salad

1 tablespoon neutral oil, such as
avocado or grapeseed

1 head purple, green, or white
cauliflower, chopped into small
florets

Kosher salt and freshly ground
black pepper

4 cauliflower leaves, kale leaves, or
collard greens, stemmed

4 cups winter frisée

1 pear, cored and sliced into
matchsticks

½ cup walnuts, toasted and chopped

¼ cup grated Parmesan cheese

Though we do get a couple of freezes every year in South Texas, they don't typically last long, which allows me to grow brassicas like broccoli and cauliflower throughout the winter. It's great to have a handful of varieties growing in the garden, because in addition to the crowns, you can eat their leaves, which I treat just like kale or collard greens. One of the reasons I love growing broccoli and cauliflower is because I can choose when to harvest the crown. I let my cauliflower grow a little longer, so the buds spread out just slightly instead of staying densely packed like the cauliflower you see at the grocery store, then harvest the crowns before they try to bolt. This gives me florets with extra nooks and crannies that brown quickly and grab the vinaigrette in this salad. In this recipe, the purple cauliflower florets are flash-seared to preserve their color, and the leaves are thinly sliced and softened by a bright, herbaceous lemon-dill vinaigrette. This beautifully layered salad offers a refreshing contrast to heavy winter braises.

1 **Make the vinaigrette:** In a small bowl, stir together the lemon juice, garlic, Parmesan, and dill. While whisking, slowly pour in the oil in a thin, steady stream, then whisk to emulsify. Taste and season with salt, pepper, and extra dill, if desired. Set aside.

2 **Make the salad:** In a large sauté pan, heat the oil over high heat. When the oil is hot, add the cauliflower in a single layer. For maximum crispiness, leave room between the pieces and work in batches as needed. Season with a pinch each of salt and pepper. Cook, undisturbed, for a minute or two, then flip and sear the other side until the florets are toasted and golden on the outside but still have a snappy texture; if you're using purple cauliflower, it should retain its color. Set aside to cool.

3 Remove the ribs from the cauliflower leaves. Stack the leaves on top of one another, tightly roll them up like a cigar, and thinly slice them crosswise. In a large bowl, toss the sliced cauliflower leaves and the seared cauliflower with a couple spoonfuls of the vinaigrette. Let stand for 15 minutes before serving to macerate and infuse with flavor.

4 Add the frisée, pear, walnuts, and Parmesan to the bowl with the cauliflower and toss to combine. Drizzle with more vinaigrette and chopped dill as desired and serve.

Fennel, Orange, and Ginger Salad

SERVES 4

Ginger–Miso Dressing

3 tablespoons rice vinegar

2 tablespoons fresh orange juice

2 tablespoons white miso paste

2 teaspoons grated fresh ginger

1 garlic clove, grated

1 teaspoon sugar

½ cup neutral oil, such as avocado or grapeseed

1 teaspoon toasted sesame oil

Salad

4 fennel bulbs, cored and shaved into thin slices, plus 1 cup packed fennel fronds

4 navel oranges, cut into suprêmes (see Note)

1 medium shallot (about the size of a golf ball), or ¼ small red onion, thinly sliced

½ cup roasted unsalted cashews, coarsely chopped

When thinking about how to organize this book, I wasn't sure where to put this recipe—where I live, you can find the ingredients during a moment of transition between the tail end of winter and the early signs of spring. But since the peak of citrus season (when we can get incredible Cara Cara oranges) hits in January, I decided it belongs in winter. This salad is especially nice to have during a season that's typically filled with heavy, hearty soups and stews. It's a beacon of light and a promise that sunnier days are right around the corner!

1 **Make the dressing:** In a small bowl, whisk together the vinegar, orange juice, miso, ginger, garlic, and sugar to combine, then add the neutral oil and sesame oil and whisk until emulsified. Set aside. (The dressing can be stored in an airtight container in the refrigerator for several days.)

2 **Make the salad:** In a large bowl, combine the shaved fennel and about half the dressing. Set aside to macerate for at least 30 minutes or up to 2 hours.

3 Place the shallot in a small bowl filled with ice water. Let stand for at least 15 minutes to soften and tone down its pungency.

4 Drain the shallot and add it to the bowl with the fennel, then mix in the orange suprêmes, shallot, cashews, and fennel fronds. Taste and add more dressing, if desired, then serve.

Note: I like to suprême the oranges for this salad, a technique you can use with any citrus fruit when you want to give it a little extra flair: Take an orange and cut a slice from the bottom so that it stands flat on your cutting board, then, following the curve of the fruit, use your knife to cut away the peel and pith (the bitter white layer under the bright, colorful zest). Holding the orange over a bowl, cut between the membranes and the flesh, letting the segments and any juice fall into the bowl as you work. Discard the membrane (might as well squeeze out any lingering juice before you do), and you're done.

Chai-Spiced Parsnip Cake with Cream Cheese Frosting

Cake

4 large eggs

½ cup neutral oil, such as avocado or grapeseed

½ cup (1 stick) salted butter, melted

1¾ cups packed dark brown sugar

2 cups all-purpose flour

1½ teaspoons baking powder

½ teaspoon baking soda

1 teaspoon coarse sea salt

1 tablespoon ground cinnamon

2 teaspoons ground ginger

2 teaspoons ground cardamom

1 teaspoon ground cloves

2½ cups grated parsnips (about 1 pound)

1 cup chopped toasted nuts, such as walnuts, hazelnuts, or pecans

Cream Cheese Frosting

1 (8-ounce) package cream cheese, at room temperature

10 tablespoons (1¼ sticks) salted butter, at room temperature

2 teaspoons pure vanilla extract

2 cups confectioners' sugar, sifted

Ground cinnamon, for dusting

Coming home from school in the afternoon to a kitchen filled with the smell of something delicious baking in the oven is among my favorite childhood memories. Our family collectively has a sweet tooth, and my mom loved to indulge us with a variety of cakes. The flavors varied, but they were *always* baked in a 9 by 13-inch baking dish. She never felt the need to layer cakes or stack them so they looked fancy; she appreciated a simpler, more humble approach.

The cake she made most often was German chocolate, my dad's favorite. As a kid, I felt strongly that shredded coconut and chopped nuts didn't belong in a cake, and I was always annoyed that we couldn't just make it plain chocolate. Luckily, I've moved far past my picky-eating days and embraced the texture. These days I swap out the coconut for shredded parsnip to make this winter variation of carrot cake, Travis's favorite. The blend of chai-inspired spices is hearty and warm, and the lightly sweetened cream cheese frosting definitely appeals to my adult taste buds.

The one thing I haven't changed is the vessel it's baked in—a humble 9 by 13-inch baking dish, just like my mother used. And although she's no longer with us, every time I bake a cake, I feel her near, smiling down on me.

1 Preheat the oven to 325°F. Lightly grease a 9 by 13-inch baking dish with butter or line it with parchment paper, folding it at the corners so that it fits snugly.

2 **Make the cake:** In a large bowl, beat the eggs, oil, melted butter, and brown sugar together until well blended.

3 In a separate bowl, thoroughly mix the flour, baking powder, baking soda, salt, cinnamon, ginger, cardamom, and cloves together.

4 Working in portions (about a third at a time), add the flour mixture to the egg mixture, using one hand to turn the bowl clockwise and the other hand to scrape the sides to gently fold it in. After the flour is mostly incorporated, use the same motion to fold in the parsnips and the nuts until combined; do not overmix the batter.

5 Bake for 55 to 60 minutes, until a toothpick inserted into the center comes out clean. Allow it to fully cool down before adding frosting.

continued

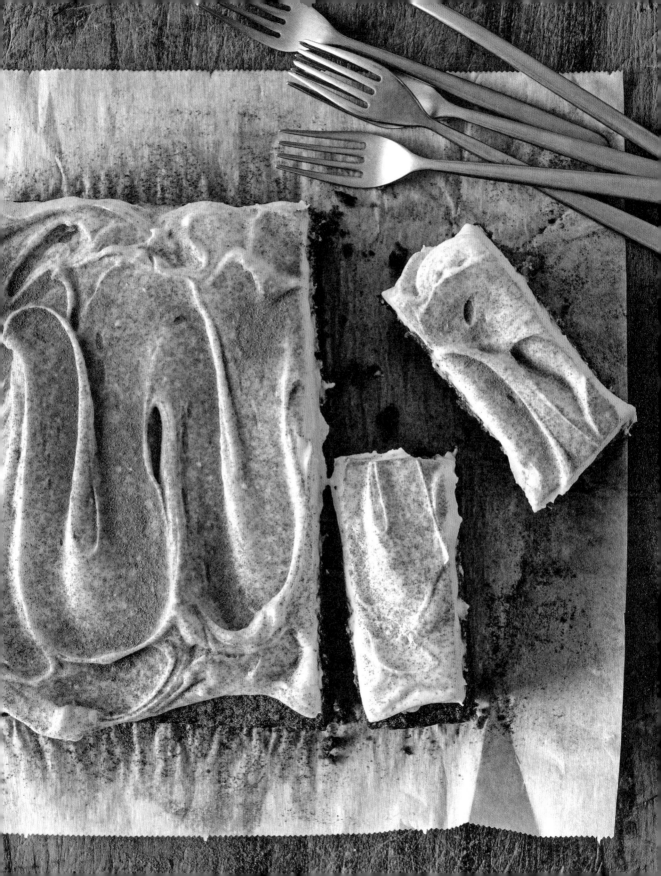

Note: If you're okay with breaking tradition and want to make a layer cake, lightly grease two 9-inch round cake pans with butter or line with parchment paper cut to fit, then divide the batter evenly between them and bake for 35 to 40 minutes, until a toothpick inserted into the center comes out clean. Let cool completely before removing from the pans, then frost the tops of the cooled cakes individually and stack the layers.

6 **Meanwhile, make the frosting:** In the bowl of a stand mixer fitted with the paddle attachment, beat the cream cheese until completely smooth. Add butter and vanilla and whip until fluffy and doubled in volume, about 3 minutes. Working in batches, add the confectioners' sugar, beating until each addition is well combined before adding the next. Transfer to the refrigerator for 20 to 30 minutes to chill and stiffen slightly.

7 Use a spatula to swipe the frosting across the top of the cooled cake. Using a fine-mesh strainer, dust the top with cinnamon. I like to eat the cake at room temperature for the best texture and to bring out the flavors of the spices, but it's equally good served cold with coffee in the morning. Store leftover cake in an airtight container in the fridge or at room temp (your choice).

Giant Duck Fat Chocolate Chip Cookies

MAKES EIGHT 5- TO 6-INCH COOKIES

1 cup all-purpose flour

1 teaspoon baking soda

½ teaspoon coarse sea salt

4 tablespoons (½ stick) salted butter, at room temperature

¼ cup chilled duck fat

1 cup sugar

1 teaspoon pure vanilla extract

1 large egg

1 cup dark chocolate chips

Flaky salt (optional)

Notes: Prefer thicker, softer, chewier cookies to thinner ones? Increase the flour to 1½ cups for a thicker dough that will spread less in the oven, and skip smacking the pan—just bake for 10 to 11 minutes straight through.

I use a stopwatch instead of a timer because it's easier for me to mark the intervals as they're counting up to 15 minutes, versus counting down from 15 minutes on a timer, but if you're not bad at math like me, use whichever method you prefer!

This started as an adaptation of my grandmother's chocolate chip cookie recipe, which our family has been using for many years. She's a serious baker, and was raised at a time when Crisco was king. Even though Crisco has lost mainstream popularity, she still loves using it in cookies because she doesn't like the way butter makes them spread. With all due respect to my grandma, I prefer to use butter and animal fats, particularly duck fat, instead of processed vegetable shortening.

One thing I've learned is that you have to embrace the inherent qualities of an ingredient. Duck fat is liquid at room temperature, which means using it in cookies would make them spread even more than those made with butter alone. I decided to use this to my advantage—and even take it to the next level—by slapping the cookie sheet against the counter to deflate the cookies as they bake (a technique that's been around for decades but reached viral status when Sarah Kieffer shared it a few years ago). The result? Thin cookies with rippled, caramelized edges and a fudgy center. The duck fat adds a savory quality that I love, and I always finish the cookies with a sprinkle of flaky salt, just to be extra.

1 Preheat the oven to 350°F. Line two baking sheets with silicone baking mats or parchment paper.

2 In a medium bowl, stir together the flour, baking soda, and salt. Set aside.

3 In the bowl of a stand mixer fitted with the paddle attachment, beat the butter, duck fat, and sugar on medium-low speed until light and fluffy, 3 to 4 minutes, scraping down the sides to incorporate everything evenly if needed. Add the vanilla and egg and beat for another minute or two, until smooth. Reduce the speed to low and add one-third of the flour; when that is nearly incorporated, add another third, and then finally the last third. Stir a few times, then add the chocolate chips and stir until just combined. Chill the cookie dough in the freezer for 20 minutes.

4 Using a measuring cup, scoop ¼ cup of dough and shape it into a ball. Place it on one of the prepared baking sheets and repeat to form

continued

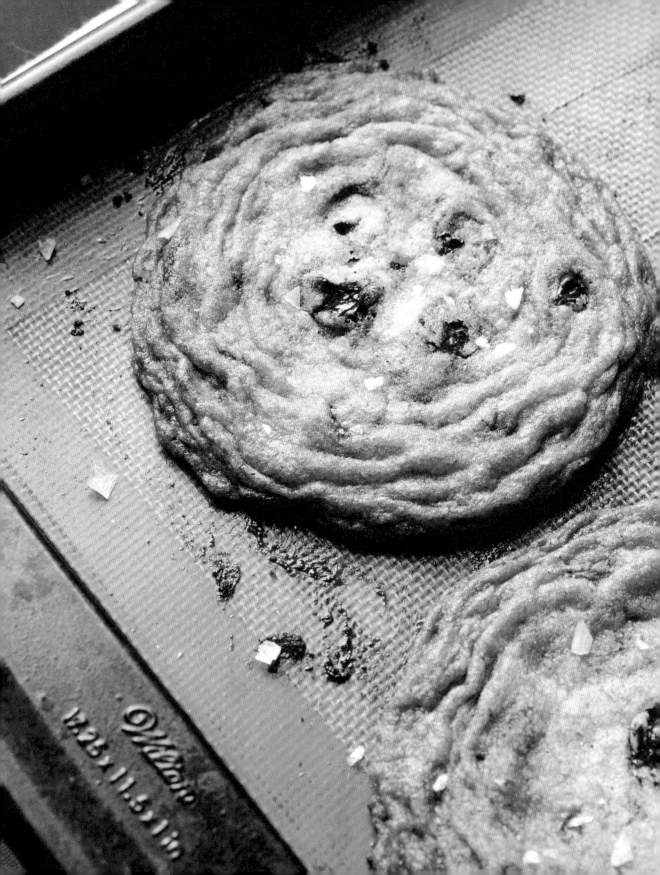

3 additional cookies; return the remaining dough to the refrigerator. Transfer the cookies to the oven and start a stopwatch, keeping a close eye on it.

5 In first few minutes, the cookies will look like melting snowmen. When they're about 50 percent melted and the centers are puffy (about 5 minutes in), remove the baking sheet from the oven and forcefully smack it on the stovetop to deflate the cookies, then immediately return them to the oven. Repeat this process at the 7-minute mark, and again at the 13-minute mark. For a soft, fudgy center, remove the cookies from the oven at 15 minutes. For crispier cookies, remove the pan at the 15-minute mark, smack it on the stovetop one last time, then bake for 1 minute more. Transfer the cookies to a wire rack and let cool completely before eating, or they'll fall apart. As the cookies cool, finish them with a sprinkle of flaky salt, if you like, and repeat to bake the remaining cookie dough.

Things Better Homemade

Mayonnaise (and Aioli)

Mayonnaise and aioli are each a blank canvas to which any combination of flavorful ingredients can be added, taking your sandwich game to the next level. These are staples in my house. Both are easy to make at home, with the added bonus that you have control over the type of oil used. I like making mayonnaise by hand using a whisk instead of using a blender or food processor. It's a bit of a workout and there's more room for error, but I find it very satisfying. You might have another opinion, so I've included a fast and ultra-easy way to make it using modern technology.

MAKES ABOUT 1 CUP

1 large egg yolk

1 cup neutral oil, such as avocado or grapeseed

2 teaspoons fresh lemon

juice, white wine vinegar, or distilled white vinegar

Coarse sea salt

1 **The hard way:** Put the egg yolk in a medium bowl. While whisking vigorously, slowly pour in about 1 tablespoon of the oil in a very fine stream. Whisk until incorporated, then repeat, pouring in more oil, about 1 tablespoon at a time, until the mixture starts to thicken (usually around ¼ to ⅓ cup). Whisk in 1 teaspoon of the lemon juice and 1 tablespoon water until fully blended to thin the mixture, then stream in the rest of the oil—keep on whisking! When the mixture is smooth and emulsified, you can add more lemon juice for acidity, a sprinkle of salt, and/or any other flavor additions you like (suggestions follow).

The easy way: Start by chilling your ingredients first; this will help keep the emulsion from breaking. Combine the egg yolk, oil, and lemon juice in a blender and blend until smooth, a minute or two. (Alternatively, combine the ingredients in a tall container or jar and whiz with an immersion blender until emulsified.) Taste and season with salt as desired.

2 Store the mayonnaise in an airtight container in the fridge for up to 1 week.

Spring Aioli

Stir the following into 1 cup mayonnaise to combine: ¼ cup grated Parmesan cheese, ¼ cup thinly sliced ramp leaves or fresh chives, 2 tablespoons minced nasturtium leaves, and 1 tablespoon fresh lemon juice.

Bacon and Pickled Pepper Aioli

Follow the mayonnaise recipe, but replace half the oil with rendered bacon fat. When the mayo is finished, stir in 6 hot banana peppers, minced; ¼ cup finely chopped cooked bacon; 1 large garlic clove, grated; and a few cranks of black pepper. (If bacon grease is unavailable, stir the ingredients into 1 cup regular mayonnaise.)

Refrigerator Pickles

I quick-pickle vegetables from the garden often to extend the life of my produce and add a bright pop of acidity to many dishes. My favorite vegetables to pickle include cucumbers, wax beans, okra, carrots, green tomatoes, peppers, zucchini, and onions.

When making refrigerator pickles, always use clean, undamaged fresh vegetables. I always stuff a few different aromatics into the jar as I'm packing in the vegetables. The type of vinegar you use is a personal choice. Each has its own flavor and acidity level, with rice vinegar being the least acidic and distilled white vinegar being the most.

The calcium chloride is optional; it helps keep vegetables crispy after they're pickled. Pickling salt is pure, non-iodized salt with no anticaking additives and is used to keep the brine clear. You can find it at Walmart and in many grocery stores, as well as online.

Aromatics are ingredients that add flavor to the pickles; examples include sliced onion, shallot, or leek; a garlic clove; a few thin slices of ginger; whole or chopped chiles; a sprig of fresh herbs; whole peppercorns or other spices; and citrus zest. Get creative and try different blends; a few of my favorite combinations are onion, jalapeño, and coriander; garlic, rosemary, and celery seed; and ginger and star anise.

MAKES ABOUT 3 PINTS

All-Purpose Pickling Brine

1½ cups vinegar (distilled white, white wine, rice, or apple cider)

⅓ cup sugar

4 teaspoons pickling salt, or 2 tablespoons coarse sea salt

2 teaspoons calcium chloride granules, such as Ball Pickle Crisp (optional)

Pickles

1 pound vegetables (Cherokee wax beans, okra, radishes, carrots), cut, sliced, or chopped

Aromatics of your choice (see headnote)

1 **Make the brine:** In a small saucepan, combine the vinegar, sugar, salt, calcium chloride (if using), and 3 cups water. Bring to a boil over high heat, stirring to dissolve the salt and sugar. Remove from the heat and let cool completely.

2 Meanwhile, pack the vegetables and aromatics into three clean 1-pint jars, dividing them evenly. Pour the brine over the vegetables, filling the jars to the rim. Let cool completely, then seal the jars and store in the refrigerator. The pickles will keep for up to a few months.

Classic Dill Pickles

Everyone needs a classic dill pickle recipe—make the brine using distilled white vinegar, and pack your jars with 1 pound of pickling cucumbers (4 to 5 inches long), cut into spears or slices; ¾ teaspoon mustard seeds; ¾ teaspoon whole black peppercorns; 6 dill sprigs; and 3 peeled garlic cloves (divide the ingredients evenly among the jars). For a different spin, sub small zucchini (cut into spears or slices) or trimmed green beans for the cucumbers.

Fresh Venison Sausage with Garlic

These are rich, fatty sausages with a 30 percent ratio of fat to meat. Use them for Chicago-inspired sausages (see page 116) or serve with a side of grilled cabbage (see page 223).

MAKES 5 POUNDS BULK SAUSAGE MEAT, OR ABOUT TWENTY 6- TO 8-INCH SAUSAGE LINKS

2 tablespoons plus 2 teaspoons kosher salt

4 teaspoons smoked paprika

1 tablespoon dried marjoram

1 tablespoon mustard powder

1½ teaspoons freshly ground black pepper

4 garlic cloves, minced

3½ pounds venison or beef, chopped into 1-inch cubes

1½ pounds pork fatback, chopped into 1-inch cubes

¾ to 1 cup ice water

12 feet fresh hog casings (see sidebar, page 252)

1 In a large bowl, combine the salt, paprika, marjoram, mustard, pepper, and garlic. Add the meat and fatback and mix until the spices are evenly distributed. If you have the room, spread the meat out over a baking sheet and chill it in the freezer for 30 minutes, until very cold, almost crunchy, but not frozen solid.

2 Set up your grinder with the large die attachment. Grind all the meat into a bowl set over an ice bath to keep cold, then switch out the plate to a small die and grind again.

3 To bind the sausage, transfer the meat to the bowl of a stand mixer fitted with the paddle attachment. With the mixer on low speed, slowly pour in the ice water (you may not need a full cup), mixing just until the meat comes together into a large ball and is no longer crumbly; the texture should be tacky and the meat should stick together. (Alternatively, stir the water into the meat by hand with a wooden spoon.) Transfer the sausage meat to the fridge to keep it cold while you clean up your meat grinder and set up your sausage stuffer.

4 Pull the meat out of the fridge and place it in the hopper of your sausage stuffer, being sure to push it down so there are no air pockets. Pull the casings out of the water and squeeze any excess liquid from inside the casings; you want the outside to remain a little wet (this helps the casings slip onto the stuffer without ripping and slide into a coil on the counter as they're filled). Feed all the casing over the tube of the stuffer, leaving a few inches hanging off at the end. Tie a small square knot at that end to close off the casing. Begin to feed the stuffing into the casing at a consistent pace. There's a Goldilocks method here: You don't want the meat to be so loose in the casing that you have lots of air pockets, but you don't want to stuff the casing so much that it pops when you go to twist it into links. As the stuffer continues to extrude meat, you can start to coil up the sausage.

5 After all the meat has been pressed into the casing, start to form links by pinching the stuffed casing at equal 6- to 8-inch intervals and twisting several times at the spot you pinched; twist the links in alternating directions (or tie them off with butcher's string). Do this along the entire length of the stuffed casing, then tie a square knot at the end. Use a sharp sewing pin or sausage pricker to poke little holes in any air pockets.

continued

Tips for Making Sausage at Home

It's hard not to love a juicy, fatty, incredibly flavorful sausage, and after you've tried your hand at making your own, you'll see why people do it. You have control over every ingredient that goes into the mix, and although they're a labor of love, you'll find the reward is worth the hard work.

If you're new to making sausages, know that it can be a little bit of a challenge, but with practice, you'll get better and better. Sausage making requires just a few pieces of equipment: First, a meat grinder. There are several types of grinder on the market, ranging from manual grinders to large electric countertop grinders to stand mixer attachments. And second, if you plan to make link sausages, you'll need a stuffer—and casings to stuff. Most fresh casings come in a bag with brine. Drain them and rinse them well with tepid fresh water. If you're using salt-packed dry casings, soak them in a bowl of tepid water for at least an hour or up to overnight, then rinse them well inside and out.

Taking a tough cut of meat and grinding it is the quickest way to make it tender, and ground meat is a versatile ingredient. There are a lot of benefits to grinding your wild game at home rather than taking it to a processor. The greatest of these is that you have control over the entire process and can decide what type of fat to use and how much of it to add. Here are some of my best tips for grinding meat:

1. Keep the meat, fat, and even the grinding equipment icy cold for the best texture. In fact, I store all the grinding parts in my freezer.

2. My standard ratio is to add 20 percent fat to plain ground meat, and 30 percent if I'm making sausage. If you like, you can add offal (like heart, liver, and kidneys) to your sausage blends in order to boost their nutritional value. I'll add up to 20 percent offal to the total weight of meat and fat.

3. Trim most of the silver skin from the meat to keep it from wrapping around the auger (the rotating shaft inside the grinder), and chop the meat into smaller pieces (roughly 1- to 2-inch cubes) before grinding.

4. Fatback (the fat from the back of a pig) is my favorite fat to add to ground wild game because its texture is soft and its flavor doesn't overpower the meat.

6 The sausages can be cooked right away but are much better after resting in the refrigerator, uncovered, overnight. This allows the flavors to meld and the casing to dry out so the sausages have that snappy texture when cooked. After their overnight rest, I cut the sausages into individual links. They can be stored in an airtight container in the refrigerator for about 5 days, or place individual links on a baking sheet and freeze until solid, then transfer to vacuum-seal bags and freeze for up to a year.

Hot Italian Sausage

This sausage has the classic hot Italian flavors, with 25 percent fat added. I never stuff it in casings, as my favorite recipes call for bulk sausage meat, but you're welcome to do so; just follow the instructions for stuffing the casings on pages 252–253. I like rolling this sausage into meatballs to serve with orzo and red peppers, adding it to spaghetti sauce, and putting it in my Midwest Cioppino (page 234).

MAKES ABOUT 4 POUNDS BULK SAUSAGE, OR ABOUT TWELVE 6- TO 8-INCH LINKS

1½ tablespoons dried oregano leaves	1½ teaspoons red pepper flakes
2 tablespoons kosher salt	3 pounds wild hog, pork, or venison, chopped into ½- to 1-inch cubes
1 tablespoon smoked paprika	
2 teaspoons whole fennel seeds, crushed in mortar and pestle	1 pound pork fatback, chopped into ½- to 1-inch cubes
1½ teaspoons granulated garlic	½ to ¾ cup ice water
	2 tablespoons red wine vinegar, chilled

Follow the instructions for making Fresh Venison Sausage with Garlic on page 251 starting with step 2, adding the vinegar with the ice water when you bind the meat in step 3. Use as bulk sausage, or proceed to stuff it into casings as instructed above. The sausage can be stored in an airtight container in the refrigerator for about 5 days or frozen for up to a year.

Texas BBQ Rub

I find that most BBQ rubs are way too sweet, which tends to make everything burn on the grill. This recipe is how I think a barbecue rub should taste. It has smoky flavors from the paprika and ancho chile, and just a touch of sugar—but not too much.

MAKES 1 CUP

3 tablespoons coarse sea salt

3 tablespoons smoked paprika

4 teaspoons coarsely ground black pepper

4 teaspoons dark brown sugar

1 tablespoon ancho chile powder

2 teaspoons granulated garlic

2 teaspoons coarsely ground mustard seeds (use a spice mill)

Stir together all the ingredients in a small bowl. Transfer to an airtight container and store in a cool, dark spot for up to 1 year.

Hot Italian Seasoning

If a recipe calls for Italian sausage and you don't have any handy, use this spice blend as a substitute to season plain ground hog, pork, or venison.

MAKES ABOUT 6 TABLESPOONS

1½ tablespoons coarse sea salt

3½ teaspoons garlic powder

2½ teaspoons fennel seeds, ground in a mortar and pestle

2 teaspoons paprika

2 teaspoons dried oregano

2 teaspoons red pepper flakes

1 teaspoon coarsely ground black pepper

Stir together all the ingredients in a small bowl. Transfer to an airtight container and store in a cool, dark spot for up to 1 year.

Ancho Chile Seasoning

This is my go-to spice blend and reflects the flavors I love in Tex-Mex foods. I use this more than any other blend. It's great for seasoning meat, fish, and vegetables.

MAKES ½ CUP

3 tablespoons coarse sea salt

3 tablespoons ancho chile powder

5 teaspoons ground cumin

5 teaspoons dried oregano

½ teaspoon cayenne pepper

Zest of 1 lime

Stir together all the ingredients in a small bowl. Transfer to an airtight container and store in a cool, dark spot for up to 1 year.

Mushroom Rub

This is great for steaks and roasts (see page 162), but it can also be used to add umami to soups and stews (like the Beef Cheek, Red Wine, and Barley Stew on page 226), season bread crumbs (as in the Turkey Cutlet with Morels and Asparagus on page 68), and even amplify the flavor of sautéed mushrooms.

MAKES A SCANT 1 CUP

2 ounces dried mushrooms (meaty varieties such as porcini, morel, shiitake, and hen of the woods)

1 tablespoon plus 2 teaspoons coarse sea salt

1 tablespoon crushed dried rosemary

1½ teaspoons coarsely ground pepper (black, mélange, or pink peppercorns)

Working in batches, pulse the dried mushrooms in a spice grinder until you reach a coarse powder. Transfer to an airtight container, stir in the salt, rosemary, and pepper and cover. Store in a cool, dark spot for up to 1 year.

Garlic and Herb Salt

This is less of a spice rub and more of a seasoned salt made with fresh garlic and herbs. The high ratio of salt means it doubles as a dry brine. In fact, I make this fresh every fall and use it to brine my Thanksgiving turkey or pheasant (see page 66). It can also be used for pork chops and seafood.

MAKES 1 CUP

¾ cup coarse sea salt

¼ cup mixed minced fresh sage, rosemary, and thyme

3 garlic cloves, minced

Stir together all the ingredients in a small bowl. I prefer to use this immediately since the garlic and herbs are so fragrant, but for long-term preservation, spread it over a baking sheet and dehydrate in the oven set to its lowest temperature or in a dehydrator until dry. Store in an airtight container in a cool, dark spot for up to 1 year.

All-Purpose Meat Stock

MAKES 4 TO 6 QUARTS

Neutral oil, such as avocado or grapeseed

4 to 6 pounds bones (venison, beef, poultry, or pork) and meat trimmings

2 tablespoons tomato paste (optional)

2 yellow onions

2 carrots

2 celery stalks

1 tablespoon whole black peppercorns

A few sprigs of thyme

A few sprigs of parsley

1 bay leaf

Coarse sea salt

2 teaspoons red wine vinegar or apple cider vinegar (optional)

Notes: Pressure canning is a great alternative to freezing for long-term pantry storage. Follow the guidelines for safe canning provided by the National Center of Home Preservation (see Resources, page 262).

You can cook the stock in a pressure cooker to cut the time in half; just roast the bones as directed, then combine the ingredients in the pressure cooker, add water to cover, seal the lid, and cook on high pressure for 3 to 4 hours; allow the pressure to release naturally.

This is the recipe I use to make stock with all manner of proteins: venison, beef, poultry, and pork. With venison and beef, it's best to take the extra step of basting the bones with tomato paste and roasting them, which will ensure you end up with a rich brown stock. You can do the same with poultry and pork, or skip that step and opt for a blond stock, which has a lighter flavor and color. The flavor of your stock is directly tied to the ratio of bones to liquid. If you cut bones into small pieces, they take up less volume in your pot, so you'll need far less water and will end up with a more concentrated stock.

1 If making a brown stock, preheat the oven to 425°F. Lightly oil the bottom of a roasting pan. Brush the bones with the tomato paste and place them in the prepared roasting pan. Roast for 30 to 45 minutes, until browned (this contributes depth and richness to the stock). If you're making a blond stock, omit this step.

2 Meanwhile, put the onions, carrots, celery, peppercorns, thyme, parsley, bay leaf, and a few pinches of salt in a large stockpot. Transfer the bones (roasted or otherwise) to the pot, then pour a small amount of water into the roasting pan and stir to scrape up the browned bits from the bottom. Pour the liquid from the roasting pan into the stockpot. Add enough cold water to cover the bones and vegetables, then pour in the vinegar (if using; the acid helps break down connective tissue and extract more gelatin).

3 Heat the water over high heat to just above a simmer, then immediately reduce the heat to maintain a gentle simmer (don't let the liquid come to a boil!). Cook, skimming the surface occasionally, until the stock is light to dark brown and very flavorful. The bigger the pot and the bigger the bones, the longer the stock will need to cook; poultry stock might take 4 to 8 hours, while venison stock could take from 8 to 12 hours or even longer. Remove from the heat.

4 Using tongs, remove the bones from the liquid. Strain the stock through a fine-mesh strainer (lined with a paper towel for a clear stock) into another large pot or container and discard the solids. Taste and season with additional salt, if desired. Let cool, then transfer to airtight containers and store in the fridge for up to 5 days, or freeze for up to 6 months.

Fish Stock

MAKES ABOUT 4 QUARTS

4 pounds fish bones and heads and/or crustacean shells (see Notes)

3 tablespoons kosher salt (optional)

1 tablespoon extra-virgin olive oil

2 small leeks, sliced and rinsed well to remove any grit

½ yellow onion, diced

4 small celery stalks, sliced

4 garlic cloves, smashed and peeled

1 cup dry white wine

1½ teaspoons whole white peppercorns

Several sprigs of parsley and/or tarragon

2 bay leaves

Notes: When making shellfish stock, I include 3 diced fresh tomatoes to add color and umami. You could also include 1 fennel bulb, roughly chopped (including the stalks).

Even if fish soup isn't your thing, don't let those carcasses go to waste—toss them in a pot with some water (nothing else) and simmer for 30 to 45 minutes, then strain and serve the flavorful liquid to your pets. My aging golden retriever, Marina, drools at the smell of fish simmering away in my kitchen, and she doesn't even realize how her body benefits from the glucosamine in the fish heads.

Throwing fish heads into a pot doesn't sound all that glamorous, but homemade fish stock is truly much better and more nutritious than anything you can find at the grocery store. Mild white fish carcasses make the cleanest-looking and cleanest-tasting stock, but shellfish and lobster add a sweetness of their own. I use seafood stock in hearty winter stews like bouillabaisse and cioppino (see page 234), but it's also a flavorful substitute for water when you're making seafood risotto or grits you'll be topping with shrimp or blackened fish.

1 Clean the fish parts well, scrubbing the fins and scales under cold water. This next step is optional, but I recommend it for a cleaner-tasting broth, especially if the fish was not bled out when caught. Fill a large stockpot with water and stir in the salt. Submerge the fish in the water and soak for 30 minutes. Drain and rinse the fish; set aside.

2 Wipe the pot clean and place it over medium heat. Pour in the olive oil, then add the leeks and onion and gently stir. Cook until the onion is soft and translucent. Add the celery and garlic and cook for 1 minute more, then pour in the wine and stir, scraping up any browned bits from the bottom of the pot. Cook until the alcohol has burned off, about 30 seconds. Add the peppercorns, herb sprigs, and bay leaves and return the fish to the pot. You want the highest ratio of fish to water, so try to break the fish bones in half and smash them to decrease their volume and release gelatin. Add enough water to just cover the fish, then increase the heat to high. When the water begins to bubble, reduce the heat to its lowest setting—don't let the water come to a full boil. Gently simmer the stock for 30 to 45 minutes, skimming off any scum that collects on the surface as necessary. When the heads and bones are falling apart, remove the pot from heat. Use tongs to fish out the bones and heads.

3 Pour the broth through a fine-mesh strainer and discard the solids. For clear stock, line the strainer with cheesecloth or a paper towel and strain the stock again. Use immediately, or let cool, then transfer to airtight containers and store in the fridge for use within 2 days, or freeze for up to 6 months.

I judge the quality of a homemade stock by whether it turns gelatinous in the fridge. When I'm butchering meat, I save the silver skin, tendons, and joints to throw in the stockpot. These bits contain collagen, which breaks down into gelatin as it cooks, making my stock more nutrient-dense and very silky in texture. And—just like Jell-O—the gelatin in the stock sets when chilled! If it wiggles when I shake the container, I know I've nailed it. If it stays liquid, I add a packet of gelatin, a trick I also use when I've exhausted my stash of homemade stock and have to opt for store-bought, which can be pretty watery in comparison.

To level up your stock, whisk a ¼-ounce packet (2 teaspoons) unflavored gelatin powder into 2 cups cold stock before using it to give it silkiness. Look for gelatin powder near the Jell-O at the grocery store.

Vegetable Stock

Vegetable stock is easily overlooked when you have a beautiful, gelatinous bone broth on hand, but it's a great substitute for water when you're cooking grains, beans, or any other vegetable dish that you want to infuse with more flavor. It's also a great way to use those produce scraps—like carrot tops, fennel stems, tomato cores, even mushrooms (whole ones or woody trimmings)—that would typically be composted. The only things you want to avoid are bitter greens and sulfurous vegetables such as broccoli or Brussels sprouts. This recipe makes a basic vegetable stock; feel free to get creative and adjust based on what you have, or include a variety of herbs for different flavor profiles. When you're adding vegetables to the pot, a good rule of thumb is to use 1 part allium (like onion and leek) to 2 or 3 parts vegetables, like carrots, parsnips, celery, or fennel.

MAKES 2 TO 4 QUARTS

1 medium yellow onion, coarsely chopped

1 leek, coarsely chopped and rinsed well to remove grit

1 tablespoon neutral oil, such as avocado or grapeseed

6 garlic cloves, smashed

4 carrots, coarsely chopped

6 celery stalks with leaves, coarsely chopped

Juice of ½ lemon

Whole black peppercorns

Fresh parsley

A few sprigs of woody herbs, such as rosemary, thyme, and/or sage

Coarse sea salt

1 In a large pot, cook the onion and leek in the oil over medium-high heat until soft. Add the garlic, carrots, and celery and cook until softened and aromatic. Add the lemon juice, some peppercorns, parsley, woody herbs, a couple pinches of salt, and enough water to just barely cover everything.

2 Bring the water to a simmer over high heat, then reduce the heat to low and simmer gently for 1 hour, until lightly golden in color and flavorful. Pour the stock through a fine-mesh strainer and discard the solids. Let cool, then transfer to airtight containers and store in the fridge for up to 1 week or freeze for up to 1 year.

All-Purpose Pie Dough

This pie dough can be used for any pie, savory or sweet. I like to use a mix of lard for flaky texture and butter for moisture and flavor. The trick to making pie dough from scratch is to be sure all your ingredients are very cold.

MAKES ENOUGH FOR 1 DOUBLE-CRUST PIE,
2 SINGLE-CRUST PIES, OR 18 TO 20 HAND PIES

2½ cups all-purpose flour

1 teaspoon kosher salt

½ cup (1 stick) unsalted butter, chilled and grated on the large holes of a box grater

½ cup rendered leaf lard (see sidebar, page 261), chilled

½ cup ice water

1 In a large bowl, whisk together the flour and salt. Using a fork, blend in the grated butter. Cut in the cold lard until the mixture takes on a crumbly texture. Use your fingers to roll the lard and flour together to coat until the lard is dispersed in pea-size pieces.

2 Add the ice water little by little, mixing with a spatula to incorporate, until you can form the dough into a mound. Be careful not to overwork the dough. It should barely be holding itself together. If it wants to fall apart, add a little more water. If it's sticky, sprinkle with a little flour. Divide the dough in half, form each half into a disk, and wrap the disks tightly with plastic wrap. Refrigerate for at least 1 hour or up to 3 days before using, or place the wrapped disks in a freezer bag and freeze for up to 6 months. Thaw in the fridge overnight before using.

Empanada Dough

This dough is similar to my All-Purpose Pie Dough but contains egg, which binds the dough, making it easier to manipulate. It's perfect for the Black Bean, Corn, and Tongue Empanadas on page 100 (of course!), but you can also use it for other pastries in place of pie dough.

MAKES ENOUGH FOR SIXTEEN TO EIGHTEEN
6-INCH EMPANADAS

3 cups all-purpose flour

½ teaspoon kosher salt

4 tablespoons (½ stick) unsalted butter, chilled and grated on the large holes of a box grater

½ cup rendered leaf lard, chilled

1 large egg, beaten

⅓ to ½ cup ice water

1 In a large bowl, whisk together the flour and salt. Using a fork, blend in the grated butter, then cut in the cold lard until the mixture takes on a crumbly texture. Use your fingers to roll the fat and flour together to coat until the lard is dispersed in pea-size pieces and the mixture has a crumbly, sandy texture.

2 Add the egg and half the ice water, then stir with a spoon until the dough comes together in a clump; resist the urge to overstir. If the dough isn't coming together, add more ice water a little bit at a time until it does (you may not need all the water). Divide the dough in half, form each half into a disk, and wrap the disks tightly in plastic wrap. Refrigerate for least 30 minutes or up to 2 days before using, or place the wrapped disks in a freezer bag and freeze for up to 6 months. Thaw in the fridge overnight before using.

Rendered Fat

When you eat as much lean wild game as I do, you start to crave animal fat. And not only does it taste good—it's valuable, too! A jar of pure duck fat or grass-fed beef tallow isn't cheap, so I find ways to save and use every bit of extra fat I can find. I save the soft caul fat and leaf lard wrapped around the stomachs of deer and hogs, and turn the belly on an acorn-fed wild sow into bacon (see page 125). I trim excess fat from bone-in pork chops and rib eyes, tear out the chunk of soft fat near the tail of a whole chicken, duck, or goose (even wild birds), reserve excess fatback or lard from sausage making, and save the fat left in the pan after searing a duck breast. The only fat I don't save is the back fat from deer and hogs, because it turns to wax the moment it cools even slightly—save it to mix with seeds as a treat for the birds.

What do I do with all that fat I've collected? I render it! This just means heating solid animal fat or tissue over low heat so the fat becomes liquid. This removes impurities, moisture, and pieces of inedible meat or skin that can affect texture, flavor, and shelf life, and leaves you with fat in a form you can easily use for cooking. Rendering fat is very easy to do, and I think you'll find endless opportunities to cook with it. Experiment a little!

I like to buy animal fat, like pork fatback and beef suet, in bulk and render it myself, which is more economical than buying rendered lard or tallow by the jar. You want to render it without browning anything in it, which would impart a meaty quality. I find this easiest to do in a slow cooker; the fat can have a strong aroma, so crack a window first or render it outside. Pour a tablespoon of water into the bottom of the crock (this is to prevent browning), then add the fat and set the slow cooker to warm, but do not cover it. Let the fat slowly melt, giving it a stir occasionally to make sure nothing is sticking to the bottom or sides, until all of it has liquefied. Strain the rendered fat to remove any gristly bits, then pour it into an airtight container and let it cool completely before covering. Rendered fat will keep at room temperature for a month or two, in the refrigerator for 6 months to 1 year, or in the freezer for over a year. It will solidify and turn opaque white when chilled.

RESOURCES

Ingredients

MEAT AND SEAFOOD

- White Oak Pastures, whiteoakpastures.com: pasture-raised meat
- Porter Road, porterroad.com: pasture-raised meat
- Grass Roots Farmers' Cooperative, grassrootscoop.com: pasture-raised meat
- Roam Ranch, roamranch.com: pasture-raised buffalo
- Fatworks, fatworks.com: animal fats
- Maui Nui Venison, mauinuivenison.com: invasive wild axis deer
- Broken Arrow Ranch, brokenarrowranch.com: nonnative wild game
- Salmon Sisters, aksalmonsisters.com: sustainably caught wild seafood
- Smart Source Seafood, smartsourceseafood.com: sustainably caught wild seafood

GRAINS AND FLOUR

- Anson Mills, ansonmills.com
- Barton Springs Mill, bartonspringsmill.com
- King Arthur Baking, kingarthurbaking.com
- Marsh Hen Mill, marshhenmill.com

SEAWEED

- Barnacle Foods, barnaclefoods.com
- Nautical Farms, nauticalfarms.com

US-MADE ARTISANAL SALT

- Jacobsen Salt Co., jacobsensalt.com
- J. Q. Dickinson Salt-Works, jqdsalt.com
- Redmond Real Salt (Redmond Life), https://redmond.life

PRODUCE

- Hungry Harvest, hungryharvest.net
- Imperfect Foods, imperfectfoods.com
- Misfits Market, misfitsmarket.com

Tools and Supplies

- LEM Products, lemproducts.com: meat processing
- Weston Brands, westonbrands.com: food preservation and meat processing
- Botanical Interests, botanicalinterests.com: vegetable seeds
- Baker Creek Seeds, rareseeds.com: vegetable seeds
- Native American Seed, seedsource.com: wildflowers and native grasses

Directories of Local Farmers

- Regenerative Farmers of America, regenerativefarmersofamerica.com/regenerative-farm-near-me: national directory of regenerative farmers
- Local Harvest, localharvest.org/organic-farms: national directory of small family farms
- Real Milk, realmilk.com/raw-milk-finder: national raw milk directory

Education

- Wild + Whole, wildandwhole.com
- MeatEater, themeateater.com
- Epic Gardening, epicgardening.com
- The Chicken Chick, the-chicken-chick.com
- *The Complete Guide to Hunting, Butchering, and Cooking Wild Game: Volume 1: Big Game* by Steven Rinella
- *The Complete Guide to Hunting, Butchering, and Cooking Wild Game: Volume 2: Small Game* by Steven Rinella
- *The Forager's Harvest: A Guide to Identifying, Harvesting, and Preparing Edible Wild Plants* by Samuel Thayer
- *Sacred Cow: The Case for (Better) Meat* by Diana Rogers, RD, and Robb Wolf
- *Nature's Best Hope* and *Bringing Nature Home* by Douglas Tallamy
- *Teaming with Microbes* and *Teaming with Nutrients* by Jeff Lowenfels

Organizations to Support

- Theodore Roosevelt Conservation Partnership, trcp.org
- The Nature Conservancy, nature.org/en-us
- National Wildlife Federation, nwf.org
- National Deer Association, deerassociation.com
- Rocky Mountain Elk Foundation, rmef.org
- National Wild Turkey Federation, nwtf.org
- Coastal Conservation Association, joincca.org
- Ducks Unlimited, ducks.org
- Delta Waterfowl, deltawaterfowl.org
- Pheasants Forever, pheasantsforever.org
- Quail Forever, quailforever.org
- North American Grouse Partnership, grousepartners.org
- Backcountry Hunters & Anglers, backcountryhunters.org
- Tall Timbers, talltimbers.org
- Regenerate America, kisstheground.com/advocacy
- Regenerative Farmers of America, regenerativefarmersofamerica.com
- Savory Institute, https://savory.global
- North American Native Plant Society, nanps.org
- Homegrown National Park, homegrownnationalpark.org

Additional Photo Credits

- Matt Gagnon: pages 133 and 195 (and photo of mushroom on back cover)
- Cody MacCready: pages 11, 41, 146–147, and 201
- Loren Moulten: page 67
- Mike Raabe: pages 17 and 107
- Danielle Prewett: pages 4–5, 21, 22, 23, 27, 48, 69, 83, 124, 132, 142, 153, 156, 159, 175, 180, 191, 198, 203, 214, 233, 238, 246, and 248
- Jonathan Vail: pages 12 and 94–95

ACKNOWLEDGMENTS

This book would not exist without my husband, Travis. Your awe-inspiring love for the outdoors taught me how to connect to my food and find deeper meaning in the meals we share together. You've always been good at talking me into hunting or fishing during the worst conditions, which coincidentally makes for good memories and a full freezer. Thank you for pushing me out of my comfort zone and for your unwavering support in this incredible journey.

To my collaborator, Ivy McFadden—I will be forever grateful for your unrelenting commitment to creating the best cookbook possible. Thank you for the countless hours spent working though the nitty-gritty details that bring a recipe to life (you are truly the best in the biz), for translating real-life stories into the beautiful words on these pages, for keeping me grounded when my head went too far down the rabbit hole, and for being a supportive friend when I needed it most.

I owe many thanks to incredibly talented chef Kevin Gillespie for making the food in these images look so delicious, helping me work through recipe ideas, and being a mentor. Your belief in me and the concept behind *Wild + Whole* has encouraged me to keep pushing forward.

To my photographer, Angie Mosier, and prop stylist, Thom Driver—you guys are a kick-ass team and such a pleasure to work with! You worked incredibly hard to make my dreams a reality, and the images in this book are more beautiful than I could have ever expected. Thank you to Matt Gagnon, Jonathan Vail, Cody MacCready, Loren Moulten, and Mike Raabe for capturing beautiful moments in the field and sharing those images with me, and to Stephanie Singleton, the talented illustrator who brought the words on these pages to life with visuals that convey my love for the natural world.

Thank you to my agent, Tess Callero, and Katie Finch at MeatEater, the catalyst behind this book. Your leadership and management of this project allowed me to focus on doing what I love: developing recipes. Thank you to Brody Henderson and Savannah Ashour, the publishing team at MeatEater, for providing valuable feedback and insight on this manuscript.

To my editor, Dervla Kelly, I can't thank you enough for believing in *Wild + Whole* and for your willingness to bring this concept to life. Thank you to the talented editorial and design teams at Penguin Random House, including Joyce Wong, Katherine Leak, and Kelli Tokos, and to designer Amy Sly. Thanks also to the marketing and publicity team of Odette Fleming, Keilani Lum, Christina Foxley, Cindy Murray, and Kelly Doyle.

While I personally hunted for many of the ingredients found in this book, I couldn't source everything alone. Thank you to Cory Caulkins for being an incredible hunting guide and helping me shoot my first mule deer. Thank you to Rhett Hall, who, without hesitation, dropped work for a week to help me procure two perfectly shot and plucked pheasants for the cover of this book. To Max Barta, who shared with me the most beautifully plucked mallard I've ever seen, and to Hayden Sammak, for teaching me how to find and identify porcini mushrooms. To Simon and Linnet Cartwright of Cartwright Truffière, for overnighting some fresh Périgord truffles. Lastly, I want to thank Will Harris and his family at White Oak Pastures for taking the time to share their beautiful farm with me and for gifting me with beautiful, regeneratively raised meat to cook.

NOTES

1. Katie Pavid, "What Is Biodiversity and Why Does Its Loss Matter?" Natural History Museum, accessed August 4, 2023, https://www.nhm.ac.uk/discover/what-is-biodiversity.html.

2. World Wildlife Fund, Living Planet Report 2022, accessed August 11, 2023, https://livingplanet.panda.org/en-us/.

3. "A Look at Agricultural Productivity Growth in the United States, 1948–2017," US Department of Agriculture, March 5, 2020, https://www.usda.gov/media/blog/2020/03/05/look-agricultural-productivity-growth-united-states-1948-2017.

4. "Why Do We Consume Only a Tiny Fraction of the World's Edible Plants?" World Economic Forum, January 15, 2016, https://www.weforum.org/agenda/2016/01/why-do-we-consume-only-a-tiny-fraction-of-the-world-s-edible-plants.

5. "Crop Biodiversity: Use It or Lose It," Food and Agricultural Organization of the United Nations, October 26, 2010, https://www.fao.org/news/story/en/item/46803/icode/.

6. "Chronic Wasting Disease (CWD)," Centers for Disease Control and Prevention, last reviewed April 17, 2023, https://www.cdc.gov/prions/cwd/occurrence.html.

7. Jack Cheney, "Buying Sustainable Seafood: A New Shopping Guide for the Grocery Store," Sustainable Fisheries, accessed August 13, 2023, https://sustainablefisheries-uw.org/buy-sustainable-seafood-grocery-store/.

8. "The Farmer's Small Share of the Food Dollar," Farm Policy Facts, accessed August 13, 2023, https://www.farmpolicyfacts.org/the-farmers-small-share-of-the-food-dollar/.

9. "Food Waste," ReFED, accessed August 13, 2023, https://refed.org/food-waste/the-challenge/#overview.

10. "Trichinellosis Information for Hunters," Centers for Disease Control and Prevention, last reviewed July 28, 2017, https://www.cdc.gov/parasites/trichinellosis/hunters.html; "Control and Prevention in Pork and Other Meat from Food Animals," International Commission on Trichinellosis, http://www.trichinellosis.org/Control_and_Prevention.html.

11. "Burning Issue: Acidifying Tomatoes When Canning," National Center for Home Food Preservation, September 4, 2013, https://nchfp.uga.edu/publications/nchfp/factsheets/acidifying.html.

12. "Bacon and Food Safety," USDA Food Safety and Inspection Service, last updated October 29, 2013, https://www.fsis.usda.gov/food-safety/safe-food-handling-and-preparation/meat/bacon-and-food-safety.

13. Andrew Spellman, "North American Grasslands Conservation Act Gaining Traction on Capitol Hill," *Project Upland* magazine, August 23, 2021, https://projectupland.com/hunting-policy/north-american-grasslands-conservation-act-gaining-traction-on-capitol-hill/.

RECILES BY TECHNIQUE

INDEX

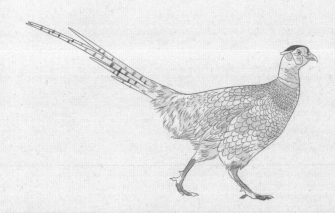